MASTER THE

GED –

SOCIAL STUDIES

2 0 0 2

UPDATED FOR THE ALL-NEW GED!

ARCO

THOMSON LEARNING

Australia • Canada • Mexico • Singapore • Spain • United Kingdom • United States

An ARCO Book

ARCO is a registered trademark of Thomson Learning, Inc., and is used herein under license by Peterson's.

About Peterson's

Founded in 1966, Peterson's, a division of Thomson Learning, is the nation's largest and most respected provider of lifelong learning resources, both in print and online. The Education Supersite^{SM} at www.petersons.com—the Internet's most heavily traveled education resource—has searchable databases and interactive tools for contacting U.S.-accredited institutions and programs. In addition, Peterson's delivers unmatched financial aid resources and test-preparation tools. Peterson's serves more than 100 million education consumers annually.

Peterson's is a division of Thomson Learning, one of the world's largest providers of lifelong learning. Thomson Learning serves the needs of individuals, learning institutions, and corporations with products and services for both traditional and distributed learning. Headquartered in Stamford, Connecticut, with offices worldwide, Thomson Learning is a division of The Thomson Corporation (www.thomson.com), one of the world's leading e-information and solutions companies in the business, professional, and education marketplaces. For more information, visit www.thomsonlearning.com.

For more information, contact Peterson's, 2000 Lenox Drive, Lawrenceville, NJ 08648; 800-338-3282; or find us on the World Wide Web at: www.petersons.com/about

ISBN 0-7689-0797-7

Printed in the United States of America

10 9 8 7 6 5 4 3 2 1   04 03 02

Contents

Acknowledgments

"Bush 2000—No More Recounts . . ." Mike Thompson from the *Detroit Free Press*

"Wonder How Long the Honeymoon Will Last?" by James Berryman. Marriage of Adolf Hitler and Joseph Stalin © CORBIS

Paul Revere Engraving, Boston. Copyright © Library of Congress

British Cartoon, published 1780. Miriam and Ira D. Wallach Division of Art, Prints, and Photographs. The New York Public Library.

From Strong Government, Weak Government. "Cartoon of Grant in Carpet Bag." © Bettman/CORBIS

"Bull in a China Shop." *San Francisco Chronicle,* February 27, 1919.

"Let's Throw Another Desert Storm." Mike Luckovich—*Atlanta Constitution,* Creators Syndicate.

"Poverty, Drugs, Ignorance." Dick Locher/Tribune Media Services.

"Parole Board." Dick Lochner/Tribune Media Services.

"The North Atlantic Tea & Origami Society." John Danziger in *The Christian Science Monitor.* © 1994.

Le Pelley; reprinted by permission from *The Christian Science Monitor.* © 1970 *The Christian Science Monitor.* © 1970 The Christian Science Publishing Society. All Rights reserved.

Introduction

Congratulations on taking the first step to advancing your academic career. Whether you are taking the GED to prepare for college entrance or looking for the career opportunities that become available after completing the GED, you are not alone. Between 1949 and 1999 an estimated 14.2 million adults earned a GED credential. It is estimated that in the United States today, 1 out of every 7 high school students will complete their education with the GED Exam.

The General Educational Development (GED) tests were originally developed to help veterans returning from service in World War II regain academic skills or complete an education that had been interrupted by the war. Many returning veterans used the knowledge from the GED Testing Services to gain jobs. Over the years, the emphasis of these tests has changed from knowledge required for industrial jobs to knowledge needed for today's information-driven world.

This book was designed to assist you with successfully passing the Social Studies portion of the GED test. Skills essential to passing all areas will be covered, key social studies concepts will be addressed, and plenty of practice with the types of questions you will encounter on the real exam will be provided.

WHAT IS GED?

The acronym GED stands for the tests of General Educational Development. The tests are a national examination created by the GED Testing Service of the American Council of Education. GED tests cover topics that are normally tested in high school: language arts, reading and writing, social studies, science, and mathematics. Each of these tests covers topics specific to that course. The ultimate goal in passing these exams is a certificate equivalent to a high school diploma.

WHAT IS COVERED IN THE GED TESTS?

The GED consists of tests in four content areas. The chart on the next page tells you what will be on each test, how many questions there will be, and how much time you will have to complete each exam.

To pass the Language Arts, Writing test, you will need to know how to communicate with the written word in today's world. Business communications are a large part of the knowledge you will need: how to write letters and memos and how to write reports and complete applications. Since all of these require proper grammar and punctuation, this skill is part of the testing process. What is not tested is "everyday" spelling, since so much writing and composition is done today on computers and other machines with spell checkers.

The test on Writing also looks for composition skills—do the thoughts flow in a normal sequence. Is there a smooth or logical transition between paragraphs? All of these are part of writing. An essay is required and will be graded.

The Language Arts, Reading test looks for comprehension and analysis of what has been read. Most of the focus will be on fiction, but there will also be some content on non-fiction, including reading a business document. The test will also see if you can apply what you've read.

The Mathematics test covers algebra, geometry, number relations, and data analysis, including statistics. The candidate should be able to look at data and statistics and analyze the numbers in relation to questions posed. Additionally, problem-solving skills will be tested. Calculators are allowed during the first part of the exam but not the second part.

ROAD MAP

- *What is GED?*
- *What is Covered in the GED Tests?*
- *What is Needed to Pass the GED Tests?*
- *What is Covered in the Social Studies GED Test?*
- *What is the Breakdown of the Social Studies Test?*
- *Test-Taking Strategies and Tips*
- *Study Skills and Tips*

Test	Content Areas	Number of Questions	Time Limit (minutes)
Language Arts: Writing I	Correction—45% Revision—35% Construction Shift—20%	50	120 minutes
Language Arts: Writing II	Essay	250 words	
Social Studies	History—40% Geography—15% Civics & Government—25% Economics—20%	50	75 minutes
Science	Fundamental Science—60% Unifying Concepts & Processes—3.5% Science as Inquiry—8% Science as Technology—3.5% Science in Personal & Social Perspective—17% History & Nature—8%	50	85 minutes
Language Arts: Reading	Poetry—15% Drama—15% Fiction—45% Nonfiction Prose—25%	40	65 minutes
Mathematics Booklet One: Calculator Booklet Two: No Calculator	Procedural Knowledge—20% Conceptual Understanding—30% Application—50%	50	45 minutes (calculator) 45 minutes (non-calculator)

The Science test requires knowledge of a wide range of subjects and is based on the National Science Education Content Standards. The topics include earth and space science, physics, chemistry, and environmental and health sciences, with an emphasis on the latter. Tested will be an understanding of concepts and problem-solving skills.

The Social Studies Test covers United States history, economics, civics and government, and geography. (The Canadian test, of course, covers Canadian history and government.) More about this later.

WHAT IS NEEDED TO PASS THE GED TESTS?

To pass the GED tests, the candidate must obtain a minimum score of 225 points over the five (5) exams, as well as a minimum score per test. The number of points received for correct answers varies from question to question, test to test. You will need to check with the GED Testing Service in your state to determine what minimum score is permitted for each test. It is essential that you keep in mind the score on each individual test as well as the overall score of the combined tests. To illustrate this more clearly, look at the chart below.

	Sally	Anton	Maria
Test 1	56	44	42
Test 2	33	46	54
Test 3	44	45	39
Test 4	49	41	45
Test 5	44	48	47
Total	226	224	227

We will assume these students took the tests in the state of Iowa. The minimum score for all five exams is 225 points. The minimum score on any one exam is 35 points. With these testing requirements, Maria would have been the only person to have successfully passed the GED requirements. Sally earned the minimum of 225 points, but she fell below 35 points on Test 2. Anton scored over 35 on all of his tests, but failed to earn a total of 225 points.

WHAT IS COVERED IN THE SOCIAL STUDIES GED TEST?

The Social Studies test examines history, economics, civics and government, and geography. Not only knowledge of these topics is covered but also the candidate's ability to read maps, charts, graphs, cartoons, and a voters' guide or a tax form.

American history covers the growth of the United States from its earliest beginnings, through the Revolutionary and Civil Wars, western expansion and the plight of the Native Americans, the Industrial Revolution, and events of the Twentieth Century. Included will be the texts of notable American documents such as the Declaration of Independence, the U. S. Constitution, and landmark Supreme Court cases.

World History covers the history of Africa, South and Southeast Asia, East Asia, Latin America, Middle East, Western Europe, the Former Soviet Union and Eastern Europe, as well as the world today.

Economics covers the laws of supply and demand, how government taxation and spending affects local, state, and national economies, and other effects on the economy of an area or country. Once again, the ability to read and analyze charts and graphs is of the utmost importance.

Civics looks at the ways citizens interact with each other, volunteer organizations and governments. Government examines our federal, state, and local setups, including the checks and balances that the Founding Fathers wrote into the Constitution. Included are political parties and their effects on day-to-day government actions and elections. Although dealing primarily with the various governments in the United States, the candidate should also be aware of the other forms of government in existence around the world.

Geography requires map-reading skills, knowledge of longitude and latitude, climate, and natural and man-made resources among other areas of study. To be successful, the candidate should be able to answer questions based on maps and charts on a variety of these topics.

WHAT IS THE BREAKDOWN OF THE SOCIAL STUDIES TEST?

The Social Studies GED test will consist of fifty (50) multiple-choice questions. Twenty of the questions will be over a graphic such as a chart, graph, map or cartoon. Twenty questions will be over a reading passage of up to 250 words. Ten questions will include both a graphic and reading passage. Also tested is your ability to think about certain ideas and concepts. This means you will have to be able to do more than simply recall an answer or locate an answer in a provided passage. The way this is tested is by following what is known as Bloom's Taxonomy. This is illustrated in the chart below.

Understanding Material	20%
Applying Material	20%
Analyzing Material	40%
Evaluating Material	20%

TEST TAKING STRATEGIES AND TIPS

GED candidates, in order to pass the Social Studies GED test, should be able to look at visual or graphic sources (charts, maps, graphs, tables, diagrams, cartoons and photographs) and use those graphic sources to obtain information, evaluate and use the information, and determine the validity of the information as well as the source of that information.

The best way to develop and practice these skills is to read a variety of different materials from a variety of sources: magazines, newspapers, and Internet Web sites. Read federal and state income tax forms. Check out other sources of local, national and international news. Look at the graphics and analyze what information each is portraying. Is the information slanted in some way (very typical of political cartoons) or is it straightforward (such as a national poll on a particular topic)? What is each one saying? How reliable or accurate is that information (a national poll that only samples 450 people is less accurate, for example than the same poll conducted with 45,000 people).

For the geography part of the test, be sure to know the difference between longitude and latitude, parallels of latitude and meridians of longitude. Where is the equator? Where is the prime meridian? Map reading is a very important skill to have.

The night before the test, eat a good dinner and get a good night's rest. The morning of the test, eat a good breakfast and get to the testing center early so that you have time to "unwind" a bit—maybe chat with other candidates—before the exam. Then take the test knowing that you have done your best to prepare for it.

STUDY SKILLS AND TIPS

Everyone has a different way to study. Some people take notes based on what they are reading and then review the notes later to reinforce the reading material. Others highlight passages in their texts and skim those passages later to reinforce the reading. Others employ both methods to ensure they get the maximum information from their reading.

Be sure to give yourself plenty of time to study before taking the exam. Many candidates find that taking a course with an instructor gives them the needed structure to accomplish their goal. Others have the self-discipline to study on a regular basis without the structure of a class.

Regardless of which method you use to study and how you accomplish that, be sure that your study area is away from distractions (such as children, television, etc.), and that you study on a regular basis.

Above all, develop and practice the skills you will need to pass the exam. This means that you need to read as much as possible from as many different sources as possible.

Practice, practice, practice!

Pretest

75 Minutes 50 Questions

Directions: Choose the one best answer for each item.

Items 1 and 2 refer to the following information.

The Eastern Woodland people of North America lived in what is now the northeastern part of the United States. The Mohawk, Oneida, Seneca, and other groups lived by hunting, farming corn and squash, fishing, and gathering berries. By contrast, people of the Northwest, including Nootka, Tillamook, and Coos, survived by fishing for salmon, cod, herring, and halibut in the crowded streams and coastal waters and by using the trees of the huge forests of the area for many of their needs.

1. Salmon was a staple in the diet of the

    (1) Tillamook.
    (2) Seneca.
    (3) Mohawk.
    (4) Oneida.
    (5) people of the Northeast.

2. The passage indicates that a native people's way of living depended on

    (1) the fish available in the region.
    (2) the proximity of streams and coastal waters.
    (3) the crops and berries that grew in the region.
    (4) the geography and resources of the region.
    (5) the proximity of large forests.

3. When you enter a grocery store, you may find that the produce section is located near the entrance. Store owners believe the smells of fresh fruits and vegetables will make you hungry, which in turn will cause you to

    (1) sample the fresh produce as you shop.
    (2) leave the store and return after you have eaten.
    (3) purchase more food items.
    (4) search the shelves for your favorite brands.
    (5) rush through your shopping so you can go home to eat.

4. Forty-nine of the fifty states have bicameral, or two-house, legislatures. Nebraska is the only state with a unicameral, or one-house, legislature. What is one possible disadvantage of Nebraska's unicameral legislative system?

    (1) Bills might pass too quickly, without adequate consideration.
    (2) Voters would have fewer choices in elections.
    (3) Fewer people would have the opportunity to run for office.
    (4) One interest group could dominate the entire legislature.
    (5) The efficiency of state government could be obstructed.

Items 5 and 6 are based on the following passage.

"The accumulation of all powers, legislative, executive, and judiciary in the same hands . . . is the very definition of tyranny"

—From *Federalist 47* by James Madison

5. The fear expressed by James Madison is the fear of

    (1) concentration of power.
    (2) division of power.
    (3) executive authority.
    (4) an independent judiciary.
    (5) checks and balances.

6. The Constitution follows through on Madison's ideas by

    (1) dividing power between state and national governments.
    (2) separating power among the three branches of government.
    (3) adopting a Bill of Rights.
    (4) making ratification very difficult.
    (5) creating a complicated amending process.

7. The Articles of Confederation framed the first government of the United States. They were replaced by the

    (1) Declaration of Independence.
    (2) Constitution.
    (3) Northwest Ordinance.
    (4) Doctrine of Nullification.
    (5) Mayflower Compact.

8. In order to further protect the people against the threat of abusive government, the Anti-Federalists demanded and won the

    (1) Bill of Rights.
    (2) life term for federal judges.
    (3) two-term presidency.
    (4) taxation power of Congress.
    (5) term limits for all federal officials.

Items 9 and 10 refer to the time zone map below.

TIME ZONES IN THE 48 CONTIGUOUS STATES

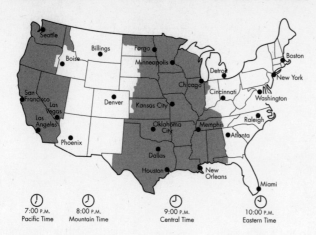

9. When it is 1 a.m. in Atlanta, what time is it in Los Angeles?

    (1) midnight
    (2) 2 a.m.
    (3) 1 p.m.
    (4) 11 p.m.
    (5) 10 p.m.

10. When it is 2 p.m. in Seattle, what time is it in San Francisco?

    (1) noon
    (2) 1 p.m.
    (3) 2 a.m.
    (4) 2 p.m.
    (5) 11 a.m.

Items 11–13 refer to the following graph.

COST OF AN AVERAGE TRADITIONAL WEDDING

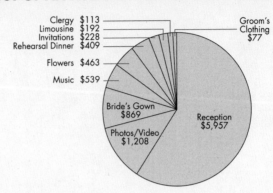

Clergy $113
Limousine $192
Invitations $228
Rehearsal Dinner $409
Flowers $463
Music $539
Bride's Gown $869
Photos/Video $1,208
Reception $5,957
Groom's Clothing $77

11. According to the graph, which two categories cost less than the limousine?

    (1) Invitations and clergy
    (2) Music and the flowers
    (3) Clergy and groom's clothing
    (4) Rehearsal dinner and invitations
    (5) Groom's and bride's clothing

12. A couple on a limited budget would save the most money by cutting back on which category?

    (1) The rehearsal dinner
    (2) The reception
    (3) The invitations
    (4) The photographs and video
    (5) The music

13. The average traditional wedding shown in the graph costs slightly more than $10,000. About what portion of that amount is the cost of the reception?

    (1) Less than 10 percent
    (2) About 90 percent
    (3) About 30 percent
    (4) A little less than half
    (5) About 60 percent

14. This president was the first to come from a western state and welcomed average people to his victory celebration, part of which was held on the White House lawn. Which president are we describing?

    (1) George Washington
    (2) Thomas Jefferson
    (3) Ronald Reagan
    (4) Andrew Jackson
    (5) James K. Polk

Items 15 and 16 are based on the following passage.

The preamble to the Declaration of Independence states in part:

"When in the course of human events it becomes necessary for one people to dissolve the political bands which have connected them with another . . . a decent respect to the opinions of mankind requires that they should declare the causes which impel them to separation."

15. Another word for preamble would be

    (1) conclusion.
    (2) introduction.
    (3) body.
    (4) appendix.
    (5) amendment.

16. The Declaration of Independence sets forth the

    (1) laws of the land.
    (2) reasons for revolting against England.
    (3) Bill of Rights.
    (4) new form of government.
    (5) reasons for the abolition of slavery.

17. In the first years of the existence of the United States, the right to vote was limited to white male landowners aged 21 or over. Since then there has been a gradual extension of this right to include women, minorities, and people aged 18 and over, regardless of economic status. Which statement best describes why this extension of rights has taken place?

    (1) The great growth in overall population has been the major cause of the extension of voting rights.
    (2) The idea has grown that all people are equal and should be treated as such.
    (3) The westward movement of white settlers in the 1800s led to the need for more voters west of the Mississippi River.
    (4) The elimination of slavery in 1865 was the main reason for this extension of rights.
    (5) More people today feel qualified to elect responsible leaders.

18. Which of the following men is best known as the leader of the American civil rights movement of the 1960s?

    (1) W. E. B. Du Bois
    (2) Jesse Jackson
    (3) Martin Luther King Jr.
    (4) Booker T. Washington
    (5) Marcus Garvey

19. In his January 1961 inaugural address, a new American president said, "Ask not what your country can do for you—ask what you can do for your country." Which president was this?

    (1) George Washington
    (2) Abraham Lincoln
    (3) Theodore Roosevelt
    (4) John F. Kennedy
    (5) Bill Clinton

Items 20–22 are based on the following cartoon.

20. This cartoon was drawn in 1874 during the era of rebuilding *after* the U.S. Civil War, known as the

    (1) Renaissance.
    (2) Reconstruction.
    (3) Reorganization.
    (4) Reformation.
    (5) Restructuring.

21. The motto above the head of the freed slaves, "worse than slavery" refers to

    (1) the work of the Freedman's Bureau.
    (2) the radical Republicans.
    (3) the development of the Ku Klux Klan and other white reactionary groups.
    (4) Southern lifestyles unfamiliar to African Americans.
    (5) service in the African American regiments of the Union army.

22. A logical conclusion drawn from this cartoon is that

    (1) the Civil War was a total success.
    (2) African American in the South had a wonderful life as a result of the Civil War.
    (3) true freedom for the African American would be a long struggle.
    (4) the Klan was able and ready to help African Americans.
    (5) Reconstruction succeeded in extending equality to the freed slaves.

Items 23–25 refer to the globe.

LATITUDE AND LONGITUDE

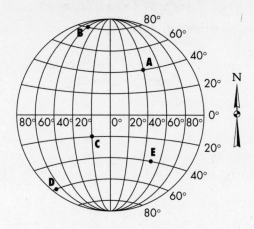

23. Which point on the globe can be found at 80 degrees north, 60 degrees west?

    (1)   Point A
    (2)   Point B
    (3)   Point C
    (4)   Point D
    (5)   Point E

24. Which point probably has the warmest year-round weather?

    (1)   Point A
    (2)   Point B
    (3)   Point C
    (4)   Point D
    (5)   Point E

25. A traveler going from point B to point E would travel in which direction?

    (1)   North
    (2)   West
    (3)   Southeast
    (4)   Southwest
    (5)   Northwest

Items 26–28 refer to the following information.

To help America recover from the Great Depression, President Franklin Delano Roosevelt's administration got Congress to enact laws that created the following programs:

Rural Electrification Administration, which provided low-cost electricity to isolated rural areas.

Civilian Conservation Corps, which provided jobs for young, single men on conservation projects for the federal government.

Works Progress Administration, which created as many jobs as possible as quickly as possible, from electrician to violinist, and paid wages with government funds.

Banking Act of 1935, which created a seven-member board of public officials to regulate the nation's money supply and interest rates on loans.

Tennessee Valley Authority, which developed natural resources of the Tennessee Valley.

26. Today's powerful Federal Reserve Board, which sets interest rates charged by the Federal Reserve Bank, is an outgrowth of which legislative initiative of the 1930s?

   (1) The Rural Electrification Administration
   (2) The Civilian Conservation Corps
   (3) The Works Progress Administration
   (4) The Banking Act of 1935
   (5) The Tennessee Valley Authority

27. A farmer in rural Oregon was probably most interested in which of the five government initiatives?

   (1) The Rural Electrification Administration
   (2) The Civilian Conservation Corps
   (3) The Works Progress Administration
   (4) The Banking Act of 1935
   (5) The Tennessee Valley Authority

28. The social legislation of the 1930s had a profound and lasting effect on American society. Today some people believe that this effect was not an entirely positive one. Which statement probably best describes those people's beliefs today?

   (1) The federal government spends too much money on foreign aid.
   (2) The federal government should take more control of public education and agencies that deal with child abuse.
   (3) The Tennessee Valley Authority was an overly ambitious project that destroyed the natural beauty of the Tennessee Valley.
   (4) Too many social programs of today are not as well administered as were those of the 1930s.
   (5) Social programs have created a nation of people who depend on the government too much for the everyday things of life.

29. From 1919 to 1933, Americans lived with a constitutional amendment that forbade the making, selling, or transporting of intoxicating liquors for drinking purposes. During that time, now often referred to as the Roaring 20s, a great deal of liquor was illegally manufactured, transported, sold, and consumed. Large, well-organized groups of violent criminals made huge profits on this illegal activity. Which of the following people may cite that national experience to support his or her point of view today?

(1) Someone who favors the decriminalization of drugs
(2) Someone who wants to increase the number of government drug inspectors at major seaports and airline terminals
(3) Someone who works for a liquor manufacturer today
(4) Someone who believes there is too much violence on TV
(5) Someone who wants much higher "sin taxes" on items such as liquor and tobacco products

30. George Washington was chosen president of the Constitutional Convention in 1787 and was then overwhelmingly elected to serve as the first president of the new republic in 1789 and 1792. Washington is associated with which of the following wars?

(1) The French and Indian War
(2) The Revolutionary War
(3) The War of 1812
(4) The Civil War
(5) The Spanish-American War

31. With which act of government is President Abraham Lincoln most closely associated?

(1) The Monroe Doctrine
(2) The Louisiana Purchase
(3) The Emancipation Proclamation
(4) The Roosevelt Corollary
(5) The Truman Doctrine

Items 32 and 33 refer to the following passage.

The removal of Native Americans from land desired by white settlers began long before Americans crossed the Mississippi River. The Indian Removal Act of 1830 gave the U.S. government authority to relocate the native people of the South and Northwest to Indian Territory, an area set aside west of the Mississippi. There they would "cast off their savage habits and become an interesting, civilized, and Christian community," said President Jackson. During the forced migration, disease, severe weather, and hardships on the trail took their toll; thousands of Native Americans died. The Cherokee had a particularly hard time. Of about 20,000 removed from their homes, 4,000 died on the journey, which came to be known as the "Trail of Tears."

32. The Indian Removal Act was a justification of the American policy of

    (1) Manifest Destiny.
    (2) expansion.
    (3) "civilizing" Native Americans.
    (4) Native American relocation.
    (5) settlement west of the Mississippi River.

33. The Cherokees' name for their journey, "Trail of Tears," suggests that they

    (1) were forced to migrate against their will.
    (2) were not as civilized as other tribes.
    (3) planned to hurt the people responsible for their move.
    (4) wept constantly on the trail.
    (5) viewed the journey with bitterness and sorrow.

Items 34 and 35 refer to the following passage.

The railroad changed the way Americans viewed time. Before, most people used the sun to set their clocks. Because the sun appears to move across the sky from east to west, a city a little to the east of a neighboring town marked noon a few minutes earlier. In the early days of the railroad, each city and each railroad had its own time. The main terminal in Buffalo, New York, had four clocks, one for each railroad using the train station and one on "Buffalo time." In 1883, an association of railroad managers ended the confusion with Standard Railway Time. They divided the nation into time zones, and every community within a time zone was on the same time. An Indianapolis newspaper noted, "The sun is no longer [the boss]. People—55,000,000 people—must now eat, sleep, and work, as well as travel by railroad time." In 1918, Standard Railway Time became federal law.

34. Standard Railway Time most likely had the effect of

(1) placing all cities in the same time zone.
(2) confusing the public.
(3) establishing two main time zones.
(4) improving railroad efficiency.
(5) making trains run faster.

35. The Indianapolis newspaper viewed railroad time as

(1) a great innovation.
(2) a dangerous move.
(3) an example of the power of the railroad.
(4) unnecessary.
(5) unnatural.

36. Mapmakers use parallels of latitude and meridians of longitude to determine the exact locations of places on earth. The exact location of any place is where

(1) the prime meridian crosses the equator.
(2) two meridians intersect.
(3) two parallels intersect.
(4) a particular parallel intersects a particular meridian.
(5) 60 degrees north latitude intersects 30 degrees west longitude.

Items 37 and 38 refer to the following information.

Other factors besides latitude may affect the climate of a region.

Ocean currents can warm or cool shorelines as they pass.

Oceans and large lakes, which do not lose or gain heat as quickly as land does, may cause milder temperatures nearby.

Mountains affect rainfall by forcing clouds to rise up and over them. As air rises, it cools. Since cold air cannot hold as much moisture as warm air, the clouds drop their moisture as they rise.

37. Inland areas, away from the coast, are likely to be

    (1)   colder in winter than places near a coast.
    (2)   warmer in winter than places near a coast.
    (3)   rainier than places near a coast.
    (4)   drier than places near a coast.
    (5)   similar in temperature and rainfall to places near a coast.

38. Although Valdez, a port in Alaska, lies near the Arctic Circle, it is free of ice all year long. The most likely explanation is that

    (1)   winds that blow over water are warmer than winds that blow over land.
    (2)   mountains block the cold winds.
    (3)   Valdez is warmed by an ocean current.
    (4)   the ocean does not gain or lose heat as quickly as land.
    (5)   Valdez is affected by prevailing winds.

39. For which of the following activities would knowledge of relative location be more helpful than information about longitude and latitude?

    (1)   Piloting a plane
    (2)   Driving a car
    (3)   Sailing on the ocean
    (4)   Surveying a state's borders
    (5)   Laying out a new city

Item 40 refers to the circle graph below.

WATER SUPPLY

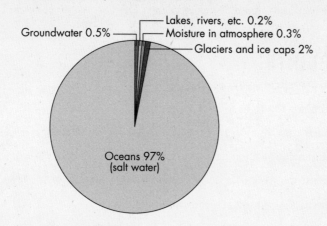

Groundwater 0.5%
Lakes, rivers, etc. 0.2%
Moisture in atmosphere 0.3%
Glaciers and ice caps 2%

Oceans 97%
(salt water)

40. The graph suggests that people could increase their fresh water supply significantly if they could find an inexpensive way to

    (1)   melt the glaciers.
    (2)   reach aquifers and other sources of groundwater.
    (3)   turn salt water into fresh water.
    (4)   channel water from places that have too much water to those that have too little.
    (5)   clean polluted rivers and lakes.

41. In the United States, power is divided among several branches of government so that no one branch has too much power. This division is called

    (1)   separate-but-equal policy.
    (2)   the system of checks and balances.
    (3)   the process of amendment.
    (4)   judicial review.
    (5)   representative democracy.

Items 42 and 43 refer to the following information.

The Constitution provides for changing times with a process for amendment, or change. Today, the Constitution includes 26 amendments. The first ten amendments, called the Bill of Rights, are outlined below.

BILL OF RIGHTS

First Amendment: religious and political freedom

Second Amendment: the right to bear arms

Third Amendment: the right to refuse to house soldiers in peacetime

Fourth Amendment: protection against unreasonable search and seizure

Fifth Amendment: the right of accused persons to due process of the law

Sixth Amendment: the right to a speedy and public trial

Seventh Amendment: the right to a jury trial in civil cases

Eighth Amendment: protection against cruel and unusual punishment

Ninth Amendment: the rights of the people to powers that may not be spelled out in the Constitution

Tenth Amendment: the rights of the people and the states to powers not otherwise given to the federal government, states, or people

42. Which two amendments provide for changes over time in the circumstances and realities of American life?

    (1) The First and Second Amendments
    (2) The Fifth and Sixth Amendments
    (3) The Third and Fourth Amendments
    (4) The Ninth and Tenth Amendments
    (5) The Seventh and Eighth Amendments

43. A family that was forced by the U.S. Army to provide housing and food for a group of soldiers could appeal to the courts based on which amendment to the Constitution?

    (1) The Sixth Amendment
    (2) The Third Amendment
    (3) The Second Amendment
    (4) The Ninth Amendment
    (5) The Tenth Amendment

When people make economic decisions, they must often give up something; for example, they give up taking a vacation in order to save for a car. The value of the thing given up is called opportunity cost. In another example, Maria is trying to decide whether to take a part-time night job that pays $200 per week or take courses for credit at the local community college. Her uncle will pay for her tuition and books if she decides to go to college. In addition, he will give her $100 per week.

44. What is Maria's opportunity cost of going to college?

(1) $100 per week
(2) College credits
(3) The $200-per-week job
(4) Payment for tuition and books
(5) Working too slowly toward her degree

45. Why does Maria's decision involve opportunity cost?

(1) She doesn't want her uncle to pay her college costs.
(2) She wants both to work and to go to school.
(3) Her resources (her uncle's money) are endless, so she can choose to take classes.
(4) Her resources (time and money) are limited, so she must make a choice.
(5) She would rather go to college than work at night.

46. In recent years, mail-order catalog sales have increased substantially over previous years. What is the best explanation for this increase?

(1) People are too lazy to shop in stores.
(2) People respond favorably to lower prices in catalogs and the convenience of ordering by mail.
(3) People respond favorably to lower catalog prices.
(4) People like the convenience of ordering by mail.
(5) People are effectively persuaded to buy from catalogs.

Items 47 and 48 refer to the following graph.

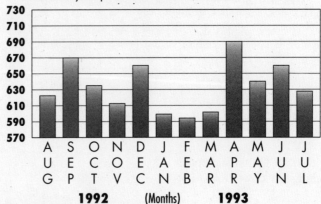

NEW HOME SALES
Seasonally Adjusted Annual Rate, Thousands of Units

Source: U.S. Department of Commerce

47. Which is the best description of the market for new homes shown in the graph?

(1) The market is on a decreasing trend.
(2) The market is on an increasing trend.
(3) Compared to 1991, the market is good.
(4) There doesn't seem to be an overall trend in the market for the time period shown.
(5) Sales of between 600,000 and 700,000 houses are pretty good for the time period shown.

48. For the period April through July 1993, the home sales trend is

(1) flat.
(2) increasing.
(3) neither increasing nor decreasing.
(4) decreasing.
(5) lower than it should be

Items 49–50 refer to the following illustration:

Purchasing Power of the Dollar

49. This illustration tells the story of the value of money in selected years. The base year, in which the dollar could buy a dollar's worth of goods, must be

(1)   2001
(2)   1976
(3)   1967
(4)   1983
(5)   1900

50. As the buying power of the dollar decreases, which economic condition becomes more likely?

(1)   Recession
(2)   Depression
(3)   Inflation
(4)   Deflation
(5)   Deficit

ANSWERS AND EXPLANATIONS

1. **The correct answer is (1). (Comprehension)** The Tillamook group lived in the Northwest, where the tribes fished for salmon.

2. **The correct answer is (4). (Comprehension)** The passage shows that the native peoples in both areas of the country relied on locally available game and plants (such as fish and berries) for food and on geographic characteristics, such as forests, for their other needs.

3. **The correct answer is (3). (Analysis)** Store owners hope that your hunger will cause you to buy more food.

4. **The correct answer is (4). (Analysis)** The system of checks and balances, which prevents one group from gaining too much power, might not operate as well in Nebraska's one-house legislature as it does in two-house legislatures. There is no evidence that bills pass too quickly in Nebraska as suggested in choice (1). Government efficiency, choice (5), might be improved with only one house, and voters might welcome fewer choices, choice (2). In a state with a small population, fewer candidates, choice (3), would be an advantage.

5. **The correct answer is (1). (Analysis)** The consequence of placing all power in the hands of one person or branch would be a concentration of power leading to dictatorship or tyranny.

6. **The correct answer is (2). (Application)** The outline of government described in the Federalist Papers was carried out in the provisions of the Constitution.

7. **The correct answer is (2). (Application)** The Articles of Confederation provided a framework of government, as does the Constitution which followed.

8. **The correct answer is (1). (Analysis)** The term Anti-Federalists describes those who were opposed to the Constitution. The only way some of these leaders would support the Constitution is through the inclusion of a Bill of Rights to guarantee limited government.

9. **The correct answer is (5). (Application)** As the map shows, the later times are in the east, and the time difference is three hours from east coast to west coast.

10. **The correct answer is (4). (Application)** A time zone covers all of one north-to-south area (a vertical strip on the map). Seattle and San Francisco both lie on the Pacific Ocean and therefore are in the same time zone.

11. **The correct answer is (3). (Comprehension)** According to the circle graph, the clergy costs $113 and the groom's clothing costs $77, which are both less than $192, the cost of the limousine.

12. **The correct answer is (2). (Application)** Since the reception is by far the greatest single expense, the greatest saving probably could be made there.

13. **The correct answer is (5). (Analysis)** If the wedding cost about $10,000 and the cost of the reception was just under $6,000, then a little more than half, or about 60 percent, of the total cost was for the reception.

14. **The correct answer is (4). (Evaluation)** We can eliminate choices (1) and (2) based on their birthplace, and choice (3) is a Westerner but not the first.

15. **The correct answer is (2). (Comprehension)** The prefix "pre" indicates "coming before."

16. **The correct answer is (2). (Analysis)** The passage indicates that the causes of separation will be discussed.

17. **The correct answer is (2). (Evaluation)** A growing belief in the essential equality of all people is the core factor that has led to an extension of voting rights.

18. **The correct answer is (3). (Application)** Martin Luther King Jr. was the great leader of the 1960s American civil rights movement. Choices (1), (4), and (5) are African American leaders of the early 1900s, and choice (2) is a leader of today.

19. **The correct answer is (4). (Application)** The sentence is probably the most famous utterance of John F. Kennedy throughout his entire presidency. A clue to the correct answer is the part of the question that tells in what year the statement was made.

20. **The correct answer is (2). (Comprehension)** A synonym for the rebuilding era is Reconstruction.

21. **The correct answer is (3). (Analysis)** The cartoon illustrates the Klan and white reactionary groups causing terror among the freed blacks.

22. **The correct answer is (3). (Application)** The struggle for equality would take more than 100 years after Reconstruction.

23. **The correct answer is (2). (Comprehension)** Point B is at about 80 degrees north latitude and 60 degrees west longitude.

24. **The correct answer is (3). (Application)** Places near the equator generally have warmer climates than places near either the North Pole or South Pole.

25. **The correct answer is (3). (Application)** A traveler would move in a south-easterly direction when going from point B to point E.

26. **The correct answer is (4). (Analysis)** The 1935 Banking Act created a group to regulate the money supply and interest rates, very much as the Federal Reserve Board does today.

27. **The correct answer is (1). (Analysis)** The nationwide spread of cheap electricity to rural areas probably would have held the most interest for an Oregon farmer, so choice (1) is correct. Choice (2) might have been involved in conservation projects nearby, but there is nothing to indicate an even national spread. Choices (3) and (4) would have had no more effect on a rural farmer than on any other person in the nation, and choice (5) was for a specific geographic region of which Oregon was not a part.

28. **The correct answer is (5). (Evaluation)** Since the programs of the 1930s created many jobs with the government and brought new services to citizens, the dependence on the government grew. Many efforts of government since the 1930s have also meant a larger role in peoples' lives for official agencies. Some people believe this growing role has led to a dependence that is not a positive factor of American life today.

29. **The correct answer is (1). (Evaluation)** The similarity of crime today because of illegal drug sales to the crime caused in the 1920s by illegal liquor sales could be cited as a possible reason to change drug laws by someone who favors such a decriminalization.

30. **The correct answer is (2). (Application)** George Washington was a general and commander-in-chief of the colonial armies in the American Revolution. The dates of his presidency are clues you can use to arrive at the correct answer (the Revolution was fought between 1775–1783). The French and Indian War was earlier in the 18th century (1754–1763), while the remaining three wars were fought in the nineteenth century.

31. **The correct answer is (3). (Application)** Abraham Lincoln issued the Emancipation Proclamation in 1865. Choices (1), (4), and (5) all include the names of other presidents, which should tell you that these choices are incorrect, even if the specific action or stance is not well known. The Louisiana Purchase, choice (2), made by President Thomas Jefferson in 1803, more than doubled the size of the United States at that time.

32. **The correct answer is (2). (Analysis)** The information in Lesson 2 and in the passage indicates that white settlers wanted more land. This passage shows that the U.S. government pursued a policy of helping the settlers take the land from the native people. Manifest Destiny, choice (1), was a feeling, not a policy. The government was interested in land, not Native American civilization, choice (3), and Native American relocation, choice (4), was an effect of the policy of expansion. Settlement west of the Mississippi, choice (5), was not an issue in 1830.

33. **The correct answer is (5). (Comprehension)** The Cherokees viewed their forced migration, choice (1), with great bitterness. There is no evidence in the passage that they actually wept, choice (4), or planned to hurt people, choice (3). Their level of civilization, choice (2), was not related to their hardships.

34. **The correct answer is (4). (Analysis)** The passage strongly implies that different times caused confusion and standard time lessened the confusion. The fact that the entire country adopted Standard Railway Time indicates that the new standard time had improved efficiency.

35. **The correct answer is (3). (Comprehension)** The writer complained that railroad time controlled fifty-five million people—an example of the railroad's power.

36. **The correct answer is (4). (Comprehension)** The grid system of intersecting parallels and meridians allows the identification of specific locations. Choices (1) and (5) each identify a specific place. Choices (2) and (3) are not possible.

37. **The correct answer is (1). (Application)** The passage refers to the effect of large bodies of water on temperature. It suggests that such bodies of water have a moderating effect on temperatures. Therefore, places inland are likely to be colder in winter and warmer in summer than places near a coast.

38. **The correct answer is (3). (Analysis)** As a port, Valdez lies along an ocean, so choice (2) is incorrect. Choices (1) and (4) are incorrect because they explain only why Valdez might have more moderate temperatures than places inland. They do not explain why those temperatures are above freezing. Choice (5) is incorrect because prevailing winds can bring warm or cold temperatures to a place.

39. **The correct answer is (2). (Analysis)** Drivers rely on landmarks to find their way. The other activities require a knowledge of absolute location.

40. **The correct answer is (3). (Evaluation)** The graph shows that most of the world's water is salt water.

41. **The correct answer is (2). (Comprehension)** Any one branch of government is prevented from growing too powerful by the system of checks and balances.

42. **The correct answer is (4). (Analysis)** The Ninth and Tenth Amendments give powers not otherwise described to the people and to the states.

43. **The correct answer is (2). (Application)** The Third Amendment protects citizens from having to house and feed troops during peacetime.

44. **The correct answer is (3). (Application)** By choosing to attend college, Maria gives up the opportunity of earning $200 per week.

45. **The correct answer is (4). (Analysis)** Maria's decision involves a choice between the part-time job and college classes. Because she can't be in two places at once or pay her college costs, choosing one means giving up the other.

46. **The correct answer is (2). (Analysis)** While people may like lower prices, choice (3), and convenience, choice (4), a combination of these reasons is a better explanation.

47. **The correct answer is (4). (Analysis)** Home sales are up one month and down the next, meaning that there is no discernible trend in this market.

48. **The correct answer is (4). (Analysis)** With the exception of the month of June 1993, there is a decreasing trend over the four-month period.

49. **The correct answer is (3). (Evaluation)** Although 1967 does not appear in the actual illustration, it is the base year which is used for comparison with the others.

50. **The correct answer is (3). (Comprehension)** The shrinking buying power of the dollar is the definition of inflation.

Introduction to the GED Test

Before we get started with the information you need to know about the GED (General Education Development) tests, you should be congratulated for the effort you have put into finishing your education. Since 1949, more than 14 million other adults have finished their education and received their GED credential the same way you are about to do. Originally the GED tests were created for returning World War II veterans whose educations were interrupted by the war. Through the years, though, the focus of the GED tests has changed and the GED tests are now suited for adults like you who either want to finish their education or complete job or college requirements.

The GED tests are standardized tests that measure skills currently required of high school graduates throughout the United States and Canada. The tests cover academic areas including writing skills, social studies, science, reading, and mathematics. To pass the tests and receive your diploma, you must show a mastery of skills equal to or greater than the top two-thirds of high school graduates in the United States and Canada.

Many times each year the GED Testing Service of the American Council on Education administers the tests throughout the United States and Canada and offers the tests in English, French, Spanish, large print, Braille and even audio tape format. To learn more about when and where the GED will be administered in your area, contact the GED Testing Service:

General Educational Development
GED Testing Service
American Council on Education
One Dupont Circle, NW
Washington, D.C. 20036
1-800-626-9433
www.gedtest.org

CONTENT AND FORMAT OF THE GED TEST

As mentioned in the earlier paragraphs, the GED tests measure skills in the areas of writing skills, social studies, science, reading, and mathematics. Each subject area is tested on a separate section of the GED. Although this book deals specifically with the Social Studies test, let's look briefly at each of the other tests you will be taking.

WRITING SKILLS

The first test is a two-part test that measures writing skills. Part One of this test contains 50 multiple-choice questions, which you have 75 minutes to complete. This part of the test covers areas of grammar including sentence structure, word usage, punctuation, capitalization, and spelling. Part Two of this test is a 45-minute essay in

ROAD MAP

- *Content and Format of the GED Test*
- *Scoring the Test*

which you are expected to demonstrate a mastery of proper grammar and usage. The essay topic will be provided for you in your test booklet.

SOCIAL STUDIES

This test, discussed in greater detail later in the next chapter, contains 50 multiple-choice questions in the area of social studies. You will have 75 minutes to complete this test. The Social Studies test includes questions from history, economics, civics and government, and geography. The questions measure skills such as comprehension, analysis, evaluation and application within the context of social studies.

SCIENCE

The third test, the Science test, contains 50 multiple-choice questions that are to be completed in 85 minutes. The science questions cover life sciences and physical sciences. Like the Social Studies test, the Science test measures skills such as comprehension, analysis, evaluation, and application but within the context of life and physical sciences.

LANGUAGE ARTS, READING

The fourth test, Language Arts, Reading, is a 40-question test that you will have 65 minutes to complete. This test contains questions that deal with popular literature, classical literature and commentary on both literature and art. More than half of the questions measures comprehension skills. Many of the excerpts used as sources will be from plays, prose, and poetry (from a variety of time periods and cultures) as well as critical reviews of literature or the performing arts.

MATHEMATICS

The Mathematics test contains 50 questions that are to be answered in 90 minutes. This test contains two test booklets. Part One of this test, in the first test booklet, allows you to use a calculator. Part Two does not allow you to use a calculator. The questions on the Mathematics test deal with geometry, algebra, and arithmetic.

SCORING THE TEST

You will receive a score report that lists six different scores. You will receive a score for each of the two parts of the Language Arts, Writing test and a score for each of the other tests (the Social Studies, Science, and Language Arts, Reading tests). The sixth and final score on your score report will be the average of the five other scores.

Because requirements vary from state to state, there is not one particular score you must achieve in order to pass. In most cases, a state will require you to receive a minimum score on each of the subject area tests in addition to a minimum average score. You should check with the GED Testing Service or your state's Department of Education to determine the score you need to pass the GED.

The Social Studies Section of the GED

As you know, this book was written specifically to prepare you for the Social Studies section of the GED. In this section, you will learn about the content areas covered on the GED Social Studies test, the skills necessary for success on the test, the types of questions you can expect to see, and strategies for being successful.

CONTENT AREAS OF THE GED SOCIAL STUDIES TEST

The Social Studies section of the GED measures your ability to use concepts in a variety of ways in four different content areas: history, economics, civics and government, and geography. You will not be tested on random facts or trivial information from these content areas. Additionally, prior knowledge of these subject areas is not essential to your success on the GED Social Studies test. Instead, you will need to use your reading comprehension and analytical skills within the context of history, economics, political science and geography.

More than half of the Social Studies test questions will be based upon various reading passages, some of which may be up to 250 words in length. The remaining questions will be based upon maps, charts, cartoons, or other items known as visuals. The Social Studies test will contain at least one excerpt from one of the following documents: the U.S. Declaration of Independence, the U.S. Constitution, the Federalist Papers, or a landmark U.S. Supreme Court case.

HISTORY

Of the 50 multiple-choice questions on the Social Studies section of the GED, over 40 percent will come from the content area of history. In fact, questions from the content area of history will make up a higher percentage of the Social Studies test than ever before. Within the area of history, most of the questions will deal with U.S. history (or Canadian if you are taking the test in Canada) and the rest will deal with world history. History can be defined as the record of past events or as the subject matter that makes up those records. The Social Studies test questions are going to require you to work with some of these records and glean information from them by using reading comprehension skills or analytical skills. Remember, the questions from this content area will not require you to recall random historical facts such as names, dates or other trivial information, so you need only be able to work within a historical context to be successful with the history questions. However, if you have a good background in history, particularly in U.S. (or Canadian) history, you will have an advantage when dealing with these questions. It is possible that some anthropology concepts may appear within the world history questions.

ROAD MAP

- *Content Areas of the GED Social Studies Test*
- *Four Skills Necessary for Success on the GED Social Studies Test*
- *Source Material for GED Social Studies Test Questions*
- *Types of Questions Found on the GED Social Studies Test and Strategies for Each Type of Question*
- *General GED Test-Taking Tips*

CIVICS AND GOVERNMENT

Political science questions will comprise 25 percent of the Social Studies test. The political science questions will deal with both civics and government. It is likely that the excerpt from one of the documents mentioned earlier (the U.S. Declaration of Independence, the U.S. Constitution, the Federalist Papers, or a landmark U.S. Supreme Court case) will appear as a source for some of the political science questions. As with the history questions, it is possible that anthropology concepts may be integrated into the civics and government material.

ECONOMICS

Economics questions, or those dealing with the study of how humans use resources to meet their material needs, will comprise 20 percent of the Social Studies test. It is possible that some psychology concepts may appear within the economics questions in areas such as advertising or consumer behavior.

GEOGRAPHY

The final category of questions found on the Social Studies test, geography, accounts for 15 percent of the total Social Studies questions. Geography questions deal with the study of the earth's physical features and the way humans adapt to the features.

BEHAVIORAL SCIENCE

On the Social Studies test prior to 2002, the behavioral sciences (anthropology, psychology, and sociology) were tested as a separate content area. Beginning in 2002, however, the behavioral sciences will not be tested as a separate content area. There will be no question or set of questions dealing only with any of the behavioral sciences. Rather, as mentioned earlier, the concepts of the behavioral sciences may be integrated into other areas of the Social Studies test, such as law, religion, culture, etc.

FOUR SKILLS NECESSARY FOR SUCCESS ON THE GED SOCIAL STUDIES TEST

To be successful on the GED Social Studies test, you will need to demonstrate proficiency in several critical thinking skill areas: comprehension, application, analysis, and evaluation. You will use these critical thinking skills throughout the Social Studies test. Let's examine each skill more closely.

COMPREHENSION

On the GED Social Studies test you will encounter reading passages, cartoons, graphs, charts, and other materials on which questions will be based. In order to successfully answer the questions, you will need good comprehension skills. In other words, you must be able to read a passage or look at a visual and understand what you read or see. Additionally, to demonstrate your comprehension of a source, you may need to identify the main idea of a paragraph or cartoon.

APPLICATION

Some questions on the Social Studies test deal with application. The application questions will require you to use information from a passage, chart, graph, or some other source in way that is different from the way it is presented to you. This critical thinking skill will help you use information you already have in a new situation.

ANALYSIS

The Social Studies test contains many questions that require analysis of information. Basically, analysis is breaking down ideas and information into more basic elements. For example, some questions may require you to use analysis to identify cause and effect. Other questions may require you to distinguish between fact and opinion or between supporting statements and a conclusion. This critical thinking skill will help you break down large amounts of information into smaller, more manageable pieces.

EVALUATION

The fourth critical thinking skill you will need to be successful on the Social Studies test is evaluation. With questions that require evaluation, you may need to determine a statement's validity or accuracy. You may also have to determine whether or not there is enough information to make an accurate evaluation of the given information. Some evaluation questions may involve points of view and statements that either reflect or oppose those points of view. This critical thinking skill will be especially important in dealing with reading passages, quotes, and historical documents.

By working through the sample questions provided in later chapters and by working through the practice tests in the back of this book, you will sharpen each of the four critical thinking skills you need to be successful on the Social Studies test: comprehension, application, analysis, and evaluation.

SOURCE MATERIAL FOR GED SOCIAL STUDIES TEST QUESTIONS

The questions on the Social Studies test will be based on a variety of sources of information, such as an article, an excerpt of a textbook, a graph, or a map. Some questions may be single questions related to a particular source. Other questions may be grouped together in sets of three or four questions, each of which are related to the source. The two basic types of sources used on the Social Studies test are called primary sources and secondary sources. Primary sources are those that are original and contemporary to whatever event or issue the source documents. A good example of a primary source is a diary entry or a newspaper article. Secondary sources are those that are based on primary sources or other secondary sources.

The Social Studies test employs a wide variety of both primary and secondary source materials, which include prose-only, visual-only, and combined sources. Prose-only sources are those such as speeches, letters, laws, articles, or textbooks, to name just a few. Visual-only sources, also referred to as visuals, include cartoons, maps, charts, tables or diagrams. Combined sources use both prose and graphics as the basis for questions. When working with these questions, remember that you will not have to recognize or identify any of the documents. Rather, you will just need to comprehend, evaluate, or analyze the source and work with the information you are given.

TYPES OF QUESTIONS FOUND ON THE GED SOCIAL STUDIES TEST AND STRATEGIES FOR EACH TYPE OF QUESTION

The questions on the Social Studies test are written in multiple-choice format. Some of the questions will be based on reading passages and some will be based on visuals. Each of the questions will require you to use at least one of the four critical thinking skills. In this section of the book, we will examine each of these possibilities and show you exactly what you need to know about how to approach each type of question.

MULTIPLE-CHOICE QUESTIONS

All of the questions on the Social Studies test will be multiple choice questions with five possible answers; each of the possible answers for each question will be numbered 1–5. When answering multiple-choice questions, it is very important that you completely read the passage or completely survey the visual that will be used as the source for the question or questions. The next step, also very important, is to read the question carefully and make sure that you understand exactly what the question is asking. After you have the first two steps complete, carefully read through each of the possible answers. If you can eliminate any of the answer choices as incorrect, mark through them and forget about them. Try to eliminate as many of the incorrect answers as possible. You may narrow your choices down to two possible choices that seem as though they could both be correct. However, only one answer is the correct answer. When you choose the correct answer, circle your choice and move on. Be confident in your answer and don't second-guess yourself. Your first choice is most probably the correct one!

READING PASSAGE ITEMS

As mentioned earlier, many of the questions on the Social Studies test, approximately 40 percent, will be based on a reading passage. The passage may be up to 250 words in length and may be an excerpt from a speech, a textbook, a law, a government document, or some other social studies work. When dealing with a reading passage, it is always a good idea to look first for the main idea of the passage. In a paragraph, the main idea is often (but not always) stated in the first sentence or two. If that is the case, the rest of the paragraph will most probably be details that support the main idea. When you find the main idea of the paragraph, underline it or circle it. This will help you remember the main idea and will help you locate it later if necessary. This is also an important step because some of the test questions may ask you to identify the main idea of a source. If the source is a list, look for the main idea in the heading. If the source is a quote, look for a sentence that summarizes the rest of the thought expressed within the quote. It is possible, though, that in some cases you will have to summarize the passage yourself and determine the main idea. Let's look at an example of a reading passage item and a question about the passage.

Item 1 refers to the following paragraph.

Line   John Adams, the second President of the United States, once remarked, "The education of our children is never out of my mind. Train them to virtue. Habituate them to industry, activity, and spirit . . . For God's sake make your children hardy, active, and industrious; for strength, activity, and industry will be their only resource and dependence."

1. Which of the following statements best sums up the passage?

   (1) It is important for the children of a President to be active.
   (2) It is important for the education of children to include such elements as virtue and work ethic.
   (3) Children of the President should be educated in a different manner than other children.
   (4) Children should be educated in such a way that they will be trained to work in major industries.
   (5) Educating children is not as important as training children to be active.

The correct answer is (2). After you have read the passage carefully and have read each of the possible answer choices, you are ready to answer the question. You can eliminate (5) because Adams indicates that education is on his mind and therefore important. You can eliminate (1) and (3) because it is not reasonable to expect the President to be speaking only of the education of his own children and not children in a broader sense. With only two options left, you can eliminate (4) because the word *industry* is not used in the passage to represent a craft, a trade, an occupation, or a business. By eliminating all of the incorrect possibilities, you have narrowed the options to (2), the correct answer. Clearly, (2) echoes the thoughts of Adams that children should be educated in such a manner that virtue and industrious activity will be important to them.

When you read the passages on the Social Studies test, you may encounter a word within the passage's text that you do not recognize or that you do not understand. If you do, don't worry. You can use context clues to figure out the meaning of the unfamiliar word. Let's refer back to the paragraph above to look at an example of word that may be confusing for a test taker. Perhaps you recognize the word *hardy* but you do not understand its meaning. Use the words around *hardy* as clues to the meaning of *hardy*. Look at the line "make your children hardy, active, and industrious." Now look at the line of text that immediately follows: "for strength, activity, and industry will be their only resource." By looking carefully at the words around *hardy* and the string of words in the line that follows, especially the word *strength*, you can conclude that *hardy* is a synonym of strong. If you follow these steps each time you encounter an unfamiliar word, you should be able to figure out the meaning of the word and then answer the question correctly.

VISUAL ITEMS

Approximately 40 percent of the questions on the Social Studies test will be based on a graphic of some kind. About 10 percent of the questions will be based on a combination of a graphic and a reading passage. These graphic-based questions are known as visuals. The graphics in the visuals may be political cartoons, graphs, charts, tables, maps, or some other type of illustration. The questions about the visuals measure your ability to interpret the meaning of the graphic. Even if you do not recognize the graphic in a question or if you don't initially understand the visual, you can still figure out the best answer by looking for clues or for things you do recognize. Let's look at an example of a visual item and a question about the item.

Based on the cartoon above, what is the cartoonist implying about President George H. Bush?

(1) President Bush likes parades.
(2) President Bush believes that a parade may lead to a victory in Desert Storm.
(3) President Bush believes that a parade will fix the problems facing America.
(4) President Bush would rather celebrate the victory in Desert Storm than tackle the problems facing America.
(5) The problems of education, economy, racial tolerance, and cities all point to President Bush.

After you have carefully looked over the cartoon and have read each of the possible answer choices, you are ready to answer the question. Before you start eliminating incorrect answer choices, let's think through what you know about the cartoon. Even if you did not recognize the person in the cartoon as President George H. Bush, you can determine that it is Bush because every answer choice refers to President Bush. Next, if you are familiar with recent United States history you may remember that President Bush tried to use the momentum from Desert Storm to win re-election as President. If you are an astute student of recent history you may remember that the four issues surrounding Bush in the cartoon were all real issues that actually faced Bush in the time before the presidential election of 1992. Now let's work through the possible answer choices and answer the question.

The correct answer is (4). You can eliminate (1) because it is unreasonable to think that may be an answer; the cartoon conveys too much information for you to think it is just portraying Bush as a simpleton. You can eliminate (2) because it is highly unlikely that Bush would have wanted to throw a victory parade before Desert Storm was complete and victory was certain. You can eliminate (5) because the arrows in the sign imply that education, economy, racial tolerance, and cities are declining. The two options left are (3) and (4). At first glance, (3) may seem like a good choice but it is unlikely that President Bush would really try to fix America's problems with a parade. However, it is conceivable that President Bush would prefer to promote the recent victory in Desert Storm than tackle tough issues facing his administration, especially if he were facing re-election. Therefore, the correct answer is (4).

Let's look at a visual that contains a different kind of graphic.

The Wartime Economic Boom, 1940-1945

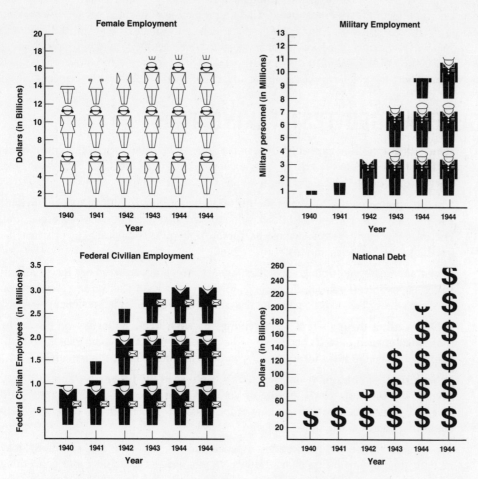

Based on the information in the chart above, which of the following is most likely a valid statement?

(1) There is a direct correlation between government spending and the number of military personnel and federally employed civilians.

(2) The national debt increased because of the number of women who went to work between 1940 and 1945.

(3) The number of civilians employed by the government in 1945 equals the number of military in 1945.

(4) The greatest increase in employment between 1940 and 1945 was among females.

(5) All of the military employed between 1940 and 1945 were males.

The correct answer is (1). After you have carefully looked over the charts and have read each of the possible answer choices, you are ready to answer the question. Even if you did not know the information before you read the charts, you will be able to figure this out by just looking carefully at each chart. Choice (1) looks like it could be correct because two of the charts above show that federal employment increased each year between 1940 and 1945. The chart also indicates that government spending increased each year because the debt increased each year. Circle choice (1) and we'll come back to it. Choice (2) probably is incorrect because we just noted that while the national debt increased, so did the number of people employed by the government, not just women. Choice (3) can be eliminated because in 1945 there were 3.5 million federal civilian employees while there were 13 million military employees. Choice (4) can be eliminated, too, because female employment actually increased less than military employment. Choice (5) can be eliminated because there is no indication in the Military Employment chart that only males were in the military. Additionally, you might have known that women were members of the military during World War II as WACs (Women's Army Corps), WASPs (Women Air Service Pilots), and more. Based on what you have seen in the charts, choice (1) is definitely the correct answer.

GENERAL GED TEST-TAKING TIPS

1. **Read each question carefully and make sure you know what the question is asking.** Look for clue words such as evaluate, main idea, analyze, true, valid, etc. These words can be clues about how to answer the question.

2. **Choose an answer that answers the question being asked.** This may seem obvious, but you should be careful not to choose an answer that doesn't even fit the question. For example, don't select an answer choice if it gives supporting facts when the question asks for the main idea.

3. **When answering multiple-choice questions, try to eliminate as many incorrect answers as possible.** If you can eliminate 2 or 3 incorrect answer choices on a question you may not know, your odds of guessing the correct answer more than double.

4. **When reading through text on a reading passage item, underline or circle the main idea of each paragraph.** This will help you remember the main idea, and it will help you locate the main idea again if you have to refer back to the paragraph later.

5. **When using graphics in visual items, be sure to read the title or caption that may accompany the map, chart, graph, or cartoon.** Many times the title or caption will give you a clue about the true meaning of the visual. You can then use this clue to help clarify the question and eliminate incorrect answers.

6. **Use common sense.** Many questions, especially about economics and geography, may be unfamiliar to you at first glance. However, you use and make decisions concerning economics and geography every day. Use your real-life, practical economics and geography skills to help you on the test.

7. **If you don't know the answer, guess!** Because there is no penalty for guessing on the Social Studies test, you should never leave a question unanswered. If you don't know the answer, guess. If you are almost out of time and have several left, go through them and guess. You have nothing to lose and everything to gain by leaving no question unanswered.

8. **Don't try to cram all the GED tests in a short period of time.** You won't be taking these tests in one sitting and you won't be required to take them all in one week. Spread them out so that you allow yourself plenty of time to prepare adequately for each one.

9. **Make sure you are well rested and well fed before you take the test.** In order for your mind to be its sharpest, you should feel fresh and not tired. Also make sure that you eat before you take the test. Like your body, your brain needs energy, too!

10. **Relax and be confident in your abilities!** Don't be nervous about taking the GED tests. These tests are practical measures of knowledge that you have gained not only through study but also through life experiences. The test is not designed to trick you or cause frustration. Therefore, find confidence and reassurance in the hard work and hours of preparation you have invested in this endeavor and do great job!

Chapter

The New World

Until the late 1400s, most of Europe depended on trade from the Far East. Much of this trade was done via land routes that made the trade slow and somewhat unreliable. In the late 1400s and early 1500s, though, European monarchs sponsored expeditions, or voyages of discovery, that crossed the Atlantic Ocean and explored the lands of North, Central, and South America. By 1700, the Portuguese, Spanish, French, and British had all established colonies in the New World. In 1607, Jamestown, Virginia, became the first permanent British settlement in the New World. Jamestown and other settlements and colonies were created as joint-stock companies. Joint-stock companies were business ventures in which a large number of people invested small amounts of money. This allowed the investors to avoid the risk of losing huge sums of money. A total of thirteen British colonies appeared on the eastern coast of North America over the next 125 years, each with its own identity. The British sponsored the colonies and the journeys of the colonists because the British hoped to make vast amounts of trade revenue from trade with the colonies. The colonists from England who sailed to the New World sought freedom of worship, a voice in their government, and a fresh start with land of their own. Some colonists, many of those in Georgia, for example, sought refuge from the law in the New World. By 1763, after an armed conflict with the French (known in the Americas as the French and Indian War and known in Europe as the Seven Years War), the British controlled a large portion of the North American continent. Unfortunately for those Native Americans who occupied the lands of North America before the arrival of the Europeans, colonization meant the end of many Native American cultures. Partly because of armed conflict and partly because of the introduction of European diseases into North America, the Europeans caused the death of many, many Native Americans.

Between the time of their arrival in the New World and the years prior to the War for American Independence, the colonists developed their own ideas about the way the colonies should be governed. Consequently, many of the colonists disagreed with the way that the British governed the colonies. Among these points of contention was the problem of taxation without representation. In other words, the colonists did not like the fact that they were being forced to pay increasing British taxes, but they were never allowed much, if any, say in the way the British governed the colonies. Many of the colonists also resented the presence of British troops throughout the colonies. These disagreements, among others, caused tension between the colonies and the British government and led to one of the most monumental events in history, the War for American Independence (also known as the American Revolution or Revolutionary War).

ROAD MAP

- *The Struggle for Independence*
- *The Early Government*
- *Expansion and Growing Pains*
- *The Civil War and Reconstruction*
- *Industrialization*
- *Twentieth-Century Turbulence and the Rise to Superpower Status*
- *The Late Twentieth Century and Contemporary Events*

EXERCISE 1: THE NEW WORLD

1. The British sponsored expeditions and colonists in the New World for which of the following reasons?

   (1) The British population explosion forced the British to seek relief from high population density by sending some of its population elsewhere.
   (2) The British encouraged the expeditions and colonists so that the colonists could escape the widespread famine facing the British Isles.
   (3) The British wanted to establish colonies and find new goods to bolster the British economy.
   (4) The British government wanted to give the colonists an opportunity to experiment with new religions.
   (5) The British government sent people to the New World who posed a threat to the stability of the British government.

The correct answer is (3). The British saw the economic benefits of establishing colonies and supporting expeditions based on the examples of the Spanish and Portuguese.

2. The colonists' main point of contention with the British government was which of the following?

   (1) Taxation without being allowed a fair voice in the government of the colonies
   (2) The brutality of the British soldiers against the Native Americans
   (3) The high taxes on tea
   (4) The slow communications between the British government and the colonies
   (5) The lack of a constitutional government in the colonies

The correct answer is (1). The colonists thought it was unfair that they paid taxes to the British government yet had no say in the way they were governed by the British.

THE STRUGGLE FOR INDEPENDENCE

Between 1765 and 1776, the British imposed a number of taxes on the colonies that the colonists viewed as unfair. Some of the items taxed by the British included sugar, playing cards, newspapers, and tea. In many cases, the colonists displayed their displeasure and anger by burning officials in effigy, tarring and feathering officials, and even throwing massive amounts of tea into harbors. In response, the British government tried to limit and control the trade of the American colonies. In further attempts to keep the colonies from straying too far from British rule, the British attempted to reduce the power of the American lawmaking assemblies. After much debate within the colonies, the colonial leaders, with the support of many of the colonists, decided to cut ties with Great Britain and declare the independence of the colonies from British rule. Some of the colonists known as loyalists, however, did not want to break away from the mother country; they still felt a sense of duty and loyalty towards England. In 1776, the colonial leaders signed the Declaration of Independence, which officially declared that the colonies were no longer under British rule. The British refused to recognize the independence of the colonies. As a result, war broke out in the colonies between the American colonists and the British soldiers.

The colonists mustered an army made up of many militiamen, or citizen soldiers, and very few professional soldiers. The British, on the other hand, fielded an army of professionally trained soldiers along with a formidable navy. Although the revolutionary army was outnumbered and perhaps outclassed, they had a few advantages. The revolutionists had great leadership, they were fighting from a defensive position, and they passionately believed in the cause for which they fought. With the aid of the French, Dutch, and Spanish, all of whom were enemies of the British, the Americans won an improbable victory over the British and won their independence. The British found themselves fighting not only against angry American colonists but also against the nations of France, Holland, and Spain. By the end of the war, the colonies were only a minor concern for the British; the British were in the midst of a global conflict. Tired of war, American and British diplomats met in Paris and signed the Treaty of Paris of 1783 in which Britain recognized the independence of the colonies. After the dust settled, the thirteen colonies stood loosely united as the United States of America.

EXERCISE 2: THE STRUGGLE FOR INDEPENDENCE

The following item is based on the map below.

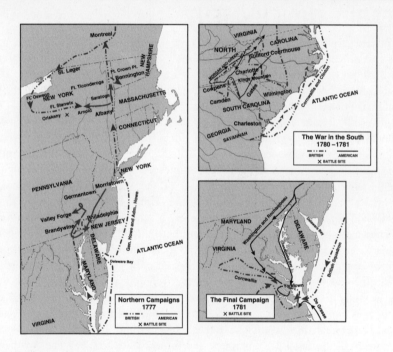

1. Which of the following conclusions can be drawn based on the map above?

   (1) Cornwallis traveled farther than either Washington or Rochambeau.
   (2) No battles occurred in either Maryland or Delaware.
   (3) Washington and Rochambeau had difficulty crossing the Potomac River.
   (4) A decisive battle occurred at Yorktown.
   (5) Yorktown lay more than 100 miles from the coastline.

The correct answer is (4). The title of the map, "The Final Campaign," is a clue that the battle at Yorktown was one of the final battles during the War for American Independence.

2. Which of the following conclusions can be drawn concerning the War for American Independence?

   (1)   The Americans may not have won the war without the aid of foreign countries.
   (2)   The British would have lost the colonies in America even if the French and Spanish had not declared war on the British.
   (3)   The emotional attachment the Americans had to their homes played little or no role in the defeat of the British.
   (4)   Every colonist wanted independence from British rule.
   (5)   Almost no colonists wanted independence from British rule.

The correct answer is (1). If France, Spain, and Holland had not supplied money and supplies and if they had not declared war on the British, the colonies may have lost the war and remained under British control.

THE EARLY GOVERNMENT

Over the next several years, the states worked hard to settle their differences and agree on a system of government that best suited all of the states. Since 1781, the colonies had operated under the Articles of Confederation, the first constitution of the United States. Under the Articles, the colonies were united as a loose union of states, the Congress held the majority of the political power and there was no executive branch of the government. The entire national government was weak. In 1787, leaders from each of the states met at the Constitutional Convention and outlined a plan for a new government. Some argued for a weak central government that was unlike the British government while others argued for a very strong central government. Eventually the states compromised. The resulting plan was the United States Constitution. Eventually, all of the states ratified, or approved, the Constitution, or plan of government; it became the official plan of government in 1789. In 1791 the United States adopted ten amendments, or changes, to the Constitution. These changes, known as the Bill of Rights, protected the rights of individuals.

About the same time, the nation's first political parties were forming as a result of disagreements over the proper political and financial policies for the new nation. The two parties that emerged were the Federalists and the Republicans. The Federalists, who were led by the wealthy and educated, sought a strong central government steered by the elite. The Republicans, on the other hand, believed in the ability of the common people to govern themselves. Republican leadership like James Madison and Thomas Jefferson wanted to limit the powers of the federal government and protect states' rights. The two parties also differed in the area of foreign policy. The Republicans supported the French Revolution while the Federalists thought that the French Revolution was a terrifying act against an established government. Disputes between the Federalists and the Republicans reached new heights in the election of 1800. The Republican candidate Thomas Jefferson was elected President. This election showed that the American people believed in the power of the people to determine the course the country would take. The Federalists never won another presidential election.

EXERCISE 3: THE EARLY GOVERNMENT

3. Those opposed to a strong central government in the early days of the United States were concerned most about which of the following?

   (1) The possibility of the government becoming oppressive the way that King George had been to the colonists
   (2) The possibility that no good candidates could be found to run such a government
   (3) The possibility that the states could not agree on a leader for such a government
   (4) The idea that the states had to be a part of a single nation instead of each forming their own country
   (5) The idea of forming a country independent of British rule

The correct answer is (1). Anti-Federalists did not want a government with the potential to oppress its constituents the way the king had done to the colonists.

2. One of the results of the disagreement over the correct path for the new government to take was which of the following?

   (1) The U.S. Civil War
   (2) The creation of the first two American political parties
   (3) The Bill of Rights
   (4) The French Revolution
   (5) The Articles of Confederation

The correct answer is (2). There were two predominant ideas about the direction that the new government should go. The politicians chose sides and those two sides became the Federalists and the Republicans.

EXPANSION AND GROWING PAINS

One of the most important decisions Jefferson made as President was to expand westward. Jefferson acquired a huge amount of land known as the Louisiana Purchase. For a bargain price, Jefferson bought all the land between the Mississippi River in the east and the Rocky Mountains in the west, from the Gulf of Mexico in the south to the Canadian border in the north. For only $15 million, the United States doubled the size of its territory. Eventually the United States would create fourteen more states in the land of the Louisiana Purchase. The growing size of the United States helped earn international respect. The westward expansion of the United States was a difficult task. Settlers faced uncharted land, harsh climates, and Native Americans who did not welcome those who might drive them out of their homeland. Nevertheless, the Americans pressed onward and gradually adopted to life on the frontiers.

As the new nation continued to grow and become more self-sufficient, it struggled with policies concerning international trade. The United States passed legislation that hurt trade between the United States, Britain, and France. The British took exception to this and responded with animosity. The British navy made it a common practice to stop American ships on the open seas and say that it was searching for deserters, or people who had illegally left the British navy. Often the British captured Americans on these ships and forced them into the British navy. They also confiscated American ships and goods. These actions, along with reports of British aid to hostile Native Americans, moved Congress to declare war on the British. Known as the War of 1812, this conflict did not settle any of the issues that started it but the United States emerged victorious. The war brought the nation together and earned the nation respect in the eyes of many European nations. The period of time that followed the war was marked by further expansion, with the addition of Florida, and an increased American role in international diplomacy and politics. President Monroe issued the Monroe Doctrine and declared that the United States would not allow any further European colonization or expansion in the Western Hemisphere.

As the United States earned a reputation as an up-and-coming nation, it was able to increase its trade with other nations. This helped stimulate the economy of the country and of each of the states. The northern states concentrated on manufacturing and production while the southern states focused on agriculture, or farming. The northern states, most of whose population was urban, or in cities, became a society centered on industry and big business. The southern states, most of whose population was rural, or in the countryside, became a society centered on plantations and the production of crops such as cotton and sugar. Large plantations grew throughout the South and became the economic backbone of the Southern economy. Although all the states maintained loyalty to the nation, the two regions were often very competitive. The two sections of the country competed for political power within the Congress and for the presidency. As a result of this competition, along with other major issues such as slavery, tensions between the North and the South grew.

In the West, the United States continued to expand by annexing Texas and Oregon. The annexation of these two regions stirred great emotion. Adding Texas to the Union meant the addition of a slave territory. This possibility angered many in the North until the situation with Oregon developed. If the United States added Oregon, a non-slave territory, they could add Texas, a slave territory, and maintain equilibrium between the slave states and non-slave states. By 1846, both territories were added to the United States. However, Mexico went to war with the United States over Texas. Eventually, the United States negotiated a treaty with Mexico that added California, New Mexico, and part of Arizona to U.S. holdings in exchange for $15 million. The issue of slavery moved front and center again as both and the North and the South argued over whether or not the new territories should allow slavery. In an attempt to divert or delay major problems between the North and the South, politicians passed legislation such as the Missouri Compromise which made sure the number of free states and slave states remained equal as new states were added to the nation. After 1850, some of the new territory, prohibited slavery, while other territories permitted the settlement of slave owners and non-slave owners alike. The United States then passed fugitive slave laws that required runaway slaves to be returned to their owners. Then the Supreme Court issued the Dred Scott decision, which opened all new territories to slavery. The South felt like the North was trying to abolish slavery, an act the southern states saw as a violation of their state rights.

EXERCISE 4: EXPANSION AND GROWING PAINS

1. The majority of new territory was added to the United States through which of the following?

   (1) Warfare
   (2) Conspiracies
   (3) Diplomacy
   (4) Purchases
   (5) Trade

The correct answer is (4). Although some U.S. territory came after war, most land was purchased from other countries. The Louisiana Purchase is a good example of such a purchase.

2. Perhaps the most controversial issue surrounding new territories that were added to the United States was which of the following?

    (1)   Whether the new territory would be rural or urban
    (2)   Whether the new territory would be Federalist or Republican
    (3)   Whether the new territory would be industrial or agricultural
    (4)   Whether the new territory would be hostile or friendly to Native Americans
    (5)   Whether the new territory would allow slavery or not allow slavery

The correct answer is (5). Slave states wanted all the new territory to be open to slavery, while non-slave states wanted slavery prohibited in the new territories.

THE CIVIL WAR AND RECONSTRUCTION

In the presidential election of 1860, the issue of slavery came to a head. The Southern Democrats split into two factions, or groups, and put forth two different candidates, each with different, yet pro-slavery, beliefs. The Republicans nominated Lincoln, a candidate that did not support the idea of slavery in the new territories. A fourth party put forth yet another candidate. With American votes scattered among the four candidates, Lincoln won the controversial election with less than 40 percent of the popular vote. After Lincoln won, South Carolina seceded, or withdrew, from the Union. Shortly thereafter ten more southern states followed South Carolina and created the Confederate States of America. In order to save the Union, the North went to war in 1861 against the southern states that seceded.

Lincoln made it clear that he had no intention of allowing any state to secede from the Union. He called up troops from the remaining loyal states and went to war to preserve the Union. The South was at a disadvantage in the war because they lacked the manufacturing power and transportation that the North had. Additionally, most of the fighting was done in the South. After four years of bloody fighting, the South surrendered in what was often known as the War Between the States. Slavery ended and the United States survived. Although America suffered heavy casualties in both the North and the South, the war resolved two important issues. First, the authority of the nation took precedence over the states. Second, slavery was abolished throughout the United States.

Lincoln, thankful that the Union was still intact, intended to allow the southern states back into the Union with relatively easy terms. However, Lincoln was assassinated before he could put his plan into action. After Lincoln's death, a vindictive Congress initiated a period known as Reconstruction, during which time the South lived under very oppressive conditions. The Union had been saved but the South harbored great resentment against the North for the harsh treatment it endured after the war. Many Southerners were especially resentful of having to allow African Americans to vote and hold public office. These feelings endured in the southern states for several generations after the war.

EXERCISE 5: THE CIVIL WAR AND RECONSTRUCTION

1. Which of the following statements is true?

    (1)   The South seceded from the Union because Southerners feared Reconstruction.
    (2)   The South seceded from the Union because of the issue of slavery.
    (3)   The South seceded from the Union because of the issue of slavery, its concern about states' rights, and other issues.
    (4)   The South seceded from the Union because the North threatened to take all political power away from the South.
    (5)   The South seceded from the Union because Southerners did not want Texas annexed.

The correct answer is (3). The issues of slavery, states' rights, the threat of new free territories upsetting the equilibrium, and other issues all played a part in the South's secession.

2. President Lincoln decided to go to war with the South for which of the following reasons?

    (1)   To end slavery
    (2)   To punish the South for having slaves
    (3)   To confiscate its wealth
    (4)   To preserve the Union
    (5)   To win the election of 1860

The correct answer is (4). Lincoln refused to allow the nation to be dissolved over any issue, so he sent troops into the South to prevent them from leaving the Union.

INDUSTRIALIZATION

In the late 1800s, the United States followed the lead of Europe and began moving toward industrialization. The number of factories and manufacturing plants across the U.S. increased and big business became a way of life for many Americans. Inventions made life easier and businesses more efficient. The cities grew as rural people flocked to the cities to find work in the factories. American citizens were not the only people who benefited from the industrialization of America. People rushed to the U.S. from all over the world in search of the jobs offered by the factories. Others left their homes abroad and rushed to the U.S. to receive free land that the government was giving away in the West. The concept of Manifest Destiny inspired Americans to expand westward all the way to the Pacific Ocean, and Americans did just that.

Railroads sprawled across the country and provided better transportation for goods and people. The construction of railroads was given special attention by the United States government. The government granted huge tracts of land to railroad companies and offered special loans to the railroad companies. The economy boomed and businesses grew into corporations. Some corporations grew so large that they became monopolies; in other words, some companies were so large that they had no competition. Even though the government passed laws against monopolies, the laws were hardly enforced. Because business was so good, this era became known as the Gilded Age. However, scandal and corruption marked this era, too. The influence of big business and the incredible amounts of money that big business had at its disposal led many politicians to make secret arrangements with companies and individuals or to overlook some violations by companies or individuals. President Grant's administration was hit especially hard by scandal.

In the years that followed the Civil War, the government took a *laissez-faire* approach toward business and industry; in other words, the government let business and industry go along with little or no regulation. It seemed toward the end of the 1800s that the government was allowing many situations and problems to go untended. Eventually the government began monitoring labor conditions and regulating big business. As scandals were discovered, Americans called for reform, or change. Reformers known as Progressives sparked sweeping reforms at the local, state, and national levels in the areas of business and labor.

During the late 1800s labor issues and disputes between workers and employers prompted workers to form labor unions. These labor unions began in the first years after the Civil War, and by the end of the century, membership numbered nearly one million workers. The unions used their power to strike and bargain for better wages, better working conditions, and better benefits for their members. Unfortunately, some of the strikes were marked by violence.

Just before the turn of the century, the United States became involved in the Spanish-American War partly over issue of the liberation of Cuba and partly in retaliation for the sinking of an American ship in Cuba. Prompted by Yellow Journalism, or sensational exaggerated journalism, America went to war with Spain after an American ship was sunk in a Havana harbor. The United States won the war in a very short amount of time. As a result of victory in the war, the U.S. gained control over several foreign lands, including Guam, the Philippines, Puerto Rico, and Cuba. By gaining control of lands outside of North America, the United States had become an imperialist nation. American imperialism brought criticism from countries around the world and from politicians in the United States.

EXERCISE 6: INDUSTRIALIZATION

1. Manifest Destiny can be summed up in which of the following statements?

    (1)   The United States is destined to stretch from the Atlantic to the Pacific.
    (2)   The United States is destined to be covered in railroads.
    (3)   The United States is destined to open its doors to immigrants from other countries.
    (4)   The United States is destined to remove Native Americans from all land that it desires.
    (5)   The United States is destined to be the greatest industrial power in the world.

The correct answer is (1). The idea of Manifest Destiny arose in the nineteenth century and suggested that the United States expand all the way to the Pacific Ocean in the West.

2. Westward expansion benefited the most from which of the following?

    (1)   Government-appointed labor
    (2)   Government loans and grants of land
    (3)   Clear maps provided by explorers
    (4)   Slavery in the new U.S. territories
    (5)   Reconstruction politics

The correct is answer is (2). The government provided land to railroad companies for laying track and provided loans to finance the construction of the railroads.

TWENTIETH-CENTURY TURBULENCE AND THE RISE TO SUPERPOWER STATUS

The beginning of the twentieth century saw more reform in many areas of life in the United States. Trusts, or combinations of companies that reduced competition, came under government scrutiny. Conditions in factories drew much attention, and the government responded by cleaning up unsanitary conditions. This made working conditions better for the factory and food-packing plant workers and made the products safer for consumers. The government set aside many acres of land for national parks and wildlife preserves. The United States also began construction of the Panama Canal to join the Atlantic and Pacific Oceans; this would allow ships to pass through the canal instead of rounding the entire South-American continent.

During the early twentieth century, the United States devoted much time and energy to international diplomacy. The American policy of "Speak softly and carry a big stick" meant that the United States let their policies and intentions be known through diplomacy, and they backed that up with military action when needed. When World War I, or the Great War as it was known then, erupted in Europe, the U.S. faced a dilemma. President Wilson wanted to maintain neutrality in the war. However, after German submarines sank the *Lusitania*, a British passenger ship that contained 128 U.S. passengers, the United States entered the war on the side of the Triple Entente (Great Britain, France, and Russia). The United States tipped the scales in favor of the Triple Entente, and the U.S. troops returned home victorious. At the conclusion of World War I, the United States led a failed attempt to establish the League of Nations as an international peacekeeping organization; the U.S. Congress refused to allow the United States to join, so the League proved ineffective.

In the years following the war, the United States enjoyed a period of terrific prosperity. Business and industry grew and expanded. Individuals invested heavily and spent large sums of money on things like sporting events, parties, movies, nightclubs, and other forms of entertainment. Politically, the United States implemented many new tariffs on imports to protect U.S. interests at home. The government began regulating public utilities and the rates they charged both businesses and consumers. The government used a Constitutional amendment to ban the production and sale of alcoholic beverages; this period was known as Prohibition. Another Constitutional amendment gave women the right to vote for the first time in the United States. Millions of immigrants flocked to the United States from war-torn Europe seeking new financial opportunities.

During this era of prosperity, many individuals purchased stocks by putting up a small percentage of the stock purchase price and borrowing the rest of the purchase price from the investor. This was a very risky investment strategy. Stock prices continued to rise and investors continued to borrow money to buy stocks. Then in 1929, the Stock Market crashed and banks failed in the United States and in Europe. In other words, panicked investors began selling off their high-priced stocks at a feverish pace. The feeling of panic struck not only the United States but also the rest of the world. By 1932, many banks had failed, factories closed, workers found themselves unemployed and mortgages were foreclosed. Facing record unemployment and economic hardships, Americans elected Franklin D. Roosevelt as president in 1932. He instituted reforms and economic recovery programs in his New Deal. Roosevelt's New Deal programs included relief for businesses and individuals, new government agencies that put people to work doing public works projects. These measures, along with the onset of World War II, eventually led the U.S. out of the Great Depression. The graphs on page 49 illustrate the impact Roosevelt's administration had on the U.S. economy.

On December 7, 1941, the Japanese attacked the U.S. military base at Pearl Harbor in Hawaii. Almost immediately the United States entered World War II on the side of the Allies (Great Britain and the Union of Soviet Socialist Republics, or USSR) against the Axis Powers (Germany, Italy, and Japan). The massive war effort stimulated the economy and created millions of jobs for Americans. In 1945, after four years of fierce fighting against the Axis Powers in Europe and in the Pacific, President Harry Truman dropped two atomic bombs on Japan. Shortly thereafter the war ended and the United States stood victorious alongside the other Allied Powers. The United States emerged from World War II not just as a legitimate world power but as a superpower. After the war, with the influence and leadership of the United States, world leaders divided Germany into different zones of influence, established the United Nations, and launched efforts to help rebuild war-torn nations. The United States joined the International Court of Justice, launched the National Security Council, and established the CIA or Central Intelligence Agency.

In the years that followed World War II, the United States found itself in an ideological disagreement with the Soviet Union and the Eastern Bloc, or eastern European nations under the influence of the communism of the Soviet Union. The United States committed itself to stop the spread of communist ideas and eventually became the enemy of the Soviet Union and its allies. For years, the United States remained deadlocked in a Cold War, or a war of rhetoric and ill will, with the Soviet Union. The fear of nuclear holocaust and communism marked the next twenty-five years.

The Economy Before and After the New Deal, 1929-1941

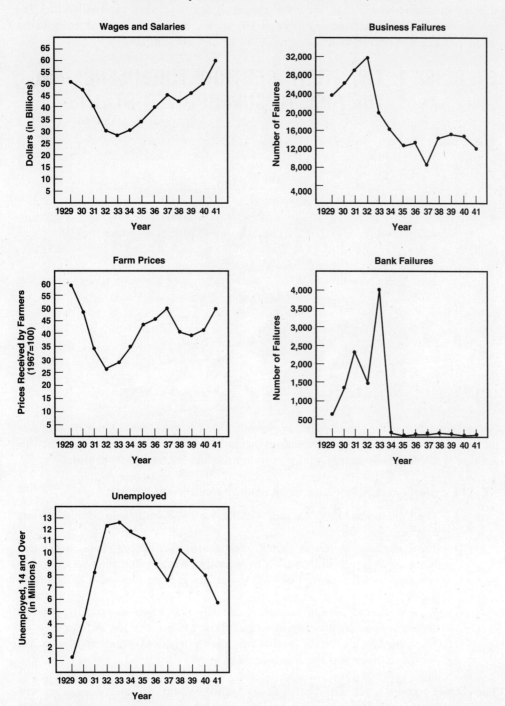

American troops did not stay home long after they returned from World War II. Only five years after World War II, American troops were deployed to South Korea to fight against the communist threat posed by the North Koreans in an undeclared war that ended with no real winner. Then in the 1960s, the United States deployed more troops to Vietnam in another controversial, undeclared war. The American troops were eventually brought home, and Vietnam fell to the communists. Each time the troops returned home from fighting in Korea and Vietnam, they had a difficult time readjusting to civilian life. The troops were not received as heroes the way World War II troops were, and many of the soldiers faced emotional problems as a result of their experiences abroad.

EXERCISE 7: TWENTIETH-CENTURY TURBULENCE AND THE RISE TO SUPERPOWER STATUS

The following item is based on the following cartoon and text.

STEP ON IT, DOC!

"After World War II, the United States implemented the Marshall Plan as a way to help ease the financial hardship of European countries that needed help rebuilding after the war. This aid was available to any country who wanted to resist the spread of communism."

1. What conclusion can be drawn based on the information above?

    (1) The United States was in a race with the Soviet Union to help rebuild Western Europe.
    (2) The United States felt as though communism may spread chaos in Western Europe if Congress did not offer assistance to Western European nations.
    (3) Communists felt as though the U.S. Congress was being reckless with its foreign policy.
    (4) Western Europe needed assistance so badly that it would open its doors to democracy and communism as long as those nations received assistance.
    (5) The United States and the Soviets were racing to get out of Eastern Europe, and Western Europe was the only safe place to go.

The correct answer is (2). The United States wanted to help rebuild Western European nations so the United States, not the Soviets, would have influence over the Western European nations.

2. The Great Depression followed an era of which of the following?

(1)   Careful financial planning by individuals but not by businesses
(2)   Widespread corruption with the Savings and Loan corporations
(3)   Carefree lifestyles, risky investing, and poor financial management on the part of brokers
(4)   World war
(5)   Industrialization

The correct answer is (3). It was an era of carefree lifestyles, risky investing, and poor financial management on the part of brokers. Investors speculated wildly, and brokers unwisely issued credit to individuals who wanted to purchase large amounts of stocks.

THE LATE TWENTIETH CENTURY AND CONTEMPORARY EVENTS

The 1950s were a tumultuous decade in the United States as many Americans reacted to the struggle for civil rights. In 1954 the Supreme Court desegregated schools in the landmark decision *Brown v. Board of Education of Topeka*. The civil rights movement built on that momentum. As people like Rosa Parks and Martin Luther King, Jr. led the civil rights movement in a dignified and peaceful manner, groups like the Ku Klux Klan promoted violence against African Americans and those who fought for the rights of African Americans, and individuals like Arkansas Governor Faubus inhibited progress toward equal rights for American citizens. In 1957 Congress created the Civil Rights Commission which investigated civil rights violations. As a result of the Commission's investigations, the government appointed officials to safeguard the voting rights of African Americans.

The 1960s saw heightened tensions between the United States and the Soviet Union reach a boiling point during the Cuban Missile Crisis. The two world powers moved dangerously close to nuclear war as President Kennedy forced the Soviets to remove missiles from Cuba. Then, in 1963, to the horror of the nation, President Kennedy was assassinated. The rest of the decade was marked by domestic problems concerning the deployment of troops to Vietnam to fight communism. Many Americans disagreed with American involvement there, and they took to the streets in protest. The civil rights situation improved during the 1960s with the passage of the 24th Amendment, which eliminated the poll tax, and the Voting Rights Act of 1965 that aided African Americans in the voting process. The 1960s ended with a cultural phenomenon known as Woodstock, a massive free concert in New York where thousands of young Americans spent days reveling in drugs, sex and rock and roll to forget about the problems that faced the nation.

Many Americans grew wary of the government as corrupt officials and oil shortages marked the 1970s. President Nixon resigned following a scandal in which several people were arrested for breaking into the Democratic National Headquarters. Nixon and his advisors knew about the break-in and about illegal wiretaps. In 1973 Vice-President Agnew was indicted for tax evasion and bribery, further damaging the people's trust in the government. The tension between the U.S. and the USSR declined in the 1970s in what is known as *détente*. Economically, the end of the 1970s brought with it further recession, an unfavorable balance of trade, high unemployment, and a very high rate of inflation.

In the 1980s, conservative Republican leadership pushed for less government and more military spending. The economy recovered, but the government's deficit spending caused, national debt to spiral. U.S. relations with the Soviets grew tense again as the United States unveiled its "Star Wars" program, a missile defense system. At the end of the decade, the U.S. and Soviet leaders agreed to reduce and end existing stockpiles of weapons.

During the 1990s, the United States enjoyed the end of the Cold War and celebrated the collapse of the Soviet Union. However, the 1990s also saw the liberal use of U.S.

military power in many places around the world including Panama, Iraq, Bosnia, and Somalia. Eventually, the government cut military spending, along with some social programs, in an attempt to reduce the national debt. President Clinton's administration was marked by scandals as the millennium drew to a close. The new millennium brought with it a presidential election unlike any that the U.S. had ever seen before. By a very controversial margin of just a very few votes, George W. Bush defeated Al Gore. Less than a year into his term, President Bush faced a crisis the likes of which few other Presidents had ever experienced. On September 11, 2001, terrorists hijacked American airliners and crashed them into the Pentagon and the World Trade Center, killing thousands. This attack roused the American spirit and resulted in an unprecedented war on terrorism, terrorists, and those who support terrorist activity. President Bush responded by mounting military attacks on terrorist bases in Afghanistan.

EXERCISE 8: THE LATE TWENTIETH CENTURY AND CONTEMPORARY EVENTS

The following item is based on the map below.

Major Events in North America and Southwest Asia, 1979-1990

1. Which of the following is most accurate based on the information in the map?

   (1) Iran was the Middle-Eastern country most hostile towards the United States during the 1980s.
   (2) Afghanistan was the only Middle-Eastern nation to be invaded by an aggressor during the 1980s.
   (3) The Middle East was a relatively peaceful region during the 1980s.
   (4) The U.S. and Soviet Union managed to stay out of affairs in the Middle East during the 1980s.
   (5) There was no time during the 1980s when the entire Middle-East region was without war or armed conflict.

The correct answer is (5). The Middle East was a hotbed of military conflict throughout the entire decade of the 1980s.

The following item is based on the cartoon below.

W. STANDS FOR "WELL-TRAINED"

1. Which of the following best sums up the meaning of the political cartoon above?

   (1)   Harris trained George W. Bush well, and now Bush does as Harris says.
   (2)   Harris does not want more recounts, and Bush already knows who won the election because the Republicans manipulated the elections.
   (3)   Because Harris does not want another recount, Harris is a Democrat who wants the election to end in defeat for Bush.
   (4)   Bush and his pet bird are ready to move into the White House.
   (5)   Bush trained Harris well, and Harris is doing exactly what she was told to do.

The correct answer is (5). The cartoon implies that Bush told Harris exactly what to say concerning recounts during the 2000 presidential election.

Civics and Government

Simply put, political science is the study of government, the methods of governing, and those who lead governments. As long as man has been organized into states, man has needed a government to maintain order. The form of government each society has used throughout history has depended on a number of factors including the size of the state and the traditions of the state. Many of the forms of government used throughout history, though, have been determined, directly affected or influenced by the means the leader used to assume the leadership of a government. Although there are many different types of government, there are a few basic political systems in which all governments may be classified.

POLITICAL SYSTEMS

One very old political system is democracy. Democracy means "rule by the people." In a democracy, the people make decisions in matters of government. Democracy dates back to ancient Greece and has changed only slightly since its birth so many years ago. There are two types of democracy that exist. In a true democracy, also called a direct democracy or pure democracy, the people make all the decisions. A true democracy is only possible within a small geographic area, such as a small country or a small town, because a large area makes the exchange of information slow and inefficient. In a representative democracy, the people elect representatives to make decisions for them. A republic is a representative democracy. The United States is a good example of a representative democracy.

Another very old political system, even older than democracy, is monarchy. Monarchy means rule by monarch, which can be either a king or queen. In a monarchy, the right to rule is hereditary, meaning that the right is passed down through a king or queen's family from generation to generation. There are a few types of monarchies that exist. An absolute monarchy is one in which the monarch controls every aspect of life within his or her kingdom. The absolute monarch controls every facet of economics, politics, diplomacy, and often religion and culture. Louis XIV of France was the epitome of an absolute monarch. A constitutional monarchy, such as Great Britain, is a monarchical government in which the power of the monarch is limited by a constitution or written laws.

Dictatorship is a third form of government. The ruler of a dictatorship, a dictator, has complete rule over his state. Often the dictator assumes control of the state after a military takeover of a government and then maintains control through military force. A dictator usually rules strictly and controls most aspects of the government, often to the point of being oppressive. Cuba under Fidel Castro and Iraq under Saddam Hussein are good examples of dictatorships.

A fourth political system is an oligarchy. Oligarchy means rule by a few. The "few" often is a group of people who lead in the style of a dictator. This group is not a group that is elected. Rather, the group usually takes control in much the same way as a dictator, after a military takeover. Also like a dictator, an oligarchy maintains control with the military. If the group takes control after a revolution, the group is referred to as junta. Ancient Sparta, a very militaristic society, maintained an oligarchy.

ROAD MAP

- *Political Systems*
- *The U.S. Government*
- *Checks and Balances*
- *The U.S. Federal System*
- *The U.S. Political System*
- *Canadian Government*

A form of government rarely seen anymore is an aristocracy. An aristocracy, ruled by aristocrats, is a system in which the best suited to rule have the power to rule. The best suited to rule, according to the aristocrats, are those who are of privileged birth and who are well educated. Usually aristocrats have great wealth and vast amounts of land. The American South before the Civil War could be considered an aristocracy.

EXERCISE 1: POLITICAL SYSTEMS

1. The most efficient form of government in a time of crisis would most likely be which of the following?

   (1) Dictatorship
   (2) Oligarchy
   (3) Democracy
   (4) Aristocracy
   (5) Monarchy

The correct answer is (1). Because one person with total control of a government can make decisions much more quickly than any other kind of government, a dictatorship is the most efficient, especially in a time of war or other emergency.

2. Which of the following political systems allows citizens the most opportunities to participate in the political process?

   (1) Dictatorship
   (2) Oligarchy
   (3) Democracy
   (4) Aristocracy
   (5) Monarchy

The correct answer is (3). Democracy is correct because this political system is built on the idea that the people should control the government.

THE U.S. GOVERNMENT

The United States government can be classified as a republic, an indirect democracy. The men who created the foundations of the U.S. government believed the government should be carefully laid out in a written plan, or constitution. According to the U.S. Constitution, the U.S. government is a federal government. In other words, the power and authority of the government is divided between the national government, state governments, and local governments. Each level of government has certain authority and responsibilities. Also according to the Constitution, each level of government is split into three branches, each with separate duties. The three branches include the legislative branch, the executive branch and the judicial branch. This is known as separation of powers. The founders of the United States deliberately divided all the power between the different levels and the different branches of government so that no one person or part of the government could assume too much power. Additionally, the founders made sure that each branch of government had the authority to limit the power of the other two branches. This, too, was a preventative measure against any one branch becoming too powerful.

THE THREE BRANCHES OF GOVERNMENT

As you have already learned, the United States Constitution divides the government into three branches, each with its own responsibilities and duties. The legislative branch makes the laws, the executive branch enforces the laws, and the judicial branch interprets the laws. Let's examine each of the three branches more closely.

The Legislative Branch

According to Article One of the Constitution, the power to make laws belongs to the legislative branch of government. The word legislative means "law making," so the legislative branch of government is the one that makes laws. The legislature, or the law-making body, is the United States Congress. The United States Congress is known as a bicameral legislature. In other words, the Congress has two parts, or houses. These are the House of Representatives and the Senate. Although their powers are practically the same, the House of Representatives, sometimes referred to as the House, is the lower house, while the Senate is the upper house of the legislature. The legislators, or lawmakers, in the House of Representatives total 435. The representatives represent each of the fifty states and the number of representatives from each state is based upon a state's population. Each state is guaranteed at least one representative regardless of population. The representatives each represent a district within his or her home state. Representatives serve two-year terms of office, and all of the representatives are elected in their states every two years. In order to run for the office of United States Congressional Representative, a person must meet three criteria or qualifications. The candidate must be at least 25 years old, the candidate must have been a United States citizen for at least 7 years, and the candidate must live in the state he or she intends to represent. There are no limits on the number of terms that a representative may serve.

The Senate is slightly different from the House of Representatives. There are 100 senators in the Senate, two from every state regardless of how large or small a state's population is. Senators serve six-year terms and one third of the senators are elected every two years. In order to be a United States Senator, a candidate must meet some stricter requirements than a candidate for the House. A candidate for the U.S. Senate must be at least 30 years old, a candidate must have been a must have been a citizen of the United States for at least 9 years, and the candidate must be a resident of the state he or she intends to represent. Currently there is no limit on the number of terms a senator may serve.

As you just learned, the legislative branch of government makes laws. Let's look at exactly how the legislature creates a law. First, a legislator must present an idea for a potential law in the form of a bill. After the legislator, either a senator or representative, writes the bill, the bill goes to either the clerk of the House or the clerk of the Senate where the bill receives a name and a number. From here, the bill travels to a committee. A committee is a small group of congressmen who specialize in a particular area of legislation. For example, the Armed Service Committee deals specifically with legislation concerning the United States armed forces. If the committee does not like the bill, it may "pigeonhole" it or "table" it by setting it aside and not dealing with it again. If this happens, the bill is said to have died in committee. If the committee likes the bill, it sends the bill to the House and Senate where the members of Congress debate the bill, make any changes they feel is necessary and then vote on the bill. If either house votes against the bill, or defeats the bill, the bill dies. If majorities of both houses approve the bill, the bill goes before the entire Congress for a vote. If a majority of Congress approves the bill, it goes before the President for his approval. The President may sign the bill and make it law or he can veto, or kill, the bill. However, another majority vote in Congress can override the veto and make the bill law. This process may seem slow and inefficient, but this slow process prevents the government from making any hasty decisions.

The Constitution grants Congress a number of powers that are clearly defined in the text of the Constitution. These powers are known as enumerated powers, expressed powers, or delegated powers. Some of these powers include the authority to tax and collect taxes from the American people, coin or print money, declare war on another country, borrow money and maintain a proper national defense with an army and a navy. Some powers of Congress are limited to only one house or the other. For example, only the House can impeach, or bring formal charges against, the president, but only the Senate can hold a trial for the president. Additionally, only the Senate can approve treaties with other countries. The Constitution granted Congress other unnamed powers through the elastic clause. The elastic clause allows Congress some amount of flexibility to deal with new issues that the founders could not foresee.

EXERCISE 2: THE LEGISLATIVE BRANCH

1. Which of the following may indicate that the Senate is the upper house of the U.S. legislature?

    (1) Senators must have graduate degrees.
    (2) Candidates must be lawyers before than can be elected to the Senate.
    (3) Requirements for senatorial candidates are a little more exclusive than requirements for those seeking a seat in the House.
    (4) There are fewer senators than there are representatives.
    (5) The Senate is located at a higher elevation than the House of Representatives.

The correct answer is (3). The fact that senatorial candidates must meet more strict qualifications indicates that the founders of the United States wanted senators to be more qualified than representatives. This indicates that the Senate must have been held in higher regard at one point in history.

2. A reason why California may have more influence than Alaska in the House of Representatives is which of the following?

    (1) California covers more square miles than Alaska.
    (2) California is located within the continental United States and Alaska is not.
    (3) Alaska has not been a part of the United States as long as California.
    (4) California has more experienced representatives than Alaska.
    (5) California has a larger population than Alaska.

The correct answer is (5). Seats in the House are appropriated to states according to population. If a state has more representatives than another state, it likely also has more influence than that state.

The Executive Branch

Article Two of the Constitution lays forth the powers of the executive branch of government. It is the responsibility of the executive branch to see that the laws of the land are carried out or enforced. The head of the executive branch is the President. Underneath the President are the Vice-President and all the departments and agencies necessary to make sure that the country's laws are enforced and administered properly.

According to Article Two, a candidate for president must meet only three qualifications or requirements. The presidential candidate must be a native-born citizen (not a naturalized citizen), the candidate must be at least 35 years of age, and the candidate must have been a resident of the United States for at least 14 years. The presidential elections are held every four years. Although the American people cast their votes for the President (and Vice-President), the Electoral College actually elects the President. The Electoral College consists of electors from each state who cast their votes for presidential candidates one month after the popular election. Originally, no law set a limit on the number of terms, although George Washington suggested that no President serve more than two terms so as not to build and maintain too much power. The 22nd Amendment, ratified in 1951, set the term limit at two terms.

The President serves in three major roles during his term in office. First, the President serves as the Chief Executive. As the Chief Executive, the President is responsible for making sure that all the laws of the land are carried out properly. Obviously, one man cannot carry out all the laws by himself. Therefore, the President must appoint officials to head executive agencies and departments to carry out and enforce the laws. The heads of the executive departments are members of the President's cabinet. The cabinet is the group of the President's closest advisors who offer advice to the President about issues within his or her department. Also as Chief Executive the President can issue executive orders. An executive order is a directive or command that has the weight of law but does not require approval of either the Congress or the Supreme Court. Most often executive orders are issued during times of war, crisis, or emergency. Second, the President serves as the Chief Diplomat. As the Chief Diplomat, the President has the responsibility of appointing ambassadors, meeting and greeting foreign dignitaries, and making treaties. The Senate must approve any appointments or treaties, though. The third major role of the President is that of Commander in Chief of the military. Although the President cannot declare war, the President can deploy troops to foreign lands or activate troops here in the United States to help in times of emergency. Additionally, during war the President is the highest commander of all the U.S. armed forces.

In addition to the major roles the President plays, the President also plays many smaller roles. As the legislative leader, the President often introduces legislation into Congress, influences the direction of legislation, and vetoes, or rejects, proposed legislation. As the party leader, the President promotes his political party, appoints leadership positions within the party, and endorses party candidates who are seeking election. As the judicial leader, the President appoints justices to the Supreme Court and other federal courts. Furthermore, the President may grant a pardon to someone convicted of a crime. Finally, as Chief of State, the President serves as a symbol of the American people. For example, the President may visit another country on behalf of the United States or issue a public statement on behalf of the United States.

The immediate assistant to the President is the Vice President. The Vice President is the only other member of the executive branch mentioned in Article II of the Constitution. If for some reason the President dies, leaves office, or becomes unable to carry out the Presidential duties, the Vice President becomes the new President. In 1947, Congress decided to lay out a plan for exactly who is next in line for the Presidency in the case of some emergency. After the Vice President, the Speaker of the House is next in line, followed by the President *Pro Tempore* of the Senate, the Secretary of State, the Secretary of the Treasury, Secretary of Defense, the Attorney General, and the other cabinet members.

As you learned earlier, the President's closest advisors are the members of his cabinet. The cabinet members are the heads of the executive departments. Some of the departments include the following: Department of State, which carries out the nation's foreign policy; Department of the Treasury, which collects taxes and prints money; Department of Defense, which controls the U.S. armed forces; Department of Justice, which heads national law enforcement; and Department of Education, which guides and provides funding for the nation's schools. In all, there are fourteen cabinet positions. The cabinet members receive appointments from the President. Then, the cabinet members choose other worthy candidates to fill positions within the executive departments that they oversee.

The last part of the executive branch is the collection of agencies known as the executive agencies. Within each Executive Department, many smaller agencies exist. Some of these agencies, known as executive agencies, include the Central Intelligence Agency, the

National Aeronautics and Space Administration, and the Environmental Protection Agency. Some of these agencies, including the Federal Reserve System and the National Labor Relations Board, are called regulatory commissions. Some agencies, the United States Postal Service, for example, are government corporations.

EXERCISE 3: THE EXECUTIVE BRANCH

1. Powers of the President include all except which of the following?

    (1) The power to introduce legislation
    (2) The power to veto legislation
    (3) The power to send troops into a country
    (4) The power to declare war
    (5) The power to grant amnesty to a criminal

The correct answer is (4). Only Congress can declare war on another country.

2. Which of the following would be the responsibility of a cabinet member?

    (1) Overriding an executive order
    (2) Heading a department within the executive branch of government
    (3) Declaring war
    (4) Approving or rejecting a presidential appointment
    (5) Making laws in their area of expertise

The correct answer is (2). Each member of the cabinet is the head of one of the executive departments within the executive branch.

The Judicial Branch

The third branch of the United States government, outlined in Article Three of the Constitution, is the judicial branch. The Constitution establishes the Supreme Court as the head of the judicial branch. The Supreme Court's main responsibility is to hear appealed cases from lower courts. However, the Supreme Court's other responsibility is to determine the constitutionality of the laws and actions of other branches of government and lower courts. This is the power of judicial review. The Supreme Court has eight justices, or judges, who were appointed by the President, and one Chief Justice, also appointed by the President. Although the President can appoint anyone to be a Supreme Court justice, the Senate has the power to reject a President's nomination. The justices maintain their seats on the Court for life.

The Supreme Court has the authority to hear, or has jurisdiction over, both criminal and civil cases that have been appealed to the high court. Criminal cases are those dealing with crimes, while civil cases are those that deal with disputes between two or more parties. The Supreme Court has original jurisdiction over cases in which a foreign diplomat is involved or in which a state is involved. In other words, these two kinds of cases may originate with the Supreme Court instead of only being appealed to the Supreme Court.

The Supreme Court is the highest court in the United States, but the lowest federal courts in the United States are known as Federal District courts. The District courts are the courts in which the trials and lawsuits begin or originate. Federal District courts hear both criminal and civil cases. If one of the parties involved in a case at the district court level believes that an error occurred during the trial, the case can be appealed to a Federal Court of Appeals. If one of the parties involved in the appealed case still believes that the case needs to be heard by a higher court, the party can appeal the case to the Supreme Court. Both the Federal Appeals courts and the Supreme Court can decide to hear a case or dismiss a case and leave it as is.

EXERCISE 4: THE JUDICIAL BRANCH

1. Which of the following is true of the Supreme Court?

   (1) The Supreme Court hears only civil cases.
   (2) The Supreme Court hears only criminal cases.
   (3) The Supreme Court is the highest court in the United States.
   (4) The Supreme Court can be overruled by a presidential veto.
   (5) The Supreme Court advises the President on legislation that should be introduced into Congress.

The correct answer is (3). Once a case has been decided by the Supreme Court, there are no more courts to which the case may be appealed.

2. The main responsibility of the Supreme Court is which of the following?

   (1) To hear and decide appealed cases
   (2) To hear and decide cases between foreign countries
   (3) To represent the United States in international court
   (4) To resolve disputes between individuals and businesses
   (5) To declare presidential acts unconstitutional

The correct answer is (1). The Supreme Court's greatest responsibility is to hear and decide cases that have been appealed from lower courts.

CHECKS AND BALANCES

As you learned earlier, the writers of the Constitution divided the United States government into three branches—the legislative, executive, and judicial—so that no one part of the government would develop too much power. The writers of the Constitution also included in the plan of government another system of safeguards against one branch dominating any other branch. This system is known as the system of checks and balances. Each branch of government has the ability to check the power of the other two branches and that helps balance the powers of the branches. Let's look at a few examples of some of the checks each branch has on the others. The executive branch can check the power of the legislative branch by vetoing legislation and can check the power of the judicial branch by appointing judges. The legislative branch can check the power of the executive branch by overriding vetoes, by rejecting presidential appointments or nominations, and by impeaching the President. The legislative branch can check the power of the judicial branch by impeaching judges and by rejecting judicial appointments. The judicial branch can check the power of the executive branch by declaring acts of the President unconstitutional. The judicial branch can check the power of the legislative branch by declaring laws unconstitutional. This system may seem like it could cause inefficiency in the government, but it helps maintain a healthy balance of power between the three branches.

THE U.S. FEDERAL SYSTEM

When the thirteen colonies first came together under the Articles of Confederation, they still governed themselves. Once they permanently united as the United States of America, the states retained many rights to continue governing themselves. The government of the country became the shared responsibility of the national government and the state governments. Things such as marriage laws, educational standards, and election laws were left to the discretion of the states. Additionally, some powers were set aside even for local governments. This division of government on different levels is known as federalism.

STATE AND LOCAL GOVERNMENTS

The powers that were set aside specifically for the states are known as reserved powers and are provided for in the Tenth Amendment. To avoid any conflict between state and federal law, the writers of the Constitution made sure to include in Article VI a provision that states that the Constitution and the laws created by Congress take priority over any state or local laws. This clause in Article VI is known as the Supremacy Clause.

The United States requires that each state have a republican form of government. In other words, each state must operate as a republic. There are no other requirements for state governments than that. Most states, however, used the U.S. Constitution as the model for their state constitutions. Therefore, most state governments are very similar to that of the United States government, even though they do not have to be. All states have a governor who serves as the head of the executive branch in his or her state. All states, with the exception of Nebraska, have two legislative houses in their legislative branch. Each state has its own court system although there are many variations of court system structures.

The Constitution requires that the state governments and the federal government work together. For example, a state law enforcement agency may work with a federal law enforcement agency on a special case. The Constitution also facilitates cooperation among states. The "full faith and credit clause" of the Constitution requires that states accept each other's legal decisions and documents. It is the "full faith and credit clause" that makes one state recognize the marriage licenses or drivers licenses from another state. States also cooperate through the process of extradition. Extradition is when a one state sends a suspected criminal back to the state in which the suspect is accused of a crime.

Although state governments tend to be very similar to the federal government, local governments vary greatly. Some local governments are headed by a mayor, or a chief executive officer elected by the people of the city or town. In these municipalities, a city council often aids the mayor in the administration of the local government. In other municipalities, a council is elected and then a city manager is hired to handle the business operations. Still other municipalities are run by elected commissioners; each commissioner is responsible for a certain area of operation such as water or public safety.

EXERCISE 5: CHECKS AND BALANCES AND FEDERALISM

1. The writers of the Constitution included in their plan of government which of the following to ensure that no branch of government grew too powerful?

   (1) Government monitors who watch for corruption
   (2) Supreme Court elections
   (3) Three separate divisions of government, each with different responsibilities
   (4) Two houses in the legislature
   (5) 9 Supreme Court justices

The correct answer is (3). With the political power divided three ways, no part of the government has the ability to dominate politically.

2. According to the Constitution, state governments must do which of the following?

   (1) Establish a pure democracy
   (2) Establish a republican form of government
   (3) Establish a federal system at the state level
   (4) Require municipalities to have a republican form of government
   (5) Prohibit all forms of government except for democracy within the state

The correct answer is (2). The only requirement a state government must meet according to the Constitution is that it have a republican form of government.

THE U.S. POLITICAL SYSTEM

Since the earliest days of the United States, Americans have had differing opinions on the way the country should be governed. These differences in opinions in the formative years of the nation led to the development of the first two political parties, the Federalists and the Republicans. A political party is a group of people who hold similar values and have similar ideas about the proper leadership of the government. Often people form or join political parties based on beliefs about how weak or strong the central government should be, how much or how little the government should tax or spend, or how federal money is spent. Both political parties and members of political parties can be classified based on their ideas about government. On the one hand, liberals, who are often referred to as being on the left, generally advocate political change and social progress. Conservatives, on the other hand, generally advocate very slow change, if any, to the existing political and social order. Those who fall somewhere in between liberal and conservative are often referred to as moderate.

The basic goal of a political party is to get its candidate elected to a public office. By doing so, the political party can influence public policy in a way that is in line with the political ideology of the party. The political parties also have another important function in the U.S. political system. In addition to influencing the policies of the government, political parties further strengthen the system of checks and balances. The parties keep a close eye on the actions of the other parties in power and help ensure that there is no abuse within the system. Furthermore, political parties give citizens a sense of belonging in the political arena and give citizens a voice in all levels of politics.

As you just learned, political parties want their candidates elected to office. In order to elect a candidate, the political party and the candidate must go through a long process. In many elections, candidates must first win a preliminary election called a primary. Each party holds a primary election in which voters choose a candidate to represent their party in the main election. For example, in a Republican primary, Republican voters choose from a list of potential Republican candidates. The winner of the Republican primary will run against candidates from other parties in the main election. Some primary elections, known as open primaries, are open to all voters. Closed primaries are primary elections in which voters must declare a party and choose from that party's candidates. One of the ways candidates get elected is by promoting their platforms. A platform is a list of beliefs, values or ideas that a particular candidate or political party holds as their own. Voters usually use candidates' platforms to evaluate and choose the candidate they want to be in office.

Individuals who are not content with simply participating in a political party often form or join pressure groups. Pressure groups are those with a particular agenda or list of needs and wants. These pressure groups diligently work to persuade legislators in the lawmaking process. This active persuasion of legislators is known as lobbying. Lobbyists often try to meet with legislators to sway the legislators one way or the other during the lawmaking process. For example, environmental lobbyists try to persuade legislators to pass only legislation that will not be harmful to the environment.

EXERCISE 6: THE U.S. POLITICAL SYSTEM

1. People may join a political party for all except for which of the following reasons?

   (1) To voice an opinion collectively instead of individually
   (2) To discover ideas of governing different from their own
   (3) To promote a particular candidate in an election
   (4) To vote in a closed primary
   (5) To associate with people who share similar political ideas

The correct answer is (2). People do not join political parties to find new and different ideas.

2. Which of the following would most likely hire a lobbyist to persuade legislators to pass a new law?

   (1) The Boy Scouts of America
   (2) A church in Georgia
   (3) A tobacco company in North Carolina
   (4) A single parent on welfare
   (5) A person convicted of a felony

The correct answer is (3). A tobacco company would want certain laws passed or certain laws changed, and they could afford to hire lobbyists to try to accomplish that goal.

CANADIAN GOVERNMENT

The Canadian Constitution establishes the responsibilities of the federal government, or a government in which responsibilities are divided between national, provincial, and municipal governments. In addition to those duties enumerated, or named, in the Constitution, the federal government also controls all issues not specifically charged to the provincial or territorial governments. Like the government of the United States, powers are divided among three separate branches of government.

GOVERNOR GENERAL

As a constitutional monarchy, Canada is governed by a monarch whose powers are defined by the Constitution. The monarch, or Head of State, is Queen Elizabeth II. The Queen, on the advice of Canada's Prime Minister, appoints a Governor General. The Governor General is traditionally appointed to a five-year term. The Governor General then fulfills all of the duties of the Head of State on behalf of the Queen.

The duties of the Governor General include executing orders-in-council and other state documents, appointing all superior court judges, and giving "royal assent" to bills passed by the House of Commons and the Senate before they can become law. The Governor General also summons, prorogues (ends a session), and dissolves Parliament.

PRIME MINISTER

The Prime Minister is the leader of the party with the most seats in the House of Commons. In addition to controlling the House of Commons, the Prime Minister advises the Queen on her appointment of the Governor General and thus enjoys quite a bit of power. The Prime Minister also oversees the Cabinet. Members of the Cabinet include the heads of the Ministries, the Prime Minister's Office, and the Privy Council Office. Canada has eighteen Ministries that cover all areas of government. Some of the Ministries are Finance, Canadian Heritage, Health, Justice, and Veteran Affairs. The Prime Minister's Office handles things related to the Prime Minister's role as Party Leader. For example, the Prime Minister's Office handles public relations and decides which matters need the Prime Minister's attention and which do not. The Privy Council Office has a number of responsibilities that range from advising the Prime Minister on national security matters to working as a liaison between the Prime Minister and the Cabinet.

PARLIAMENT

Canada has a bicameral legislature, or a legislature with two houses. The two houses include the House of Commons and the Senate. The House of Commons, also called the Green Chamber, is made up of 301 members who are elected in general elections at least every five years. The number of members is based on population. At any given time, several different political parties may be represented in the House of Commons. However, the party with a majority of seats in the House of Commons is asked to form the government of Canada. If no party holds a majority, then the parties are asked to form a partnership to form a minority government.

The Senate, or Red Chamber, was created to protect regional, provincial, and minority interests. Unlike the House of Commons, senators are appointed by the Governor General on the basis of "equal representation" and are not elected based on population. There are 105 seats in the senate. To be appointed as a Senator, one must be at least thirty years old, be a Canadian citizen by birth or naturalization, have a net estate worth at least $4,000, own property in the province for which they are appointed worth $4,000, and be a resident of the province he or she is appointed to represent.

THE JUDICIARY

The Supreme Court consists of a Chief Justice and eight justices. Each is appointed and holds office until the age of 75. A justice may be removed from office for incapacity or misconduct by the Governor General (on address of the Senate and House of Commons). The Supreme Court issues judgments and advises on questions concerning constitutional interpretation, the constitutionality of legislation, and the powers of Parliament and the Provinces. Another important branch of the Judiciary is the Tax Court. Created in 1983, the Tax Court is the first level of appeals for taxpayers.

Below the Supreme Court and the Tax Court is the Federal Court. A superior court of record with both civil and criminal jurisdiction, the Federal Court of Canada is divided into the Federal Court of Appeal and the Federal Court, Trial Division. The trial division hears lawsuits and applications to review government actions. The Court of Appeal hears appeals from the Trial Division and supervises the decisions of government tribunals. Appeals from the Court of Appeal are made to the Supreme Court.

THE PROVINCIAL AND TERRITORIAL GOVERNMENT

Each of the ten provinces and the three territories has its own capital in which its government is centered. Each province is headed by a Lieutenant Governor and each territory by a Commissioner. Generally speaking, provinces and territories differ in a few ways. All land in a province is controlled by the province itself while land in a territory is controlled by the federal government. Also, provinces are included in the Constitutional amendment process while territories are not. The governments of both provinces and territories are responsible for the education and welfare of their inhabitants, the administration of justice, and the protection of natural resources within the boundaries.

THE MUNICIPAL GOVERNMENT

Below the provincial and territorial governments are the municipal governments. Within each province and territory there exist many municipalities in the form of regions, counties, and districts called "Upper Tier" municipalities. "Lower Tier" municipalities are cities and townships. The provincial and territorial governments have the power to create and modify the municipal, or local, governments. Also, the provincial and territorial governments have the power to assign certain responsibilities to the townships. These may include things such as animal control, water and sewage management, and economic development.

EXERCISE 7: THE FEDERAL GOVERNMENT OF CANADA

1. Which of the following statements concerning the Canadian federal government is true?

   (1) The Canadian government has loose ties with Great Britain, most notably its association with the Sovereign.
   (2) The Judiciary clearly has more power than the other two branches of Canadian government.
   (3) Because of the structure of the Canadian government, it would be relatively easy for one person or one party to abuse powers and take control of the government.
   (4) The municipal governments have nearly the same amount of authority as the provincial and territorial governments.
   (5) The government of Canada stands in stark contrast to the government of the United States.

The correct answer is (1). Because the Sovereign is still the highest position in the order of precedence in Canada.

2. Which of the following government positions indicates the importance of political parties in the Canadian government?

   (1) Mayor
   (2) Governor General
   (3) Queen
   (4) Prime Minister
   (5) Chief Justice

The correct answer is (4). The Prime Minister is the leader of the party with the most seats in the House of Commons.

Economics

The study of economics is the study of the way society uses limited resources to meet its material needs. To be more specific, economics deals with the production, distribution, and consumption of goods. The field of economics can generally be divided into two major areas, microeconomics and macroeconomics. Microeconomics, also known as price theory, examines how supply, demand, and competition cause differences in prices, profits, wages, and other aspects of economics. In the area of microeconomics, economists assume that proprietors or entrepreneurs seek to make the most profit possible and that consumers spend their money to seek the most pleasure possible. Macroeconomics looks at the larger picture of economics and examines such things as employment and national income. Macroeconomics developed after the publication of a book called *The General Theory of Employment, Interest, and Money* in 1935 by a British economist named John Maynard Keynes.

Although economics has been a vital part of the life of every state in history, the academic field of economics did not take on a life of its own until a brilliant Scottish moral philosopher, Adam Smith, wrote *Inquiry into the Nature and Causes of the Wealth of Nations* in 1776. Smith's landmark work is still used today by economists and students of economics. Paramount to Smith's economic theory was the idea of the "invisible hand." Smith believed that the government should be directly involved in the economy as little as possible. He argued that if consumers were left alone to act in their own interests and on their own behalf, a natural force, an invisible hand, so to speak, would point the national economy in a direction that would benefit the greatest number of people. As a result, Smith was a critic of the economic policy of mercantilism. Mercantilism, a popular government practice during the time, was a system in which all national economic policy was directed by the goal of national self-sufficiency. In other words, a mercantilist nation sought to make its economy better by becoming less and less reliant on other nations' goods. Mercantilist nations sought to stockpile gold and silver, to keep wages as low as possible, and to keep the population growing. Smith disagreed with this policy of government manipulation of the economy.

A group of French economists, known as physiocrats, reacted to the mercantilists by advocating free trade and a *laissez-faire* approach to the economy. *Laissez faire* is a term that means the government takes a "hands off" approach to economic policy. Free trade means that the government allows both imports and exports to come and go freely. The physiocrats believed in a single tax to raise money for the state instead of the manipulation of the economy; Smith agreed with their ideas.

Other notable economists include Thomas Malthus, David Ricardo, and John Stuart Mill. Although these economists had some philosophical differences, they all basically agreed on some major principles. They all believed in a free market economy, the right to own private property, and the ability of competition to drive an economy. Another economist was Karl Marx. Marx took a different approach to economic theory, though. Marx, a socialist, believed that those who owned the means of production historically had exploited the working class. Therefore, Marx advocated the elimination of private property and the collective ownership of both property and industry. Marx outlined his economic theories in the historic *Communist Manifesto*, co-authored by Frederick Engels.

ROAD MAP

- *Economic Systems*
- *Capitalism*
- *Socialism*
- *Communism*
- *Mixed Economics*
- *Factors of Production*
- *Supply and Demand*
- *Government and Economics*
- *Money, Monetary Policy, and Financial Institutions*
- *Labor Relations*
- *Foreign Trade*

ECONOMIC SYSTEMS

The study of economics is the study of the way society uses limited resources to meet its material needs. Because material needs are often unlimited and because material resources, or capital, are limited, governments must make decisions about the manner in which the resources will be used or distributed throughout the society. The manner in which a government distributes capital is a factor that determines which economic system a government will use. Other determining factors are the values held by the government and the freedoms the government extends to the society it governs. The most common economic systems are capitalism, socialism, and communism.

CAPITALISM

Capitalism is an economic system in which private ownership of material resources, or capital, is not only allowed but also encouraged. In fact, a key characteristic of a capitalist system is the fact that both land and capital is privately owned. Also key is the belief that there is practically no limit to the wealth that can be created through a capitalist system. Another key characteristic of a capitalist system is that consumers in free markets drive economic activity. Individuals make their own financial decisions without interference by the government. Individuals are free to save, invest, and spend as they will. In addition, all parties involved are free to use their income to seek maximum pleasure and are free to seek maximum profits in business ventures. In the business sector, businesses also compete in a free market. In other words, prices, production, and distribution are determined by the competition within the market instead of by the government. Government intervention occurs in a capitalist economy only when the best interest of the public is at stake. For example, the government may intervene in the market in cases of monopolies or price gouging. Another vital role of government in a capitalist system is to protect the nation from foreign attacks or intervention. The United States is a good example of a capitalist economy, also referred to as a market economy.

SOCIALISM

In the economic system known as socialism, the government is in charge of the redistribution of wealth, and the major industries are either owned publicly or cooperatively. The major industries controlled by the government include health care, transportation, heavy industry (steel production, manufacturing, etc.), and banking. In addition, natural resources, public utilities, and finance corporations are nationalized. Competition is reduced to a minimum in these industries with the goal of creating an egalitarian, or equal opportunity, economic environment. Although there is some limited private ownership of capital, individuals work with the government to determine goods and services that should be produced and the manner in which they are distributed. Only smaller interests are left to individuals. The goal of a socialist economic system is the formation of a classless society. A key characteristic of a socialist economy is a very high tax rate. The high taxes provide revenue to fund things such as free public education and health care. Sweden is a great example of a socialist economy. Although socialism and communism were once thought of as very similar, modern socialists would be quick to point out that communism now often denotes an oppressive, authoritarian regime.

COMMUNISM

In a communist economic system, the government does not permit private ownership of either capital or the means of production. A communist government owns the property within the state and determines the way the goods and services should be distributed. The goal of a communist government is to distribute goods and services in a manner that serves the common good, or in a manner that benefits everyone the most, so that private interests are sacrificed for the welfare of the majority. Theoretically, a communist society is a classless society in which everyone in it works according to his or her ability and is provided for according to his or her need. Also theoretically, a communist society eventually will need no official state government. Critics of communism will point out that pure communism is practically impossible, though. The former Soviet Union is the most striking example of a modern communist economy, also referred to as a command economy. However, the communism under leaders like Lenin and Stalin did not even remotely resemble the communism as described by Marx and Engels.

MIXED ECONOMIES

Economists are quick to point out that there is no economic system that is purely capitalist, socialist, or communist. In every economic system, there are some elements of other economic systems present. In most cases, the term mixed economy is used to describe an economy that has elements of multiple economic systems. The United States, although generally capitalistic, is a good example of a mixed economy. The United States is, for the most part, capitalist. However, there is some government operation or subsidy of industries, such as health care and transportation. For example, the New Deal economic recovery program under President Franklin Roosevelt contained many elements of socialism, as did the social reform of President Lyndon Johnson.

EXERCISE 1: ECONOMIC SYSTEMS

1. Which of the following is a characteristic of communism?

    (1)   Less government intervention in the economy than in socialism
    (2)   Less government intervention than in capitalism
    (3)   Free market economy
    (4)   More government intervention than in capitalism
    (5)   More prosperous economy than capitalism

The correct answer is (4). In communism, the government controls every facet of the economy.

2. An individual investor would be most free to manage his money in which of the following economic systems?

    (1)   A capitalist economy
    (2)   A socialist economy
    (3)   A communist economy
    (4)   An economy with socialist and communist elements
    (5)   An economy with capitalist and communist elements

The correct answer is (1). Capitalism encourages investments and allows more economic freedom than other economic systems.

FACTORS OF PRODUCTION

When economists talk about production within an economic system, they must consider the three factors of production. These factors are natural resources, capital, and labor. Usually the factors of production cannot fully meet the demands of the consumers, or people who use the goods produced. Natural resources are the raw materials necessary for the production of goods. For example, trees are necessary for the production of houses, paper, and wooden furniture.

Capital can be any equipment, factories, or property necessary for the conversion of raw materials into finished goods. This type of capital is referred to as fixed capital. Capital can also refer to money that is invested to support the production of goods. This type of capital, called circulating capital, can be wages paid to laborers or raw materials used in production. Any capital that can be sold for cash is considered liquid capital, while capital that cannot be easily converted to cash is known as frozen capital.

In economics, the term labor is used to describe the work it takes to convert raw materials into goods and services. Labor may refer to the people who actually do the work manufacturing the raw materials and producing the goods. Laborers may be factory assembly line workers, truck drivers, sales agents, or other people involved in the production and distribution of goods. Labor may even refer to people in a service industry, such as doctors or teachers that provide services for others.

When considering productivity, economists also consider the law of diminishing returns. The factors of production, when used together in the correct proportions, will produce an end result sufficient for a society. However, according to the law of diminishing returns, at a certain point any additional resources (raw materials, labor, or capital) fails to produce any additional product. In fact, according to the law, at a certain point, additional resources may even result in less production than before the additional resources were added.

EXERCISE 2: FACTORS OF PRODUCTION

1. The natural resources required to build a log home include which of the following?

    (1) Trees, land, and construction workers
    (2) Land and construction workers
    (3) Trees
    (4) Trees and land
    (5) Land

The correct answer is (3). *Trees* is the correct choice because land is considered capital and construction workers are considered laborers.

2. The law of diminishing returns could be applied to which of the following situations?

    (1) Salaries of factory workers are raised.
    (2) New raw materials are supplied to a factory to produce a brand new product.
    (3) The number of assembly line workers in an efficient factory is cut in half to reduce company spending.
    (4) The number of assembly line workers in an efficient factory is doubled while the amount of raw materials remains the same.
    (5) A human-operated assembly line is replaced by a new, computerized assembly line to run more efficiently.

The correct answer is (4). With twice as many workers in an already efficient factory, the workers will probably get in each other's way and reduce efficiency and production.

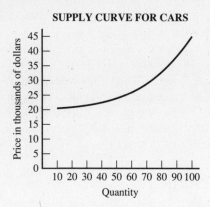

SUPPLY CURVE FOR CARS

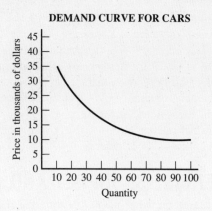

DEMAND CURVE FOR CARS

SUPPLY AND DEMAND

The primary force and one of the basic principles of economics is that of supply and demand. Supply can be defined as all the goods available regardless of price. Demand can be defined as the desire of the consumers to purchase goods. Producers supply goods with the hope that consumers will demand goods. Producers must set prices on the goods high enough that they still make a profit after paying for all the costs of production. Consumers seek to pay the lowest price possible for goods. Producers must set the amount of production based on the demand for goods. The price and the availability of goods determine the demand. These factors working together make up the principle of supply and demand.

If a given item, a car for example, has a high profit yield, a great number of producers will be interested in production of the good. The producers of the cars will compete for a share of the market. If the market is flooded with cars, or if there are too many cars on the market, and the supply of cars is greater than the demand, buyers either cannot or will not buy all of the supply of cars. If this happens, there will be a surplus that will then cause car prices to fall. This may increase the demand for the cars. If an item, such as a car, has a price that is low enough to make consumers want the item, it will be in demand. If the price of the car falls too much, there may be such a demand that producers cannot supply the item fast enough to meet the demand. If the demand exceeds the supply, the prices will rise.

To make a market stable, producers must figure out exactly the amount of goods that consumers will demand and the price that the consumers will pay for the goods. When this point is reached, it is called equilibrium. On the chart below, the point of equilibrium is the point at which the two curves intersect. When the price for goods rises above equilibrium, there is a decreased demand and, therefore, more goods than consumers want. This creates

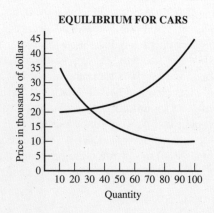

EQUILIBRIUM FOR CARS

a surplus. If the opposite happens, that is if the price falls below equilibrium, the demand increases, and there is a shortage. These are the laws of supply and demand.

It should be noted that the laws of supply and demand are only valid in an economic system in which the markets are relatively undisturbed by the government. Because supply and demand depend on market conditions, an economy in which the government controls the market would not follow the laws of supply and demand. For example, during times of war in the United States or at any given time in the former USSR, the markets were somewhat manipulated by the government. That invalidated the supply and demand mechanisms in those places.

EXERCISE 3: SUPPLY AND DEMAND

1. Based on the principles of supply and demand, what conclusion can be drawn?

   (1) The lower the profit an item generates, the more producers will be interested in producing that item.
   (2) The higher the price of an item, the higher the demand will be for that item.
   (3) The more consumers demand an item, the lower the prices will go.
   (4) The more consumers demand an item, the higher prices will go.
   (5) The fewer items produced, the lower the price will be on those items.

The correct answer is (4). If there is a high demand among consumers for an item, the producer can charge a higher price and consumers will still pay for the item.

2. Market stability will occur when which of the following occurs?

   (1) Prices rise above the point of equilibrium
   (2) Producers produce the amount of goods that consumers want at the price that consumers want to pay
   (3) A surplus is created
   (4) A shortage is created
   (5) Prices fall below the point of equilibrium

The correct answer is (2). Stability occurs when producers produce the amount of goods the consumers want at a price that consumers feel is fair.

GOVERNMENT AND ECONOMICS

The United States has a free market economy, yet the government still plays a vital role in steering the economy. Through the use of taxation, the government can create revenue for its own use or to control inflation. Inflation can be defined as a rise in prices or a devaluing of money, resulting in decreased buying power for consumers. By reducing government expenditures or by adjusting the tax rate, the government can help control or correct inflation. Taxation can also be used to increase or decrease consumer spending. By increasing the tax rate, the government can discourage consumer spending thereby slowing the economy. By decreasing the tax rate, the government can stimulate or encourage consumer spending, investing, and business transactions because people have more money to spend and invest. It should be noted that not all inflation is bad, though. Slow and gradual inflation is normal and even good for an economy. Inflation of 10 percent annually coupled with high price increases would cause concern for economists. The government also controls social programs like welfare, unemployment benefits, Medicare, and Social Security. The government manages the funds used to operate these programs and distributes the funds to citizens who have need of assistance. All of these practices are part of the government monetary policy known as the fiscal policy. The practice of increasing taxation or restricting public spending is called the contractionary fiscal policy. The practice of reducing taxation and stimulating public spending is known as the expansionary fiscal policy.

MONEY, MONETARY POLICY, AND FINANCIAL INSTITUTIONS

The use of money is the method of exchange employed in economic systems in lieu of bartering. Whatever currency an economic system uses is its money. The money supply of a nation is mostly coins and paper money, or bills, along with deposits made to banks. The use of money in an economic system is controlled through monetary policy. In the United States, the Federal Reserve Board controls the monetary policy. The Federal Reserve Board, currently chaired by Alan Greenspan, directs the monetary policy by regulating the money and credit available for use in the country. It does this by setting the reserve ratio and setting the discount rate. The reserve ratio is the amount of money that lending institutions can lend and the amount of money they must hold in reserve. By setting the reserve ratio, the Federal Reserve Board controls the supply of money that is available for banks and savings and loan associations to lend to consumers. The Federal Reserve Board tightens the supply of money by raising the reserve ratio. On the other hand, the Federal Reserve Board loosens the supply of money by dropping the reserve ratio. The discount rate is the interest rate that the Federal Reserve Board charges to member banks to borrow money. Banks then charge consumers a higher interest rate on loans than they pay to the Federal Reserve. The more money that banks want to borrow, the more it costs to borrow the money. The hike in the cost discourages banks from borrowing more and reduces bank demand for extra reserve money. The Federal Reserve Board also sets the margin requirement that determines the amount of cash a purchaser must pay up front when buying stocks; this helps deter speculation, as in the kind that led to the Great Depression.

LABOR RELATIONS

As you learned earlier, when speaking within the realm of economics, labor refers to the people who actually do the work manufacturing the raw materials and producing goods, or the people who provide services for others. All dealings between labor and management over labor issues are called labor relations. Many years ago, laborers fought constantly for better wages and working conditions, often with no success. One reason for the lack of success during pre-industrial America was because employers dealt directly with individual employees. As industrialization took over, though, employers faced many employees instead of just a few individuals. Government regulations eventually set limits on the number of hours workers had to work and the minimum wages workers could receive. These regulations helped curb dangerous working conditions. Labor, however, remained largely unorganized.

In the 1930s, the Wagner Act allowed laborers to organize and negotiate with management concerning disputes. The labor organizations became known as unions, and these negotiations became known as collective bargaining. Collective bargaining occurs when leaders of the labor unions meet with employers and management to negotiate wages, hours, conditions, benefits, or other issues. Collective bargaining is often successful. Many times independent arbitrators handle the negotiations between the two sides. However, when collective bargaining does not work, laborers may go on strike. When workers strike, or stop working, the government may intervene and end the strike or the government may help facilitate successful negotiations. The threat of a strike is most successful during negotiations when the unemployment rate is relatively low. If there are plenty of unemployed workers who are willing to replace the strikers, the strike loses its effectiveness.

To help prevent such situations from occurring, the government regulates wages, hours, and working conditions.

EXERCISE 4: THE GOVERNMENT'S ROLE IN ECONOMICS

1. Government can control aspects of the economy by controlling which of the following?

    (1)   Unemployment
    (2)   Checking and savings accounts
    (3)   The value of money
    (4)   Salary caps
    (5)   Taxation

The correct answer is (5). *Taxation* is the correct choice because a higher tax rate slows the economy, while a lower tax rate stimulates the economy.

2. The Federal Reserve Board is vital to the economy because of its policies concerning which of the following?

    (1)   Labor disputes
    (2)   Social Security
    (3)   Interest rates
    (4)   Minting of new coins and bills
    (5)   Unemployment

The correct answer is (3). The Federal Reserve Board's policies on the reserve ratio and discount rate directly affect the nation's interest rates.

FOREIGN TRADE

A major part of any economic system is foreign trade. Few nations are completely self-sufficient and isolated from the rest of the world. Therefore, countries must trade with other countries for raw materials, goods, and services they need. Often countries specialize in goods that create a high demand in other parts of the world. Specialization in a particular good may occur because of a country's expertise in that area or because a country can produce that good cheaply or efficiently. Adam Smith recognized that economic specialization led to an increase in output, and he encouraged foreign trade in specialized goods. Smith went even further and said that a country should specialize in goods that it could produce more cheaply and efficiently than its trade partners. David Ricardo modified this theory when he advocated specialization in goods, not just when a country could produce goods more cheaply than competitors, but also when a country can sell those goods for a better price abroad than at home.

Goods that are shipped out of a country to another country are known as exports; goods brought into a country from another country are called imports. To maintain a healthy economy, the goal of a country is to export more goods than it imports. Economists call this occurrence a favorable balance of trade. In order to protect domestic goods, countries often add a special tax, called a tariff, to imports so that domestic goods are more competitively priced. If the tariffs are too high, the country whose imports are being taxed will retaliate with tariffs on goods of their own. Another way that countries protect their interests is through the use of import quotas. Import quotas limit the number of particular foreign goods that may enter a country. Quotas are often very successful in reversing trade imbalances. On occasion, government health or safety standards prevent foreign goods from entering the domestic market. Government support of domestic industries provides additional advantages for domestic industries and puts foreign competitors at a disadvantage. It is very important that governments carefully manage their overseas trade; many workers in each country depend on producing goods for overseas trade.

EXERCISE 5: FOREIGN TRADE

1. Which of the following might occur if a country's tariffs were set too high?

    (1)   The country would become very rich.
    (2)   The country's trade partners would retaliate with high tariffs of their own.
    (3)   The country would go bankrupt.
    (4)   The prices of domestic goods would plummet.
    (5)   The prices of domestic goods would skyrocket.

The correct answer is (2). Many nations have become involved in tariff wars when one country raises tariffs only to have its trade partner do the same.

2. Concerning foreign trade, the goal of a country is which of the following?

    (1)   Produce and sell more goods domestically than internationally
    (2)   Import more goods than it exports
    (3)   Export more goods than it imports
    (4)   Charge wealthy countries higher prices than third-world countries
    (5)   To not export any goods

The correct answer is (3). This favorable balance of trade allows a country to make more income than it spends on importing goods.

Introduction to Geography

Geography is more than states and capitals or latitude and longitude. Geography is the study of the earth's physical features and the way man has adapted to these physical features. Geography is concerned not only with physical geographic features but also with cultural geographic features. Physical geographic features include things such as land, water, mountains, and plains. Cultural geographic features include things such as human architecture or man-made changes to the earth's physical features. The science of geography can be divided into two branches, systematic and regional. Systematic geography deals with individual elements of the earth's physical and cultural features. Regional geography, on the other hand, deals with the physical and cultural features within a particular region, or area, of the earth's surface.

Systematic geography includes a number of different fields within the realm of physical geography. Part of physical geography is cartography, or mapmaking. Another important part of physical geography is oceanography, or the study of the earth's oceans; climatology examines the earth's weather patterns; and geomorphology looks at the way the surface of the earth has changed. Other areas of physical geography include biogeography, or the study of the distribution of plants and animals, and soil geography, or the study of the distribution of soil and soil conservation. Systematic geography also includes a number of fields within the realm of cultural geography, or the study of how human social and cultural life affects geography. Economic geography, for example, examines how business and industry have affected the geographic environment. Political geography looks at nations, states, cities, and other man-made areas and examines how geography influences these political units; political geography often involves some political science, too. Military geography is the study of how the geography of a particular area may affect military operations. Military geography is especially important today in light of the events in the Middle East.

Regional geography deals with similarities and differences between various regions of the earth. Regional geographers look closely at the unique combinations of features that make regions similar or different. Sometimes regional geography includes the study of places as small as cities. This special type of regional geography is called microgeography. On the other hand, regional geography also includes the study of entire areas like the Arctic Circle or the Pacific Rim. These large areas are called macrodivisions and are part of macrogeography. Within macrodivisions, geographers may study smaller regions that make up the larger division of land based on such features as language, climate, or religion.

THE ROLE OF GEOGRAPHERS

The role of geographers, or those who study the earth's physical and cultural features, is twofold. First, a geographer studies geography. A geographer may use any number of sources to study a particular area of geography. A geographer may use maps, pictures, satellite information, or surveys to collect information. A geographer may also go directly to the area he or she is studying to get information directly from the

ROAD MAP

- *The Role of Geographers*
- *Themes of Geography*
- *Globes and Maps*
- *Latitude and Longitude*
- *Time Zones*
- *Topography and Climate*
- *Environmental Issues*

source. The second role of a geographer is to describe the earth's physical features. A geographer may help create maps or analyze data for businesses or the government. The use of computers has aided geographers in their work in the last twenty years. Each year, geographers continue to find more practical applications for their work.

THEMES OF GEOGRAPHY

Vital to the study of geography is a working knowledge of the themes of geography, the ability to use maps and globes, an understanding of topography and climate, and an understanding of environmental issues. The National Council for Geographic Education developed five themes of geography. Those who study geography, called geographers, study the earth's surface within the context of these five themes. The first theme is *location*. In geography, *location* means an exact and precise position on the earth's surface. Any place on Earth can be marked as an exact position on a globe. This exact position is known to geographers as an *absolute location*. Because of the imaginary grid of horizontal and vertical lines that is placed over the globe, any position on Earth can be marked with pinpoint accuracy. These lines are known as latitude and longitude. *Relative location* is described by landmarks, direction from or distance from another location, or by associating one location with another location.

Geographers refer to the second theme of geography as *place*. *Place* has a special meaning within the context of geography, and means not only where a location is but also what a location is like. In other words, *place* deals with the physical features that make a particular location similar to or different than another location. These features can be natural features such as climate, terrain, or wildlife; man-made features such as buildings or dams; or human characteristics such as economics or culture.

The third theme of geography is *environment*. The *environment* of an area includes the area's natural surroundings. Geographers study not only an area's *environment* but also the way that humans interact with it. For example, humans have reacted to mountainous environments by building roads over the mountains or tunnels through them. In addition, geographers study not only the way humans adapt to and modify the *environment* but also the extent to which humans depend on it.

Geographers study the relationship between places through the theme called *movement*. *Movement* is concerned with the ways humans interact with other humans in other places. It can deal with the trade of imports and exports, travel, or even communication between humans. For geographers, *movement* pertains to the movement of humans, goods, or ideas.

The final theme of geography is known as *region*. A *region* is any area, regardless of size, that contains common characteristics. To a geographer, a *region* may be as small as a city block or as large as a continent. Common characteristics, not size, determine *region*. The characteristics that determine *region* can be natural physical features such as climate or landscape or man-made features such as religion, culture, or political boundaries. In the field of geography, there are three different kinds of regions. First, *formal regions* are those defined by some type of governmental or political boundaries. Second, *functional regions* are those defined by a service of some type. For example, a television service area is an example of a *functional region*. Once a service is ended, the *functional region* no longer exists. Finally, *vernacular regions* are those that are loosely defined by people's ideas about the region. An example of a *vernacular region* would be the Midwest or the Middle East.

EXERCISE 1: THEMES OF GEOGRAPHY

1. Which theme of geography would a geographer be concerned with while studying a winding desert highway?

    (1) Location
    (2) Place
    (3) Environment
    (4) Movement
    (5) Region

The correct answer is (3). The geographer is studying a highway, which is a means of travel or transportation.

2. The region theme of geography would most likely apply to which of the following?

    (1) An area 200 miles square
    (2) An area that averages a daily temperature of 37 degrees Fahrenheit during the winter months
    (3) An area marked by a diverse population
    (4) An area that is home to a diverse collection of wildlife species
    (5) An area that used to be a wetland but was partially drained and converted to farmland

The correct answer is (2). It has a similar characteristic, winter climate, throughout the entire area.

GLOBES AND MAPS

Vital to the study of geography are the geographer's tools, the globe and the map. A *globe* is a spherical representation of a map of the earth. Because the earth is round, a flat representation of the earth is inaccurate; therefore, a globe is the most accurate way to study the earth's surface. However, a globe is not the most efficient or convenient vehicle for geographical information. Therefore, geographers most often rely on the flat representations of the earth's surface known as maps.

Maps come in all shapes and sizes and convey a wide variety of information. There are as many different kinds of maps as there are kinds of information that a map can illustrate. For example, a *political map* shows political borders or boundaries between countries, states, counties, etc. A *topographical map* illustrates physical features such as mountains, hills, valleys, rivers, or prairies. A *contour map* illustrates the elevation of physical features. A *population map* illustrates population density or how many people live in a particular area. A *weather map,* or *climate map,* illustrates the forecasted or current weather for an area.

So that geographers can understand the information on a map, mapmakers, or cartographers, usually include a legend somewhere on the map. A *legend* is like a key that contains the meanings of the symbols used on the map. A legend may also contain a scale that shows distance relative to the map. By using the legend and the scale, geographers can use a map for the purpose it was intended. The illustration below is an example of a map legend.

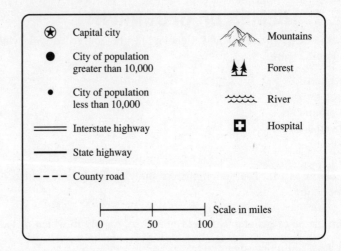

EXERCISE 2: GLOBES AND MAPS

1. The most likely use of a globe would be which of the following?

    (1) To determine the elevation of a plateau in Asia
    (2) To study the climate of Antarctica
    (3) To find all the cities in Texas with a population over 100,000
    (4) To use as a guide while traveling through Canada
    (5) To get an accurate picture of the land around the North and South Poles

The correct answer is (5). Because a flat map cannot accurately illustrate a round surface, a globe is the most accurate representation of the earth's surface, especially around the poles.

2. Which of the following maps would be the best choice to discover the capital of Albania?

    (1) Political map
    (2) Topographical map
    (3) Contour map
    (4) Population map
    (5) Weather or climate map

The correct answer is (1). A political map illustrates political boundaries, city populations, capital cities, and more.

LATITUDE AND LONGITUDE

Geographers use an imaginary grid to determine the absolute location of any place on Earth. The horizontal lines that run east and west and encircle the earth are known as lines of latitude. The latitude lines are used to measure distances north and south of the equator. The equator is an imaginary line that divides the earth into two halves, or hemispheres, and is located halfway between the North Pole and the South Pole. The equator is located at 0 degrees latitude. A line located at 60 degrees north latitude, written as 60°N, would be a line 60 degrees north of the equator just as a line located at 50 degrees south latitude, written as 50°S, would be a line 50 degrees south of the equator. Each of the poles is located at 90 degrees, the North Pole at 90 degrees north latitude, written as 90°N, and the South Pole at 90 degrees south latitude, written as 90°S.

LONGITUDE AND LATITUDE

Lines of Latitude | Lines of Longitude

The vertical lines that run north and south around the earth are known as lines of longitude. Longitude measures distances east and west of the Prime Meridian, which is the vertical line located at 0 degrees longitude that runs from pole to pole through the city of Greenwich, England. On the opposite side of the world is the International Date Line, which is located at 180 degrees longitude. A line located 120 degrees west of the Prime Meridian would be written as 120°W, while a line located at 70 degrees east of the Prime Meridian would be written as 70°E.

The lines of latitude and longitude cross over each other and form an imaginary grid on the earth's surface. The point at which a line of latitude and a line of longitude intersect is known as a coordinate. A coordinate is the way a geographer notes an absolute location. For example, the map below shows the intersection of the 45 degrees north latitude line and 100 degrees west longitude line in the state of South Dakota. The coordinate for that intersection would be written as 45°N 100°W.

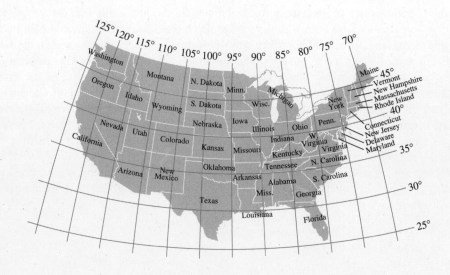

EXERCISE 3: LATITUDE AND LONGITUDE

The following items are based on the map above.

1. Which of the following lines is located closest to the equator?

    (1) 45°N
    (2) 125°W
    (3) 70°W
    (4) 25°N
    (5) 95°W

The correct answer is (4). The line is only 25° away from the equator; therefore, it is closer to the equator than the other latitude lines on the map.

2. In which state would you be standing if you were standing at 35°N 120°W?

    (1) Tennessee
    (2) California
    (3) Arizona
    (4) Florida
    (5) Nevada

The correct answer is (2).

3. Which of the following coordinates is located in the state of Arkansas?

    (1) 35°N 110°W
    (2) 35°N 98°W
    (3) 93°N 35°W
    (4) 25°N 98°W
    (5) 35°N 98°W

The correct answer is (5).

TIME ZONES

Another important set of imaginary vertical lines divides the earth into 24 geographic regions. These regions are known as time zones. Each time zone represents one hour of the day and measures a distance of approximately 15 degrees across. All clocks within the same time zone should be set to the same time and generally are one hour later than those of the time zone to the immediate west. The 0 degrees longitude line, known as the Prime Meridian, runs north and south through the Royal Greenwich Observatory in Greenwich, England. Each of the twelve time zones to the west of the Prime Meridian decrease in time by one hour, while each of the time zones to the east of the Prime Meridian increase in time by one hour. The International Date Line lies on the opposite side of the world from the Prime Meridian and is located at 180 degrees longitude. The time zones on each side of the Date Line are actually in different days. If a person crosses the International Date Line heading west, he will lose a day; if a person crosses the International Date Line heading east, he will gain a day.

TIME ZONES ACROSS THE UNITED STATES

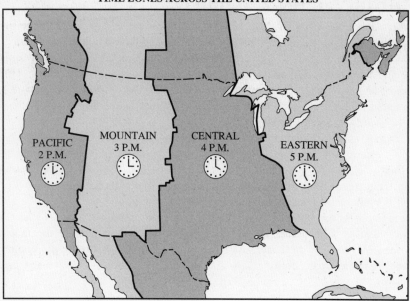

Travel and weather forecasting during the 1800s made standard time zones necessary as scheduling conflicts arose. After railroad systems in North America adopted the four time zones assigned to North America, the British helped gain support for time zone usage around the world. The continental United States and Canada are within four time zones: Eastern, Central, Mountain, and Pacific. While most time zones remain standard, there are a few exceptions. China, for example, spans about 50 degrees of longitude and several time zones. However, China operates under a single time zone, that of the eastern part of the country. Also, the International Date Line bends at the Bering Strait, between Russia and Alaska, so that all of Russia falls within the same day's time.

EXERCISE 4: TIME ZONES

The following item is based on the map above.

1. Based on the information in the map, the sun would rise first in which of the following time zones?

    (1)   Pacific
    (2)   Mountain
    (3)   Central
    (4)   Eastern
    (5)   None of the above

The correct answer is (4). The sun rises in the east; therefore, the eastern time zone would see the sun first.

TOPOGRAPHY AND CLIMATE

Geographers define the study of the earth's physical features as topography. The four main landforms that make up the earth's surface are plains, hills, mountains, and plateaus. The definition of each landform is dependent on both its shape and elevation above sea level. Plains are generally low flatlands. Plateaus are flatlands at high elevations. Hills have elevations of less than 1,000 feet above sea level and have gently sloping sides with rounded tops. Mountains have elevations of more than 1,000 feet above sea level and have steep sides and generally pointed tops or peaks.

The topography of a region plays a direct role in the climate, or long-term weather, of that region. Plains, for example, generally experience warm or hot, dry weather in the summer and cold, windy weather in the winter. Hills and plateaus often have climates similar to the plateaus they are near. Mountains generally have cool climates and often act as natural borders or boundaries between other climate regions.

Cartographers use tools called contour lines to illustrate various elevations of landforms on maps. The higher an elevation is, the closer together on the map are the contour lines. Conversely, the lower an elevation is, the farther apart are the contour lines. Cartographers often create entire maps that illustrate elevation. These maps are called contour maps.

EXERCISE 4: TOPOGRAPHY AND CLIMATE

1. Which of the following would a topographer be least interested in studying?

    (1)   A skyscraper in Paris
    (2)   A valley in California
    (3)   A mountain range in South America
    (4)   A plateau in Mexico
    (5)   The hills of central Texas

The correct answer is (1). Topography is concerned with the earth's physical features, and a skyscraper is man-made.

2. One might expect to find the coolest summer climate in which of the following areas?

    (1)   A large prairie
    (2)   A plateau west of a hilly region
    (3)   A mountain range
    (4)   A hilly region
    (5)   A valley between two mountains

The correct answer is (3). Because a mountain range has a high elevation, it is reasonable to expect that it would have a cool climate, even in the summer months.

ENVIRONMENTAL ISSUES

As humans interact with the physical features of the earth's surface, they often make changes to those features. Many times, those changes have an impact on the environment. The impact of human interaction on the environment often has far-reaching and lasting effects. These effects raise a number of environmental issues and concerns. One of the most pressing environmental concerns is the rate at which the tropical rain forests are disappearing. Every minute between 30 and 50 acres of rain forest are cut down. This is a serious concern because the rain forests help supply oxygen for the earth, and they help supply great amounts of the world's medicines.

Another serious concern is the water supply in southwest Asia and North Africa. Industrialization, irrigation demands, and population explosion are placing heavy strain on the water supply there. There is speculation that in less than fifteen years there will not be enough water to meet the people's needs in those regions.

In many parts of Africa, the process known as desertification is claiming many acres of land. Desertification can be defined as the process of creating deserts. A lack of soil conservation due to uncontrolled use of trees and shrubs for firewood allows desert winds to blow away valuable topsoil. The trees and shrubs are important because their roots hold the soil in place.

A problem that faces many places around the world is habitat loss. Because of the draining of wetlands, the cutting of forests, and the plowing of grasslands, natural habitats are being lost at an alarming rate. Habitat loss leaves countless animal species homeless. Many of these homeless species are forced to then interact with humans. Interaction of this nature often leads to injury, death, or extinction for many such species.

EXERCISE 5: ENVIRONMENTAL ISSUES

1. The most serious threat to the rain forests is which of the following?

    (1) Parasites
    (2) Flooding
    (3) Erosion and desertification
    (4) Human adaptation of the earth's physical features
    (5) Warfare

The correct answer is (4). Humans are cutting down the rain forests every day— making humans the greatest threat to the future of the rain forests.

2. Desertification could possibly be prevented if African governments took what action?

    (1) Irrigation of land after it has become desert
    (2) Replacement of lost topsoil after it has blown away
    (3) Replanting of trees and grasses to prevent valuable topsoil from eroding
    (4) Prohibition of the use of trees and shrubs for firewood, or prohibit fires altogether
    (5) Passage of laws restricting topsoil use

The correct answer is (3). Without trees, shrubs, and other vegetation to hold the soil in place, the topsoil will blow away. Therefore, if vegetation were replaced before the erosion occurred, desertification might be prevented.

Historical Documents on the GED Social Studies Test

As you learned in Chapter 2, the Social Studies test will contain an excerpt from at least one of the following historical documents: the Declaration of Independence, the United States Constitution, the Federalist Papers, or landmark Supreme Court cases. So that you will be more familiar with each of these, this chapter breaks down each of those important documents for you. Before you take the Social Studies test, take time to read some of each of these documents just to familiarize yourself with the language and the style of each one.

ROAD MAP

- *The Declaration of Independence*
- *The U.S. Constitution*
- *The Federalist Papers*
- *Landmark Supreme Court Cases*

THE DECLARATION OF INDEPENDENCE

On July 4, 1776, the members of the Philadelphia Congress adopted a motion that "The united colonies are, and of right ought to be, free and independent states . . ." Thomas Jefferson led a committee appointed to write a statement declaring the thirteen colonies officially free of British reign. The resulting document was the Declaration of Independence. Jefferson's task was not an easy one, however. He needed to clarify the colonies' purpose in fighting Britain. He succeeded, and by doing so, he appealed to other colonies to declare their independence and encouraged other nations to support the colonies against Britain.

Jefferson begins the Declaration of Independence by asserting that all people have rights to which they are entitled by nature. He states that governments are established to protect those rights and when a government fails to do so, people should abolish it and create a new government that will protect the rights.

The Declaration of Independence then takes on a more personal tone, stating that the King of Great Britain, George III, has misused his power in a number of specific ways. Basically, half of the Declaration is devoted to listing the ways in which King George abused his power. Pointing out that their previous attempts to compel the king to respect human rights had failed, Jefferson asserts that logically the Americans did the only thing they could do to preserve the rights of all people—they declared independence from Great Britain. The Declaration, a moving document, had the desired effect and enticed great support for the war against Britain.

THE U.S. CONSTITUTION

The Preamble

"We the people of the United States, in order to form a more perfect union, establish justice, insure domestic tranquillity, provide for the common defense, promote the general welfare, and secure the blessings of liberty to ourselves and our posterity, do ordain and establish this Constitution for the United States of America."

A preamble is a statement of purpose. The Preamble to the Constitution paraphrases the purpose of the Constitution. It answers the question of why the Constitution was created.

Articles of the Constitution

The Articles of the Constitution outline the plan for the government under which we currently live. As discussed in Chapter 4 three branches of government, the executive, legislative, and judicial, divide the power and keep any one part of the government from dominating another. Each branch keeps a check on the others, thus the terms "separation of powers" and "checks and balances." To balance the power of the three branches of government, each has a "check" to limit the powers of the other two. For example, although Congress may pass a bill, the president has the power to veto it. Congress may, however, override a presidential veto by a two-thirds majority vote. Finally, the Supreme Court may declare a law unconstitutional. These powers are named, or enumerated, in Articles I, II, and III of the Constitution. Let's look more closely at each of these Articles.

Article I. Legislative Department

The legislative branch is outlined in Article I of the Constitution. The U.S. legislature, called Congress, is made up of two houses—the House of Representatives and the Senate. Both houses are made up of representatives elected from the states. The House representation is based on state population, while the Senate consists of two senators from each state. The representatives are elected to two-year terms, while the senators are elected to six-year terms. The legislative branch "creates" the law under which we are governed.

Article II. Executive Department

Article II of the Constitution details the executive branch of government. The executive branch consists of the president, vice president, and various agencies and departments that administer and enforce the laws.

The president serves a four-year term and cannot serve more than two terms. The president and the vice president are elected by a vote of the people. However, there is a process known as the Electoral College, through which the results of the popular election must be certified. A president can, although it is rare, receive a majority of the popular vote and still lose the election because of the Electoral College vote. The executive branch "enforces" the laws under which we live.

Article III. Judicial Department

Article III of the Constitution provides that the "judicial power belongs to the federal courts." It is in this Article that the Supreme Court and inferior, or lower level, courts are created. As you've already learned, the Supreme Court "checks" the other two branches of government by declaring certain laws unconstitutional. **The Supreme Court has the power to rule on cases involving a state and a citizen of another state, disputes between states, between citizens of different states, between a state and its citizens, or between a foreign state and U.S. citizens.** It also may consider conflicts arising at sea or regarding patents and copyrights. Most of the time, the Supreme Court hears "appeals" of decisions made by "inferior" courts. However, the Court does have "original" jurisdiction, or the right to hear an original case and not an appealed case, in some instances. These include cases involving ambassadors or other public ministers, consuls, and those cases in which a state is a party.

Although originally created with a Chief Justice and five associate judges, the Supreme Court is now composed of nine justices, each appointed for life by the president with approval from the Senate. The Court acts by issuing opinions that explain why the Court makes particular rulings. A majority of the Court must agree before the ruling becomes law. The judiciary "interprets" the law.

Article IV. Relations of the States to One Another

The goal of this article is to promote respect between the states, also known as "full faith and credit." It requires that the citizens of different states be treated similarly. It also requires states to honor the legal decisions and legal documents of other states.

Article V. The Process of Amendment

This article explains the manner in which the Constitution may be amended or changed.

Article VI. General Provisions

Article VI notes that the United States took on debts of the Confederacy, confirms that the Constitution, federal laws, and treaties "are the supreme law of the land," and requires federal and state officers to take an oath to support the Constitution.

Article VII. Ratification of the Constitution

The authors of the Constitution wrote this article with an eye toward putting the Constitution into action. Article VII provides that the Constitution becomes effective when ratified by the conventions of nine states.

THE AMENDMENTS

In the years following the ratification, or approval, of the Constitution, many leaders wanted to make sure that the rights of individuals were protected. The Constitution did not specifically list those protected rights, so the states' leaders decided to add amendments, or changes and additions, to the Constitution. The first ten amendments are known collectively as the Bill of Rights. The other amendments were added periodically as the need arose throughout the course of American history. Let's look at each one of those amendments.

The Bill of Rights

The first ten amendments to the Constitution are known as the Bill of Rights. Many states ratified the Constitution only because they believed it would be amended to include the rights implemented in the Bill of Rights.

First Amendment—Religious and Political Freedom

The First Amendment prevents Congress from interfering with the freedom of religion, speech, and the press. It also incorporates the right to assemble and to petition the government.

Second Amendment—Right to Bear Arms

This amendment gives citizens a limited right to arm themselves, or keep weapons. There is some debate over whether this right is intended to be the right of the states or the right of individuals.

Third Amendment—Quartering of Troops

The purpose of the Third Amendment was to stop soldiers from taking over homes for their own use without the consent of the owner. The amendment provides that such "quartering," or "room and board," may occur "in a manner to be prescribed by law."

Fourth Amendment—Searches and Seizures

The Fourth Amendment forbids "unreasonable searches" and the issuance of warrants without "probable cause," or good reason.

Fifth Amendment—Right to Life, Liberty, and Property

The Fifth Amendment guarantees a citizen's rights while on trial as well as the rights to life, liberty, and property. When someone refuses to testify at trial and "takes the Fifth," they are said to be invoking their rights as established in the Fifth Amendment. It is also called a right against self-incrimination. The Fifth Amendment also provides that an individual must not be held for committing a crime without being "indicted." In addition, the Fifth Amendment protects against "double jeopardy," or the risk of being tried twice for the same offense. The Fifth Amendment also ensures individuals' "due process" rights, or the right to be moved through the criminal justice system in a proper fashion.

Sixth Amendment—Protection in Criminal Trials

Citizens are guaranteed a right to a speedy trial, an impartial jury, and the right to an attorney in the Sixth Amendment. The accused also has a right to "confront witnesses" against him or her at trial.

Seventh Amendment—Suits at Common Law

If there is a dispute over something valued at $20 or more, then the Seventh Amendment provides that citizens have a right to a jury trial in federal court. However, this type of case is not normally heard in federal court now.

Eighth Amendment—Bail and Punishment

The Eighth Amendment prohibits fines and punishments which, in essence, "don't fit the crime." It is said to be "cruel and unusual" to sentence someone unfairly and the Eighth Amendment prohibits this.

Ninth Amendment—Considering Rights not Enumerated

Fearing that the enumeration of certain rights would lead to the exclusion, or omission, of other rights, the authors of the Bill of Rights included the Ninth Amendment that establishes that citizens are not limited to the rights specifically listed in the Constitution.

Tenth Amendment—Powers Reserved to States and to People

Similar to the rationale behind the Ninth Amendment, the Tenth Amendment was created to reassure the states that they would retain power in those areas not specifically granted to the Federal Government.

THE REMAINING AMENDMENTS

Eleventh Amendment—Suits against a State

The Eleventh Amendment clarifies the original jurisdiction of the Supreme Court concerning a suit brought against a state by a citizen of another state.

Twelfth Amendment—Election of the President and Vice President

The Twelfth Amendment explains how the Electoral College chooses the president and vice president. It also states that the two should work together, and that the vice president should become president if the president can no longer stay in office.

Thirteenth Amendment—Slavery Prohibited

Slavery was abolished in the United States by the addition of the Thirteenth Amendment.

Fourteenth Amendment—Civil Rights for Ex-Slaves and Others

The Fourteenth Amendment ensures that all citizens of all states enjoy rights on the state level as well as the federal level. It has also been interpreted as providing for "due process" at the state level.

Fifteenth Amendment—Suffrage for Blacks

This amendment prohibits the use of race as a requirement or disqualification for voting.

Sixteenth Amendment—Income Taxes

The Sixteenth Amendment authorizes the collection of income taxes.

Seventeenth Amendment—Direct Election of Senators

Prior to the Seventeenth Amendment, senators were selected by the legislatures of the various states. Now, they could be elected by the vote of the citizens.

Eighteenth Amendment—National Prohibition

This amendment prohibits the sale or manufacture of alcohol in the United States. It was later repealed by the Twenty-first Amendment.

Nineteenth Amendment—Woman Suffrage

Just as the Fifteenth Amendment prohibits the use of race as criteria for voting, the Nineteenth Amendment prohibits the use of gender as a requirement or disqualification for voting.

Twentieth Amendment—Presidential and Congressional Terms

The Twentieth Amendment sets new start dates for congressional terms and also addresses what to do if a president dies before he is sworn into office.

Twenty-First Amendment—Prohibition Repealed

The Twenty-first Amendment repealed The Eighteenth Amendment which had prohibited the sale or manufacutre of alcohol in the United States.

Twenty-Second Amendment—Anti-Third Term Amendment

This amendment limits a president to two four-year terms in office. There is an exception for a vice president who takes over because the president is unable to continue. In that case, the limit is a total of ten years as president.

Twenty-Third Amendment—District of Columbia Vote

This amendment gave Washington D.C. representation in the Electoral College.

Twenty-Fourth Amendment—Poll Tax

The Twenty-fourth Amendment prohibits charging a tax for placing a vote in a federal election.

Twenty-Fifth Amendment—Presidential Succession and Disability

This amendment states the order of succession should the president be unable to continue holding office.

Twenty-Sixth Amendment—Lowering Voting Age

Citizens over 18 years old could vote after the passage of this amendment.

Twenty-Seventh Amendment—Congressional Pay Increases

The Twenty-seventh Amendment requires that any law that increases the pay of legislators may not take effect until after the next election.

THE FEDERALIST PAPERS

The Federalist Papers are a collection of eighty-five essays written by John Jay, James Madison, and Alexander Hamilton. They are considered one of the most important contributions made to American political thought. The papers were intended to influence states, particularly New York, to adopt the Constitution.

The delegates who signed the Constitution stipulated that it would take effect only after approval by ratifying conventions in nine of thirteen states. Because New York and Virginia were big and powerful, a vote against ratification from either of them would have been disastrous. The New York governor, George Clinton, clearly was opposed to the Constitution.

Hoping to persuade the New York convention to ratify the Constitution, Jay, Madison, and Hamilton wrote a series of letters defending the Constitution to New York papers under the pseudonym *Publius*. These letters are known collectively as the Federalist Papers. Clinton Rossitor said, "The message of *The Federalist* reads: no happiness without liberty, no liberty without self-government, no self-government without constitutionalism, no constitutionalism without morality—and none of these great goods without stability and order."

LANDMARK SUPREME COURT CASES

The Supreme Court has issued many cases of historical significance, which have directly affected our rights as individuals. Let's look at a summary of some of those "landmark" cases that deeply affected rights in America.

Plessy v. *Ferguson*—1896

Homer Adolph Plessy was a resident of Louisiana and a citizen of the United States. He was of partial African descent. He paid for a first class ticket on the East Louisiana Railway, a passenger train that ran through Louisiana. When he boarded the train, Plessy found a seat in a car that was filled with white people and was designated for white passengers. The train conductor informed him that he would have to find a seat in a car not designated for white people or he would be forced to leave the train. Plessy refused and was arrested.

Plessy was found guilty of violating a state statute which required passenger trains to provide "separate, but equal" accommodations for white and black people. The statute also imposed criminal punishment on those passengers who refused to comply. Plessy brought suit challenging the Louisiana statute as an unconstitutional violation of his due process rights under the Fourteenth Amendment. The Supreme Court held that the statute requiring "separate but equal" facilities was constitutional, rationalizing that separate facilities for blacks and whites satisfied the Fourteenth Amendment so long as they were equal. In other words, the Court found that segregation does not in itself constitute unlawful discrimination.

Brown v. *Board of Education of Topeka, Kansas*—1955

Linda Brown, a black third grade student, walked a mile everyday to get to her "black" school, even though a school designated for white children was much closer to her home. Linda's father tried to enroll her in the "white" school, but the school refused to accept Linda as a student. The Browns got help from the NAACP (National Association for the Advancement of Colored People) and sued the school board. The Supreme Court, hearing the case on appeal, ordered oral arguments in the case twice before reaching a decision. The question before the court: "Does segregation of children in public schools solely on the basis of race, even though the physical facilities and other "tangible" factors may be equal, deprive the children of the minority group of equal educational opportunities?"

Thus, the question of "separate but equal" was once again before the court. The Court's decision in *Plessy v. Ferguson*, a finding that separate facilities are not unconstitutional as long as they are equal, seemed to hold the answer in this case as well. However, fifty-nine years had passed, and this time the Court's ruling was quite different. Significantly, the opinion of the Court was unanimous. The decision: "We conclude that in the field of public education the doctrine of 'separate but equal' has no place. Separate educational facilities are inherently unequal."

The *Brown* decision did not abolish segregation in any areas other than public schools, but it was a start toward integrating the races in many areas of life. The Court did not overrule *Plessy* v. *Ferguson*, because it limited the decision in *Brown* to public schools. The ruling did, however, have a significant impact on the segregation of the races in many public facilities. Slowly, integration began. That was only forty-six years ago. We can only imagine how different integration might have been if the Court's decision in *Plessy* over 100 years ago had held separate facilities to be "inherently unequal."

Dred Scott v. *Sandford*—1857

Dred Scott was a black slave who lived on free (non-slavery) land with his owner for several years. He tried, unsuccessfully, to sue in state court for his freedom. He then filed suit in federal court. The basis of his claim to establish his freedom was that he had lived on free soil for more than five years in an area of the country where the Missouri Compromise of 1820 forbade slavery.

The Supreme Court ruled that Scott was a slave and not a citizen and therefore did not have the right to sue in federal court. The right to file suit is a right limited to citizens in Article III of the Constitution. A majority of the Court held that, because a slave was private property of his master, the Missouri Compromise unconstitutionally took the slave owner's property without due process of law. Thus, a slave could be taken into any territory and held there. The reason? The Fifth Amendment clearly forbids Congress from depriving people of their property without due process. To allow Scott his freedom would be to deprive his owner of his "property." The Court found the Missouri Compromise unconstitutional and Dred Scott remained a slave.

Marbury v. *Madison*—1803

Prior to his death, President John Adams attempted to fill a number of judicial vacancies. Some of the commissions were not delivered to the appointees prior to Adams's death. One of the appointees who did not receive his commission, William Marbury, sued Secretary of State James Madison to get his commission as Justice of the Peace.

This issue came before the Court on its "original jurisdiction," *i.e.*, it was not on appeal from an inferior court, and placed the Court in a difficult position. If the Court were to issue a writ of mandamus, or order, forcing Madison to turn over the commission, and he refused, the power of the Court would be weakened. On the other hand, to refuse to issue the writ of mandamus could be perceived as weakness or fear of the executive branch.

Ultimately, the Court's decision declared that Madison should have delivered the commission to Marbury but held that it did not have the power to issue a writ of mandamus. The Court declared that such power exceeded the Court's authority as granted in Article III of the Constitution. The writ of mandamus authority had been given to the Court by the Judiciary Act of 1789, a congressional act. Thus, the Court held an act of Congress unconstitutional. Ironically, by declaring that it did not have the power to order Madison to turn over the commission, the Court effectively strengthened its power over the other two branches of government.

This case exemplifies the Court's power as the "last word" on the meaning of the Constitution. It established the judicial branch as an equal power in the three branches of government. The power to declare acts of Congress unconstitutional is one that the Court has used sparingly over the years. The legislature is, however, always aware that the Court *could* declare a law unconstitutional. This awareness alone helps maintain the constitutionality of newly created laws.

Roe v. *Wade*—1973

Roe was a single, pregnant woman who brought suit to challenge the constitutionality of the Texas laws that made getting an abortion or performing an abortion illegal. The laws did except those abortions performed on medical advice to save the mother's life.

The Court held that the law violated the due process clause of the Fourteenth Amendment, which protects the right to privacy against state action. This right, the Court found, includes a woman's qualified right to terminate her pregnancy. The Court acknowledged that the state has a legitimate interest in protecting both the pregnant woman's health and the potentiality of human life, and placed those rights on a scale that tips further to the state's interests as the pregnancy progresses.

During the first trimester, the Court stated, the decision should be left to the attending physician. After that, the state could regulate the abortion procedure in ways "reasonably related" to the mother's health. Subsequent to "viability," or the ability of the child to live outside of the womb, the Court held that the state could regulate abortion and even prohibit it except where necessary to save the life of the mother. Many abortion cases have followed

Roe, but this was the first to hold a woman's right to privacy, outweighing the state's interest in protecting her health and the unborn child.

Nixon v. United States—1974

During the presidential election of 1972, burglars broke into the Democratic National Committee's headquarters in Watergate. A federal grand jury indicted the Attorney General and others, alleging conspiracy and obstruction of justice. The grand jury named President Richard Nixon as a co-conspirator.

Investigations revealed that Nixon taped many conversations that took place in the oval office. The tapes were subpoenaed, and Nixon released edited transcripts but refused to release anything more, claiming "executive privilege." Executive privilege protects the president from being compelled by the judicial branch to turn over confidential executive branch material.

The question before the Court: Does the president have the right under executive privilege to refuse to surrender material to federal court? In a unanimous (8–0, Justice Rehnquist did not participate) decision, the Court held that Nixon had to turn over the tapes. The Court stated: "[N]either the doctrine of Separation of Powers, nor the need for confidentiality of high-level communications, without more, can sustain an absolute, unqualified Presidential privilege of immunity from judicial process under all circumstances. The President's need of complete candor and objectivity from advisors calls for great deference from the courts. However, when the privilege depends solely on the broad, undifferentiated claim of public interest in the confidentiality of such conversations, a confrontation with other values arises. Absent a claim of need to protect military, diplomatic, or sensitive national security secrets, we find it difficult to accept the argument that even the very important interest in confidentiality of Presidential communications is significantly diminished by production of such material for *in camera* inspection with all the protection that a district court will be obliged to provide." With this decision, the Court limited the president's use of "executive privilege" to the need to protect military secrets, diplomatic secrets, or national security. The rationale is based on the idea that the courts will protect the information and treat it as confidential.

Miranda v. Arizona—1966

Ernesto Miranda was arrested for raping an 18-year-old girl. The police arrived at Miranda's home at night and asked him to go with them to the police station. Miranda, claiming he did not realize he had a choice, went with the police. After two hours of interrogation, Miranda confessed to the crime.

On appeal to the Supreme Court, Miranda argued that he would not have confessed to the crime if he had been advised of his right to remain silent and to have an attorney. In a 5–4 opinion, the Court determined that a suspect must be warned prior to custodial interrogation of his right to remain silent, that any statement he does make may be used against him, and that he has a right to an attorney. Specifically, the Court stated: "He must be warned prior to any questioning that he has the right to remain silent, that anything he says can be used against him in a court of law, that he has the right to the presence of an attorney, and that if he cannot afford an attorney one will be appointed for him prior to any questioning if he so desires." Thus, the infamous "Miranda" warnings.

Boy Scouts of America v. Dale—2000

The Boy Scouts revoked Dale's position as assistant scoutmaster in a New Jersey troop after learning that he was homosexual. Dale sued, claiming violation of a state statute prohibiting discrimination on the basis of sexual orientation.

The Supreme Court held that the Boy Scouts could not be required to include Dale in its organization. The Court stated that to require mandatory inclusion of unwanted individuals into the organization would violate the Boy Scouts' First Amendment right of "expressive association." Forced membership, the Court found, is unconstitutional if it affects the group's ability to advocate its collective viewpoints. Because the Boy Scouts believed that a homosexual lifestyle conflicted with its philosophies, the inclusion of Dale would have hindered the Boy Scouts' ability to teach its views. Thus, to protect the Boy Scouts' First Amendment rights, it could not be forced to include Dale in its membership.

Hustler Magazine, Inc. v. *Falwell*—1988

Reverend Jerry Falwell filed suit against *Hustler* magazine because the magazine published a cartoon that portrayed Falwell as engaging in an incestuous relationship with his mother in an outhouse.

The Supreme Court held that, in order to protect the free flow of ideas and opinions, the First and Fourteenth Amendments prohibit public figures and public officials from recovering for "intentional infliction of emotional distress" when the speech that causes the distress could not reasonably be taken as implying the truth. In essence, because the cartoon was obviously a joke, and because Falwell was a "public figure," *Hustler* had the right to print the cartoon under the First Amendment to the Constitution. If an individual places himself in a position to be known by the public, then he takes on the risk of being the topic of jokes.

Canadian History

THE EARLIEST CANADIANS

The earliest inhabitants of Canada most likely traveled from Asia to North America across a land bridge that spanned the Bering Strait. The nomadic hunters probably followed large game into North America at least 10,000 years ago. Once in North America, they scattered across the continent and formed their own communities, each with its own distinct language. A new wave of nomads probably migrated to North America about 4,000 years ago. Although the earliest Canadians settled across North America, the greatest concentrations of people were located along the Pacific Coast and in what is now Ontario. Over the centuries, the inhabitants of Canada developed a number of languages and cultures unique to Canada, including the Algonquian and the Athapaskan language groups. These groups, and others, interacted only with each other until 985 AD.

THE ARRIVAL OF EUROPEANS

In approximately 985, the first Europeans, the Vikings, landed on, explored, and settled Greenland. They also explored the northeastern coast of Canada. About fifteen years later, the famous Viking Leif Ericson sailed from Greenland to a place he called Vinland, which was probably modern-day Newfoundland. Although exploration and trade continued along the northeast coast of Canada, the Viking colonies did not last long, and by the early fifteenth century, Europeans no longer maintained contact with North America.

Toward the end of the fifteenth century, European explorers began exploring North America's eastern coast again. John Cabot unsuccessfully searched the coast for the Northwest Passage, a sea route that Europeans believed would lead to the wealthy Asian trade empires. In the sixteenth century, France sponsored Jacques Cartier to continue the search for the Northwest Passage. Cartier was also unsuccessful in locating a sea route to Asia and was later unsuccessful at establishing a colony in North America.

Later attempts at colonization also met with little success. However, the Europeans discovered the vast wealth of fish and whales available to commercial fishermen off the coast of Labrador, in the Gulf of St. Lawrence, and in the Grand Banks. Fishermen from Spain, France, England, and Portugal took advantage of the bountiful catch found here. Eventually the English explorer Sir Humphrey Gilbert claimed Newfoundland for England. After the Spanish and Portuguese left the area, the English settled the northern part of Newfoundland, and the French settled the southern part. These settlers entered into a trade relationship with the natives. The bulk of the trading was done with furs, especially beaver furs. The European demand for beaver products, particularly hats, launched an industry in Canada that remained a vital part of its economy for many years to follow.

The indigenous, or native, peoples of Canada traded with the European settlers and formed many alliances with the Europeans. Because of the large amount of

ROAD MAP

- *The Earliest Canadians*
- *The Arrival of Europeans*
- *Early Canadian Colonies*
- *Conflict with the British*
- *Early British Rule*
- *Westward Expansion and Immigration*
- *Radicals, Reformers, and the Act of Union*
- *Confederation*
- *Industrialization and Immigration*
- *Canada, the British Empire, and Problems in Quebec*
- *The Twentieth Century after World War I*

Canadian territory and the relatively small number of Europeans in Canada, few conflicts emerged between Europeans and the indigenous nations they encountered in Canada. The Europeans made some attempts to Christianize the natives, but they found little success. The greatest negative effect of the trade relationship was the transmission of European diseases to the indigenous people of Canada. Diseases in epidemic proportions spread quickly and decimated vast numbers of natives wherever the Europeans went. The indigenous population of Canada continued to decline even into the twentieth century.

EXERCISE 1: THE EARLIEST CANADIANS AND THE ARRIVAL OF EUROPEANS

1. Which of the following is most likely true of the first inhabitants of Canada?

    (1)   The first inhabitants of Canada were probably civilized.
    (2)   The first inhabitants of Canada were probably of Asian descent.
    (3)   The first inhabitants of Canada settled in permanent shelters as soon as they arrived in Canada.
    (4)   The first Canadians were indigenous to North America.
    (5)   The first Canadians probably were great farmers.

The correct answer is (2). The first people in Canada likely crossed the land bridge between Asia and modern-day Alaska.

2. Which of the following best describes the relationship between the Europeans who explored North America and the natives of Canada?

    (1)   The two groups were involved in nearly incessant warfare.
    (2)   The two groups formed a military alliance.
    (3)   The two groups had a relationship based on trade.
    (4)   The two groups freely exchanged information about cultures and farming techniques.
    (5)   The two groups never had contact with one another.

The correct answer is (3). The Europeans and the natives exchanged many goods and generally maintained a good relationship.

EARLY CANADIAN COLONIES

As France began to see the huge dividends paid by the fur trade in Canada (which was known as New France), it officially claimed and began defending the area. England, a perennial enemy of France, disputed the claim. France realized that new, permanent settlements needed to be built if the claim to New France was going to be legitimate. Therefore, France used the fur trade to finance the construction of new forts and settlements. France settled at Quebec, an inland site well protected from foreign aggression. France then employed an economic policy known as mercantilism. Under mercantilism, a trade company was given control over New France. In exchange, the company agreed to ship all exports to France and to purchase all of its raw materials and supplies from France. The French also created strong alliances with the Huron and the Algonquian, two local nations of indigenous peoples. With the help of these two peoples, the French colony grew and prospered. The French also created many maps of the area, and in the 1630s and 1640s, they established colonies at Trois-Rivières and Montreal. The colonies remained dependent upon the fur trade and their relationship with the natives. This presented a problem in the mid-1600s, though, when the French aided the Huron in a losing effort against the Iroquois. The devastation of the Huron nearly cost France the colonies.

CONFLICT WITH THE BRITISH

In the second half of the seventeenth century, the French increased their defenses and population in New France. Also during the late seventeenth century, the French sponsored significant exploration of North America, both westward across Canada and southward along the Mississippi River in the Louisiana territory. The English re-entered the picture during this same time period when the Hudson Bay Company, an English trade company, began competing with the French for the fur trade. The French responded by building more forts in French territory and along the frontier.

In the 1680s the French found themselves in conflict with the British in several parts of the world, including North America. In King William's War during the 1690s, the French and British troops in North America exchanged guerrilla raids and attacks for nearly a decade before signing a treaty that returned North America to the way it was before the war. In 1702, Queen Anne's War erupted between the two powers and later ended with France giving up some of its territory. The next half-century or so was a period of high tensions but no war. France continued to expand its fur trade and its relationship with the indigenous peoples in and around New France.

However, in 1754 the French and Indian War broke out between the French and the British. Many natives fought on both sides of the conflict. The French held their ground well against the British, who greatly outnumbered the French. However, at the war's end in 1763, France ceded its territory to Great Britain. Quebec, Nova Scotia, Newfoundland, and Rupert's Land were now under British control. Great Britain immediately sought to ease tensions between the British and the natives in Canada by signing treaties with them.

EXERCISE 2: EARLY CANADIAN COLONIES AND CONFLICT WITH THE BRITISH

1. The French and the English competed most for which of the following in Canada?

   (1) The fur trade
   (2) Indian alliances
   (3) The western territories
   (4) Influence over the colonial government
   (5) Access to the Mississippi River

The correct answer is (1). Both nations wanted control of the lucrative fur trade, which brought about fierce competition between the two rivals.

2. Which of the following is true about the situation after the end of the French and Indian War?

   (1) No indigenous peoples had become involved in the conflict between France and Great Britain.
   (2) The French territories remained unchanged from the beginning of the war.
   (3) The French added to their territories much land formerly under British rule.
   (4) The French and the British signed a treaty that allied the two powers against the indigenous peoples of Canada.
   (5) France lost much land to Britain.

The correct answer is (5). Rupert's Island, Quebec, Nova Scotia, and Newfoundland all went to Great Britain after the war.

EARLY BRITISH RULE

At first, Britain hoped to institute British customs and British-style government in its new territory. However, that plan did not work because of the resistance of the Canadian people, most of whom were originally French. With the Quebec Act of 1774, Great Britain allowed French law, French customs, and even Catholicism to continue in Canada. This went a long way toward reconciliation between the French Canadians and the British government. The Quebec Act also returned some land to Quebec and saved Montreal's fur trade, the backbone of its economy. The Canadian colonies grew, but they remained only loosely linked to each other.

With relative peace and security in Canada, the bulk of British forces left Canada. This opened the door for trouble with the thirteen British colonies to the South. In 1775 and 1776, the thirteen British colonies along the Atlantic coast (now known as the United States) decided to break away from British control. During the time the colonies fought the British, they also invaded Quebec and Montreal. The British eventually drove the Americans out of Canada, but they failed to prevent the colonies from winning their independence. During and after the war, many loyalists—those Americans still loyal to Great Britain—fled the colonies and sought refuge in Canada. The British government rewarded these refugees for their loyalty by granting them land and other financial benefits.

The loyalists who settled in Canada expected they would be living in a British land, but what they found was an unfamiliar and uncomfortable French-style society. By 1791, these loyalists had voiced their displeasure with the situation on many occasions. The British government responded by dividing Quebec into two separate colonies called Upper Canada and Lower Canada. Each colony received a new constitution. The predominantly French Lower Canada retained its French culture and laws while the mostly British Upper Canada received new English laws that favored both the English nobility and the Protestant religion.

When the United States declared war on Great Britain in 1812, the United States thought it might be able to take advantage of the perceived vulnerability of Canada. U.S. troops invaded Upper Canada but were soundly defeated by British forces and natives allied with the British. This act of aggression created an anti-American sentiment throughout much of Canada, particularly in Upper Canada.

EXERCISE 3: EARLY BRITISH RULE

1. For which of the following reasons might the Canadian people have been resistant to British rule?

    (1) Most of the people in Canada liked the government that they had already established there.
    (2) Most of the people in Canada did not like people who spoke English.
    (3) Most Canadians at the time were of French descent, and the French and British generally have never gotten along very well.
    (4) The British refused to allow French customs and traditions to be practiced in Canada.
    (5) The British established a cruel, oppressive government in Canada.

The correct answer is (3). The French and British had a long history of disputes.

2. What steps did the British take to give aid to refugees from the thirteen colonies during the War for American Independence?

(1) The government gave them safe passage back to Great Britain.
(2) The government granted them tracts of land in Canada.
(3) The government refused to give them any aid and encouraged them to return to America.
(4) The government took land and wealth away from the natives and gave it to the refugees.
(5) The government made them enlist in the British army to fight against the rebels in the colonies.

The correct answer is (2). The British government wanted to reward the loyalists for their loyalty to Great Britain.

WESTWARD EXPANSION AND IMMIGRATION

In the late eighteenth and early nineteenth centuries, two companies battled for control of the fur trade and sparked westward expansion in Canada. The Hudson Bay Company had been granted a monopoly on the fur trade, but a company founded by French-Canadian fur traders defied the monopoly. The North West Company explored, mapped, and tapped the natural resources of Canada all the way to the Pacific Coast. Both companies struggled for influence throughout the western territories. Friction between the two companies often resulted in outbreaks of violence in frontier towns. Finally, in 1821 the two companies merged and the Hudson Bay Company assumed control of the Canadian fur trade. However, by the end of the nineteenth century, the timber industry replaced the fur trade as the leading industry in Canada.

During the nineteenth century, millions of Europeans migrated to North America to seek new opportunities. Perhaps between one and two million of these migrated to Canadian territories. These immigrants came primarily from England, Ireland, and Scotland. They were willing to take the risk of moving to the frontier because of the promise of free farmland. Upper Canada grew faster than any other part of the Canadian territory. Relatively few immigrants, on the other hand, moved to the far north or the far west. Not until the gold rush in the second half of the nineteenth century did a significant number of settlers move to the Pacific region. As the immigration continued, the native peoples of British North America gradually became the minority of the population.

EXERCISE 4: EXPANSION AND IMMIGRATION

1. Which of the following statements could be made concerning the competition between the two trade companies in Canada?

(1) The competition between the two companies nearly caused a civil war.
(2) The indigenous people were caught in the middle of the war between the two trade companies.
(3) The two trade companies encouraged good, healthy competition in the marketplace.
(4) The competition between the two companies ultimately led to the mapping and exploration of some of the western parts of Canada.
(5) The revenue produced by the two trade companies provided a major boost for the French, British, and Canadian economies.

The correct answer is (4). In order to find more resources and stay competitive with the Hudson Bay Company, the North West Company moved westward, exploring and mapping as it went.

2. Which of the following was the primary reason for the massive immigration to Canada during the early 1800s?

    (1) The government offered land grants to anyone who wanted to settle on the frontier.
    (2) World War in Europe drove millions from their homes.
    (3) The prospects of finding a job in the factories of Canada prompted many Europeans to immigrate.
    (4) The gold rush made many people seek their fortunes.
    (5) Oppressive governments in the United States and Great Britain created a large number of political refugees who sought safety in Canada.

The correct answer is (1). Immigrants to Canada received large tracts of land on which they could settle and build homes.

RADICALS, REFORMERS, AND THE ACT OF UNION

Because most of the non-indigenous inhabitants of Canada during the early 1800s were hardworking farmers and fishermen, the traditional British aristocratic system of government did not please many of the Canadians. In the early 1800s, two groups called for a change in the government. The moderate group of people who sought change was known as reformers. The reformers liked the British system of government, but they wanted a parliamentary system with an elected legislature instead of one that was appointed. The radicals, the more liberal of the two groups, sought publicly elected officials within a republic modeled after the governments of France and the United States. Many in Canada, especially in Lower Canada, pointed to Britain as the root of many of the social, political, and economic problems that Canada faced. These feelings erupted in an armed rebellion in 1837 that eventually ended in victory for the British. The political climate in Lower and Upper Canada convinced Great Britain that something needed to be done in order to maintain peace.

In 1841, the British passed the Act of Union, which created the province of Canada. This province had two sections, Canada East and Canada West (formerly Lower Canada and Upper Canada, respectively). The act gave Canada West the same representation as the larger Canada East, and it made English the official language. Eventually, the government that the Act of Union created was dissolved. The Canadian provinces won the right to local self-government, and Britain retained the right to manage foreign affairs, defense, and the appointment of provincial governors.

During this time, a two-party system emerged in Canadian politics. Also during this time, industry began to grow in Canada. Trade restrictions and tariffs were eased, and North American trade flourished. Railroads were built across Canada that carried both passengers and cargo. Telegraph lines connected many parts of Canada and North America. Shipbuilding reached an all-time high in British North America. For some parts of Canada, this period was a golden age.

CONFEDERATION

During the 1850s, talk of unifying the Canadian provinces was a topic of great debate. In the 1860s, when the Southern states of the United States tried to secede from the United States, talk of Canadian unification intensified. Canada, Nova Scotia, New Brunswick, Prince Edward Island, and Newfoundland met to discuss unification, or Confederation, as it came to be known. The legislative leaders approved the Seventy-two Resolutions, which was a draft of a constitution.

Under the Confederation, the governmental responsibilities would be split between a national government and provincial governments. The Confederation was not a move toward independence, though. Leaders wanted to maintain ties with Britain to prevent aggression from the United States. After ratification of the Seventy-two Resolutions, the Dominion of Canada was created in 1867. The new Canada had four provinces: Quebec, Ontario, New Brunswick, and Nova Scotia. Ottawa was chosen as the national capital. Great Britain did not repeal the Confederation, so in 1871, the last British troops left Canada.

The new nation moved immediately to expand westward. In 1869 Canada added the Northwest Territories, land that Canada purchased from the Hudson Bay Company. In 1871, British Columbia joined Canada, followed by Prince Edward Island two years later. Canada later added the Arctic Archipelago, Newfoundland, and Labrador. Two other important steps taken by the new Canada were the creation of the Royal Mounted Police and the beginning of the transcontinental railroad.

EXERCISE 5: RADICALS, REFORMERS, THE ACT OF UNION, AND CONFEDERATION

1. One of the major concerns about the Act of Union was which of the following?

   (1) It did not preserve the heritage and culture of Quebec.
   (2) It gave two areas the same vote even though the populations of the two areas were not the same.
   (3) It allowed for no more than two parties in the Canadian political system.
   (4) It officially blamed Great Britain for all the problems in Canada.
   (5) It united all of Canada under a new government and not under the British monarch.

The correct answer is (2). Upper and Lower Canada received equal representation, but the populations of the two were not equal, thus making the representation unfair.

2. Which of the following statements best defines confederation?

   (1) Confederation meant that Canada would no longer have ties with Britain.
   (2) Confederation meant that Britain and Canada would become united as one nation under God.
   (3) Confederation meant that the Canadian provinces would be loosely united but still under the monarch.
   (4) Confederation meant that some of the Canadian provinces would secede from the British Empire the way the Southern states did in the United States.
   (5) Confederation meant that Canada would form an alliance with the United States.

The correct answer is (3). The provinces would be united but they would remain under the control of the British monarch.

INDUSTRIALIZATION AND IMMIGRATION

The late 1800s proved to be a time of industrial growth for many parts of Canada. Many cities along the railroad benefited by having their goods shipped by rail. The main areas of industrial growth were in Montreal and Ontario. The populations in those two cities grew as people flocked to the cities in search of work. Many people made the transition from rural workers to urban wage laborers. This brought with it organized labor in the form of unions. The Atlantic cities, however, suffered during this time because their wooden ships were becoming obsolete due to the new steel ships. The government also implemented tariffs during this time to help boost the Canadian economy. Another economic boost to the Canadian economy was the discovery of gold in the Yukon Territory just before the turn of the century. People rushed by the thousands to the Yukon Territory to seek their fortunes. Further economic boosts came with the development of Canada's natural mineral and hydroelectric resources in central Canada.

As the economy boomed in Canada at the turn of the twentieth century, immigrants flocked to Canada. Many of these immigrants moved to Canada from Britain and the United States. However, for the first time many immigrants moved to Canada from other European nations, particularly from Eastern Europe. The Canadian government granted many tracts of land in the far west to the immigrants, and the immigrants began to develop the frontier. Many Canadians distrusted the immigrants who did not come from Britain, though. This fear and distrust caused backlash against the immigrants several times in the late 1800s and the early 1900s.

CANADA, THE BRITISH EMPIRE, AND PROBLEMS IN QUEBEC

In the 1890s, a new Prime Minister adopted the popular Conservative political view that Canada should stand by the British Empire no matter what, even in matters of imperialism, or expansion into other lands. This policy was popular with most of the Canadians of British descent, but many of the French-speaking Canadians strongly opposed the policy. When Great Britain entered the Boer War in South Africa, many Canadians were ready to fight alongside the British. However, the French-speaking population opposed the popular policy because they were not willing to fight in Britain's wars on other continents. Furthermore, the French-speaking Canadians, most of whom were in Quebec, felt like the rest of Canada did not respect them, which caused a deep rift between Quebec and the other provinces.

The Canadian government felt pressure from both French and British Canadians over the extent to which Canada should help the British Empire. In 1910, Britain expected Canada to contribute to its navy. Instead of contributing, Canada built a small fleet of its own to sail alongside the British navy. Popular opinion turned to outrage again when Canada ratified a treaty with the United States that reduced tariffs and duties, a treaty that U.S. officials saw as a step toward the annexation of Canada. The people of Canada expressed their displeasure, which led to the Conservative Party winning the election of 1911.

In 1914, the British declared war on Germany. This meant that all British holdings, including Canada, were at war, too. Canada responded quickly to Britain's call and sent tens of thousand of Canadians to help with the war effort. The war had a huge impact on Canada. The government imposed Canada's first income tax in 1917. Also, women replaced men in the factories and consequently earned the right to vote. Another result of the war was the increased tension between Quebec and the rest of Canada. One of the biggest points of contention was the conscription, or draft, that began in 1918. This draft practically split the country because it proved to Quebec that English-speaking Canada would ignore French-speaking Canada in matters of national importance.

After the war, Canadians felt a deeper sense of nationalism than they ever had before due mostly to the large number of Canadian casualties in the war. Canada began to act as an independent, sovereign nation during treaty negotiations. In 1926, the British government acknowledged Canada's equality with Great Britain. Then, in 1931, Canada was declared a sovereign state; however, it remained under the British monarch.

EXERCISE 6: INDUSTRIALIZATION AND PROBLEMS WITH THE BRITISH EMPIRE AND QUEBEC

1. Which of the following was a result of industrialization in Canada?

    (1) People moved from urban areas to rural areas in search of jobs.
    (2) People moved from rural areas to urban areas in search of jobs.
    (3) Railroads were built after Canada completed all of its factories.
    (4) Millions of people lost their jobs because machines replaced humans at work.
    (5) The western territories became the financial center of Canada.

The correct answer is (2). People moved from the country into cities to find work in factories.

2. Which of the following was a major concern of Quebec during the late eighteenth and early nineteenth centuries?

    (1) Quebec feared that the United States would annex its territory.
    (2) Quebec feared that the rest of Canada did not respect its heritage and culture and, therefore, did not respect Quebec in important matters.
    (3) Quebec feared that French would be outlawed within its own borders.
    (4) Quebec feared that all its inhabitants would be drafted for World War I.
    (5) Quebec feared that the rest of Canada would not allow Quebec to participate in the government.

The correct answer is (2). English-speaking Canada often ignored the needs and wants of French-speaking Quebec.

THE TWENTIETH CENTURY AFTER WORLD WAR I

Canada faced many problems after the First World War. Returning soldiers had a difficult time returning to a normal life in Canada. The economy did not boom during the 1920s in Canada as it did in the United States. Industry had difficulty making the transition from wartime production to peacetime production. Unemployment was high, and labor unrest loomed large, especially in the Atlantic regions. To make matters worse, Canada felt the effects of the Great Depression immediately. Many of Canada's trade partners closed their doors to Canadian goods, and foreign investors no longer had money to invest in Canada.

Even though the economic decline slowed in the 1930s, the economy did not fully recover until World War II. Canada was initially hesitant to become involved in the war, but the government felt it had no other choice. As the war progressed, the government put the issue of conscription to a vote by the people. All of Canada except Quebec favored the draft. Canada launched a major war effort, and the economy bounced back and did well during the war years.

After the war, the Canadian government moved more and more toward governmental control of the economic and financial aspects of the country. Government spending increased to compensate for the lack of business investments in Canada. A number of major social programs, including medical insurance and health care, were launched in the twenty years after the war. The economy boomed because Canada suddenly found itself with a seemingly endless number of markets for Canadian goods in Europe. Both industry and the population increased greatly after the soldiers returned from the war. Also after the war, Canada joined the North Atlantic Treaty Organization (NATO) and played an increased role in international politics.

Problems in Quebec refused to go away, even after World War II. Many in Quebec wanted to break away from English-speaking Canada. Quebec wanted self-government and reduced Canadian control over affairs within Quebec. The situation in Quebec came to a head in the early 1970s when terrorism, kidnappings, and mass arrests occurred as a result of the Quebec dispute. Other provinces and indigenous peoples followed the lead of Quebec and demanded more provincial control and less national control over provincial affairs.

In 1982, Canada cut its final formal legislative ties with Britain by earning the right to amend its constitution. In 1987, the subject of Quebec came up again. Quebec asked for special legislation that would protect its special culture and heritage. The accord, however, did not survive. Again in 1992 Canada had an opportunity to recognize Quebec as a "distinct society," but that, too, failed to succeed. Throughout the 1990s, Quebec talked of secession, but the highest court in the land declared secession unconstitutional.

Indigenous peoples did reap one reward in the late 1990s as a new province, Nunavut, was added. In addition, Canada established a Healing Fund to help apologize to the indigenous peoples for many years of injustice. Even today, the subjects of indigenous peoples' rights and an independent Quebec are at the forefront of Canadian issues.

EXERCISE 7: THE TWENTIETH CENTURY AFTER WORLD WAR I

1. Which of the following can be said of Canada after World War I?

   (1) Canada strengthened its ties to Great Britain.
   (2) Canada moved to cut all ties with Great Britain.
   (3) Canada cut some of the last ties with Great Britain.
   (4) Canada had the strongest military in the Western Hemisphere.
   (5) Canada gave women the right to vote long after most modern nations.

The correct answer is (3). Although Canada did cut some ties, it remained under the British monarch and remains so even today.

2. Which of the following is true of Canada immediately after World War II?

   (1) The Canadian economy declined tremendously because of the Canadian war efforts.
   (2) The Canadian economy boomed because of an increase in foreign markets for Canadian goods.
   (3) Canada's role in international politics dwindled until Canada no longer had any input in the international political arena.
   (4) Canada's population doubled because of Eastern European immigration.
   (5) Canada's indigenous people were granted an apology from the government along with their own province.

The correct answer is (2). Canada shipped many of its goods to the war-torn countries of Europe.

Glossary

A

abolish—to end.

abolition—the movement in the nineteenth century to end slavery in America.

absolute location—an exact position on the surface of a globe.

absolute monarchy—a monarchy in which the king or queen has total control over all aspects of life in the kingdom.

Allied Powers—World War II alliance of Great Britain, Russia, and the United States.

amendment—a change or addition.

annex—to take over or acquire.

aristocracy—a government in which the right to rule lies with those theoretically best suited to rule, often the nobility.

Articles of Confederation—the first constitution of the United States that held the states together in a loose union.

Axis Powers—World War II alliance of Italy, Germany, and Japan.

B

bicameral—having two houses, as does the U.S. Congress.

bill—a proposed law.

Bill of Rights—the first ten amendments to the U.S. Constitution.

C

cabinet—the group of advisers who work closely with the president and who head each of the executive departments.

capital—material resources needed to convert raw materials into finished goods.

capitalism—an economic system in which private ownership of material resources, or capital, is not only allowed but also encouraged.

cartographer—a mapmaker.

checks and balances—the system in which each branch of government has some power over the other two, so as not to allow any one branch to become too powerful.

Chief Diplomat—the role of the president in which he meets and greets diplomats and works on treaties.

Chief Executive—the role of the president in which he acts as head of the executive branch of government.

circulating capital—capital such as wages or rent payments that are distributed.

climate—weather patterns over an extended period of time.

closed primary—a preliminary election in which voters may vote only for candidates of the party with which they are registered.

collective bargaining—when leaders of the labor unions meet with employers and management to negotiate wages, hours, conditions, benefits, or other issues.

colonization—the formation of colonies for the purpose of creating revenue for the sponsoring country.

colony—a group of people who live in a new territory but retain ties with the parent country.

Commander in Chief—the role of the president in which the president acts as the commander of all U.S. armed forces.

committee—a small group of legislators that deal specifically with a particular area of legislation.

communism—economic system based on collective ownership of property; private ownership of both capital and means of production are prohibited.

conservative—a term used to describe those with political ideas generally supporting very slow change to the existing political and social order.

constituents—citizens who are entitled to participate in the election of a representative.

constitution—a written plan of government.

constitutional convention—meeting of leaders to outline a plan of government.

constitutional monarchy—a monarchical government in which the power of the king or queen is limited by a constitution.

continent—one of the seven major land masses on earth including North America, South America, Europe, Asia, Africa, Australia, and Antarctica.

contour lines—lines that illustrate various elevations of landforms on maps.

contour map—illustrates the elevation of physical features.

contractionary fiscal policy—when taxation is increased and spending is slowed.

coordinate—the point at which a line of latitude and a line of longitude intersect.

D

demand—the desire of the consumers to purchase goods.

democracy—a government in which the people make the decisions.

desegregation—the process of ending racial segregation.

deserters—soldiers who run away to escape life in the military.

desertification—the process of creating deserts.

détente—the easing of Cold War tensions between the United States and the USSR.

dictatorship—a government in which one person, a dictator, has total control of the government; usually a dictator assumes control through military force.

diplomacy—the conduction of negotiations between nations.

direct democracy—a democracy in which all the decisions are made directly by the people; also known as a pure democracy or a true democracy.

discount rate—the interest rate that the Federal Reserve Board charges to member banks to borrow money.

E

economics—the study of the way society uses limited material resources to meet its needs.

effigy—a crude representation of a person, often burned as a sign of protest.

elastic clause—allows the government to be flexible in the application of it powers in order to handle situations that the founders of the nation could not foresee.

Electoral College—the group of electors that actually elect the president.

enumerated powers—powers specifically named in the Constitution.

environment—one of the five themes of geography, meaning an area's natural surroundings.

equator—latitude line located at 0° latitude, which divides the earth into the Northern and Southern Hemispheres.

equilibrium—the point at which supply and demand meet to form a stable market.

executive branch—the branch of government responsible for administering, enforcing, and carrying out the laws.

expansion—the act of adding territory.

expansionary fiscal policy—when taxation is reduced and/or spending is stimulated.

expedition—voyage of discovery.

exports—goods shipped out of a country.

F

faction—a group or sect.

factors of production—natural resources, capital, and labor.

favorable balance of trade—when the amount of a country's exports exceed the amount of its imports.

Federal Reserve Board—controls the monetary policy in the United States.

federalism—the division of governmental powers and responsibilities between national (or federal), state, and local governments.

Federalists—early American political party that favored a strong central government.

fixed capital—capital such as land or buildings that is not distributed.

formal regions—regions created by government or political boundaries.

frontier—a region beyond the border of settled territory.

frozen capital—capital that cannot easily be converted to or sold for cash.

full faith and credit clause—the clause in the Constitution that requires states to respect the legal documents and decisions of other states.

functional region—region within a particular service area, such as a television service area.

G

geography—the study of the earth's physical features and the way man has adapted to these physical features.

Gilded Age—a name given to the post-Civil War era.

globe—a spherical representation of a map of the earth.

hemisphere—half of a globe.

H

hills—landforms that have elevations of less than 1,000 feet above sea level and have gently sloping sides with rounded tops.

holocaust—the mass slaughter of Jews, gypsies, homosexuals, and other people by the Nazis during World War II.

I

impeach—to bring formal charges against a public official.

imports—goods shipped into a country.

indirect democracy—a democracy in which the people elect representatives to make decisions for them.

industrialization—the move from an agricultural to an industrial, or manufacturing-oriented, society.

inflation—a rise in prices or a devaluing of money, resulting in decreased buying power for consumers.

International Date Line—line of longitude located at 180° longitude.

J

joint stock company—business venture in which a large number of people invest small amounts of money in order to reduce risk.

judicial branch—the branch of government that interprets the law; made up of courts.

judicial review—the power of the Supreme Court to determine the constitutionality of laws and actions.

junta—a group that takes control of a government after a military takeover.

L

laborers—the workers needed to turn raw materials into finished goods.

laissez-faire—when the government allows business and industry to operate with little or no government intervention.

latitude lines—horizontal lines that run east and west around the earth and measure distances north and south of the equator.

law of diminishing returns—law that states at a certain point any additional resources (raw materials, labor, or capital) fail to produce any additional product.

legend—a key that contains the meanings of the symbols used on the map.

legislative branch—the branch of government that makes the laws.

legislator—a member of a lawmaking body.

legislature—a lawmaking body.

liberal—a term used to describe those with political ideas generally supporting change and social progress.

liquid capital—capital that can easily be converted into cash.

lobbyist—one who meets with legislators to attempt to sway them to vote in the interest of the lobbyist's cause.

location—one of the five themes of geography, meaning an exact and precise position on the earth's surface.

longitude lines—vertical lines that run north and south around the earth and measure distances east and west of the Prime Meridian.

Louisiana Purchase—massive expanse of land stretching from Canada to the Gulf of Mexico and from the Mississippi River to the Rocky Mountains; purchased by Thomas Jefferson from France; practically doubled the size of American territories.

loyalists—American colonists who did not want to break away from Britain.

M

macrodivisions—large areas, sometimes entire regions, that share similar characteristics.

macroeconomics—economics concerned with the overall economy and greater issues such as national income or unemployment.

Manifest Destiny—the idea that expansion all the way to the Pacific Ocean was an inevitable part of the destiny of the United States.

margin requirement—set by the Federal Reserve Board, the amount of cash a purchaser must put toward the purchase of stock so as to curb speculation.

Marshall Plan—an economic assistance plan for European countries after World War II.

mercantilism—economic policy in which the government seeks stockpiles of gold and silver and a much higher amount of exports than imports, so as to strengthen the national economy.

microeconomics—economics dealing with price theory, supply, demand, and equilibrium.

microgeography—the geographic study of small or specific areas.

militia—citizen soldiers who are not members of a permanent army.

mixed economy—an economy in which elements of several economic systems exist.

monarchy—a government ruled by a king or queen; the right to rule is usually hereditary.

monetary policy—the policy set by the government that controls the use of money and the amount available.

monopoly—situation that occurs when a business has no competition.

Monroe Doctrine—declaration that the United States would not allow further colonization or expansion in the Western Hemisphere.

mountains—landforms that have elevations of more than 1,000 feet above sea level and have steep sides and generally pointed tops or peaks.

movement—one of the five themes of geography; concerned with the ways humans interact with other humans in other places.

N

Native Americans—also referred to as Indians, those people who lived in the Americas before the arrival of Europeans.

New Deal—President Franklin Roosevelt's economic and social program that helped spur the economy and lead the United States out of the Great Depression.

New World—the land in the Western Hemisphere explored and colonized by Europeans during the fifteenth, sixteenth, and seventeenth centuries.

O

oligarchy—a government ruled by a few, often in a manner similar to a dictatorship; often those who rule assume control after a military takeover.

open primary—a preliminary election in which any voters are allowed to participate.

P

physiocrats—opponents of mercantilism that advocated free trade and a *laissez-faire* government economic policy.

pigeonholing—setting aside a bill so that it dies and does not become a law.

place—one of the five themes of geography, means not only where a location is but what a location is like.

plains—low flatlands.

plateaus—flatlands at high elevations.

platform—the set of values or ideas upon which a political party is based.

political map—illustrates political borders or boundaries between countries, states, counties, etc.

political party—a group of people who share similar political ideas.

political science—the study of government, the methods of government, and those who govern.

population map—illustrates population density or how many people live in a particular area.

pressure group—a political group with a specific agenda whose goal is to sway legislators in one direction or another.

primary—a preliminary election in which voters choose a candidate to represent their party in the main election.

Prime Meridian—line of longitude that runs through Greenwich, England, and is located at 0° longitude; it divides the earth into the Eastern and Western Hemispheres.

Progressives—reformers in nineteenth and twentieth century America.

Prohibition—period of time in the United States when the sale and consumption of alcohol was illegal.

R

ratify—to approve.

reform—a political or social change; progress.

republic—a government in which representatives are elected to make decisions for the people.

Republicans—early American political party that believed the American people were capable of governing themselves.

recession—a period of slowed or reduced economic activity.

region—one of the five themes of geography, meaning any area, regardless of size, which contains common characteristics.

regional geography—deals with the physical and cultural features within a particular region, or area, of the earth's surface.

reserve ratio—is the amount of money that lending institutions can lend and the amount they must hold in reserve.

revenue—the income produced by a particular source.

S

secede—to withdraw from.

separation of powers—the division of governmental power between the executive, legislative, and judicial branches.

socialism—an economic system in which major industries are owned either publicly or cooperatively; the government is responsible for the redistribution of wealth.

strike—a work stoppage.

supply—all the goods available to consumers regardless of price.

systematic geography—deals with individual elements of the earth's physical and cultural features.

T

tariff—a tax placed on imports.

tarring and feathering—a form of public humiliation in which a person was covered with tar and then rolled in feathers.

taxation without representation—being forced to pay taxes to a government that does not allow taxpayers to have a voice in the government.

time zone—1 of the 24 equal zones of the earth's surface representing 1 hour of the 24-hour day.

topographical map—illustrates physical features such as mountains, hills, valleys, rivers, or prairies.

topography—the study of the earth's physical features.

Treaty of Paris, 1783—treaty in which Britain recognized the independence of the American colonies.

Triple Entente—World War I alliance of Great Britain, France, and Russia.

trust—a combination of businesses or corporations that reduces competition.

V

vernacular regions—regions that hold a loose association given to them by humans, for example, the Middle East.

veto—a presidential act that kills a bill; it may be overridden by a congressional vote, though.

W

weather map—illustrates the forecasted or current weather for an area.

Y

Yellow Journalism—sensational and exaggerated journalism.

Practice Test

75 Minutes 50 Questions

> **Directions:** The Social Studies test consists of multiple-choice questions intended to measure general social studies concepts. The questions are based on short readings that often include a graph, chart, or figure. Study the information given and then answer the question(s) following it. Refer to the information as often as necessary in answering the questions.

You should spend no more than 75 minutes answering the questions. Work carefully, but do not spend too much time on any one question. Be sure you answer every question. You will not be penalized for incorrect answers.

Do not mark in this test booklet. Record your answers on the separate answer sheet provided. Be sure all requested information is properly recorded on the answer sheet. To record your answers, mark the numbered space on the answer sheet beside the number that corresponds to the question in the test.

Do not rest the point of your pencil on the answer sheet while you are considering your answer. Make no stray or unnecessary marks. If you change an answer, erase your first mark completely. Mark only one answer space for each question; multiple answers will be scored as incorrect. Do not fold or crease your answer sheet.

ROAD MAP

- *Practice Test*
- *Answers and Explanations*
- *Analysis Chart*

FOR EXAMPLE

Early colonists of North America looked for settlement sites that had adequate water supplies and were accessible by ship. For this reason, many early towns were built near

    (1) mountains.
    (2) prairies.
    (3) rivers.
    (4) glaciers.
    (5) plateaus.

①②●④⑤

The correct answer is "rivers"; therefore, choice (3) would be marked on the answer sheet.

Directions: Choose the one best answer for each item.

Items 1–4 refer to the following table.

IMPORTANT JOB FACTORS

Job Factor	Percentage Who Rated It "Very Important"
Open communication in company	65%
Effect of job on personal/family life	60%
Supervisor's management style	58%
Job security	54%
Job location	50%
Family-supportive policies	46%
Fringe benefits	43%
Salary/wages	35%
Management/promotion opportunities	26%
Size of company	18%

1. According to the table, which aspect of their jobs do workers consider most important?

   (1) Job security
   (2) Fringe benefits
   (3) Open communication
   (4) Management opportunity
   (5) Salary/wages

2. According to the table, which job factor is least important to employees?

   (1) Family-supportive policies
   (2) The supervisor's style of management
   (3) The size of the company
   (4) The effect on personal/family life
   (5) Fringe benefits, such as health insurance

3. Which of the following combinations might be most likely to make employees unhappy enough to consider leaving their jobs?

   (1) Few management opportunities and few fringe benefits
   (2) An uncommunicative supervisor and a company atmosphere of secrecy
   (3) A small number of total employees and an out-of-the-way office location
   (4) Policies that are not family supportive and few fringe benefits
   (5) Lack of management opportunities and a large number of staff members

4. If you are the owner of a small business and you are trying to hire a potentially valuable employee away from a large multinational competitor, what should you stress in interviews?

   (1) That you expect the size of your business to grow rapidly
   (2) That the lines of communication will always be open between the two of you, both formally and informally
   (3) That the prospective employee will never be fired or terminated
   (4) That you cannot offer many fringe benefits now, but you have great plans for such things in the future
   (5) That you plan to move the business to a newer building

Items 5 and 6 refer to the following cartoon.

5. Which choice best summarizes the cartoonist's point?

   (1) Poverty, drugs, and ignorance are root causes of gangs.
   (2) Gangs are the root cause of poverty, drugs, and ignorance.
   (3) Experts agree that poverty, drugs, and gangs are the major causes of ignorance.
   (4) Drugs are the major cause of gang violence.
   (5) Few people believe that poverty, drugs, and ignorance are root causes of gangs.

6. With which point of view would the cartoonist most clearly agree?

   (1) The only way to end gang violence is to eliminate poverty.
   (2) Gang violence can be ended only by implementing a law that puts repeat offenders in jail permanently.
   (3) Drugs are the major cause of gangs.
   (4) Only by eliminating poverty, drugs, and ignorance will we be able to end gangs and their violence.
   (5) The government has spent too much money trying to eliminate poverty and drugs.

7. Who would most immediately feel an adverse effect of inflation?

   (1) An investor in enterprises involving real estate
   (2) A retired individual living on an insurance annuity
   (3) An individual who has most of his capital invested in common stock
   (4) A union member who has an escalator clause in his contract
   (5) A government worker about to negotiate a new contract

8. Which of the following did *not* happen in the aftermath of the 1990–1991 Gulf War?

   (1) The Iraqi leader was removed from power.
   (2) Economic sanctions were imposed on Iraq.
   (3) Two no-fly zones were established inside of Iraq.
   (4) The United States periodically bombed targets inside Iraq.
   (5) The United States and Iraq continued to have strained diplomatic relations.

9. The War Powers Act of 1973 states that

   (1) the president has the power to send combat troops overseas without consulting Congress.
   (2) the president can unilaterally declare war through executive order.
   (3) Congress can require a president to bring combat troops home after sixty days.
   (4) Congress can prevent a president from sending combat troops overseas through a two-thirds vote of each house.
   (5) Congress may not declare war under any circumstances.

10. After World War II, all of the following nations were divided between Communist and non-Communist spheres of influence EXCEPT

   (1) Korea.
   (2) Germany.
   (3) Japan.
   (4) Vietnam.
   (5) China.

Items 11–13 refer to the following map.

TIME ZONES IN THE
CONTINENTAL UNITED STATES

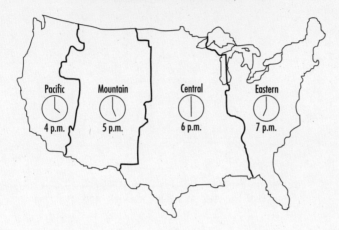

11. When it is 1:00 p.m. in San Francisco, what time is it in New York City?

    (1)   2 p.m.
    (2)   3 p.m.
    (3)   4 p.m.
    (4)   1 p.m.
    (5)   1 a.m.

12. A government worker in Washington, D.C., has to make a phone call to a Portland, Oregon, business that opens at 9:00 a.m. What is the earliest time in Washington, D.C., that the government worker can reach the Portland business?

    (1)   9 a.m.
    (2)   10 a.m.
    (3)   9 p.m.
    (4)   8 a.m.
    (5)   Noon

13. Time zones came into use in the United States in the late 1800s. What event or invention was the greatest cause of this innovation?

    (1)   The end of the Civil War
    (2)   The completion of the transcontinental railroad
    (3)   The widespread use of tin cans for preserving food
    (4)   The inauguration of the Pony Express
    (5)   The growth in the number of European immigrants to the United States

Items 14–16 refer to the following information and graph.

PROFITS FOR GARCIA'S GOODIES

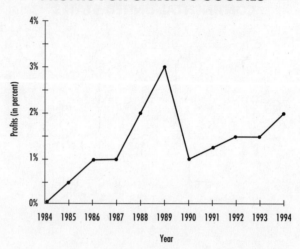

Mr. Antonio Garcia owns Garcia's Goodies, a gourmet grocery store he started in 1984. The line graph above shows the after-tax profits the store generated in each year of the first decade the store was in business.

14. According to the line graph, the year of highest profits was

    (1) 1984.
    (2) 1987.
    (3) 1989.
    (4) 1993.
    (5) 1990.

15. When profits fell in 1990, Mr. Garcia could have successfully rectified the situation by

    (1) reducing the number of full-time store employees.
    (2) getting a large loan from a nearby bank.
    (3) asking some of the store's managers to take long paid vacations.
    (4) giving cost-of-living salary increases to minimum-wage employees only.
    (5) working with owners of similar, nearby stores to raise prices on most items.

16. In which year did Mr. Garcia probably hire the most employees?

    (1) 1986
    (2) 1984
    (3) 1989
    (4) 1991
    (5) 1993

Items 17 and 18 refer to the following illustration.

LATITUDE AND LONGITUDE

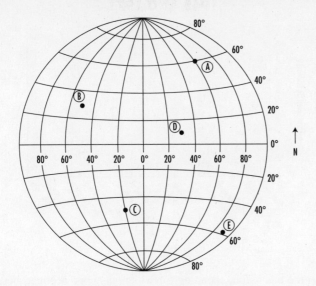

17. According to the illustration, which of the lettered points is found at 50 degrees south latitude and 20 degrees west longitude?

    (1)   Point A
    (2)   Point B
    (3)   Point C
    (4)   Point D
    (5)   Point E

18. What direction is point B from point D?

    (1)   West, northwest
    (2)   East, southeast
    (3)   East, northeast
    (4)   West, southwest
    (5)   South

Items 19 and 20 refer to the following bar graph.

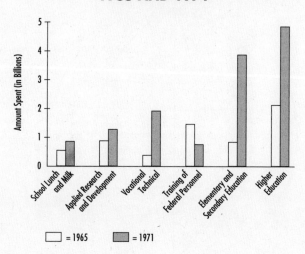

FEDERAL SPENDING ON EDUCATION 1965 AND 1971

□ = 1965   ▨ = 1971

19. According to the bar graph, spending for which category declined between 1965 and 1971?

(1) School lunch and milk
(2) Applied research and development
(3) Vocational technical
(4) Training of federal personnel
(5) Elementary and secondary education

20. Which of the following statements can be verified by information in the graph?

(1) The federal government spent a relatively small amount of its funds on education in both 1965 and 1971.
(2) The food served in most school lunch rooms did not adequately meet federal nutrition guidelines.
(3) Applied research and development was a relatively small part of the overall education budget in both 1965 and 1971.
(4) In 1971, most Americans believed federal funds for education were not being wisely spent.
(5) The number of Americans in college included a greater percentage of African Americans in 1971 than in 1965.

21. Which of the following is a *true* statement regarding UN peacekeeping efforts?

    (1) The frequency and number of peacekeeping missions have declined during the last decade.
    (2) Most peacekeeping troops have been supplied by smaller non-aligned nations.
    (3) American troops have become a common part of the UN peacekeeping missions.
    (4) In nearly all cases, UN peacekeeping missions have been able to establish a "permanent" peace.
    (5) Each nation pays an equal share of peacekeeping expenses.

22. All of the following are specifically found in the U.S. Constitution EXCEPT

    (1) the establishment of the Electoral College.
    (2) a prohibition against bills of attainder.
    (3) a statement creating national political parties.
    (4) a provision that establishes an "Acting President."
    (5) the establishment of a federal system of government.

23. "A man who lived from 1865 to 1945 would have witnessed developments which in European history occupied several centuries: absolute monarchy, constitutional monarchy, liberalism, imperialist expansion, military dictatorship, totalitarian fascism, foreign occupation." The above description best fits

    (1) India.
    (2) China.
    (3) Japan.
    (4) Egypt.
    (5) Russia.

24. The increased use of executive agreements by U.S. presidents has

    (1) actually increased congressional influence over the foreign policy process.
    (2) reflected the increase in overseas American commitments and responsibilities.
    (3) basically meant that U.S. presidents no longer use executive orders as much as in the past.
    (4) had little impact upon Congressional-presidential relationships in the area of foreign policy.
    (5) been declared unconstitutional by the Supreme Court.

Items 25 and 26 refer to the following cartoon.

25. Which statement best describes the cartoon's meaning?

   (1)   Repeat offenders are a problem in American society.
   (2)   Parole boards should carry malpractice insurance as doctors do.
   (3)   Only high wage earners such as doctors can afford to carry malpractice insurance.
   (4)   Parole boards should be held more accountable for those they release from prison.
   (5)   Parole boards should have more minority members.

26. If this cartoonist could speak to the parole board, what would he probably ask them to do?

   (1)   Be less lenient with probable repeat offenders
   (2)   Spend more time reviewing each case
   (3)   Grant paroles to first-time offenders only
   (4)   Work with state legislators to increase the funds available for building more prisons
   (5)   Grant more paroles to drug dealers

Items 27–30 refer to the following circle graph.

IMMIGRATION TO THE UNITED STATES
1900–1910

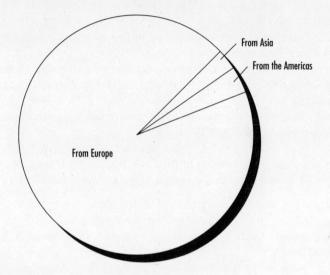

From Asia

From the Americas

From Europe

27. The period from the late 1800s to the early 1900s was a time of discrimination against people from Japan and China who wanted to immigrate to the United States. Which statement concerning the circle graph describes an effect of that discrimination?

   (1)   All of the immigrants to the United States came from Asia, the Americas, and Europe between 1900 and 1910.

   (2)   More immigrants came from Europe than from any other continent.

   (3)   According to the chart, no immigrants came from Africa or Australia.

   (4)   In the chart, "the Americas" refers to all those nations of the Western Hemisphere except the United States.

   (5)   Only a very small percentage of the total number of immigrants to the United States came from Asia, which includes China and Japan.

28. According to the graph, what percentage of the total number of immigrants came from Europe?

   (1)   About 10 percent

   (2)   About 30 percent

   (3)   About 50 percent

   (4)   About 70 percent

   (5)   About 90 percent

29. The early 1900s were a time when most immigrants traveled by boat to the United States. European immigrants landed at and were processed through Ellis Island in New York Harbor. Asian immigrants landed at and were processed through Angel Island in San Francisco Harbor. Based on the information in the circle graph, which of the following statements is true?

    (1) Many more immigrants were processed through Ellis Island than through Angel Island in the early 1900s.
    (2) Asian immigrants were often forced to live at Angel Island for several months when they first arrived.
    (3) Ellis Island was the port of entry for passengers who did not travel first class.
    (4) Immigrants at both Ellis Island and Angel Island had to pass brief medical examinations.
    (5) Most immigrants from the rest of the Americas were refused entry to the United States between 1900 and 1910.

30. Racial tensions and the aftermath of the Civil War in the United States probably had what effect on immigration to the United States between 1900 and 1910?

    (1) They led to heavier immigration from Europe.
    (2) They led to virtually no immigration from Africa.
    (3) They caused Asian immigrants to reconsider their decisions to move to the United States.
    (4) They made available to immigrants from the Americas places for legal immigration to the United States.
    (5) They caused the United States to follow the foreign policy of isolationism.

31. "I believe it must be the policy of the United States to support free peoples who are resisting attempted subjugation by armed minorities or by outside pressures . . ." is a statement taken from the famous 1947 proclamation known as the

    (1) Marshall Plan.
    (2) Baruch Plan.
    (3) Eisenhower Doctrine.
    (4) Truman Doctrine.
    (5) Four Freedoms Address.

32. "The political system of the allied powers is essentially different from that of America. We should consider any attempt on their part to extend their system to any portion of this hemisphere as dangerous to our peace and safety." This statement is representative of the ideas expressed in the

    (1) Freeport Doctrine.
    (2) Manifest Destiny.
    (3) Constitution of the Confederacy.
    (4) Monroe Doctrine.
    (5) Articles of Confederation.

Items 33–36 refer to the following map.

EXPANSION OF THE CONTINENTAL UNITED STATES

33. According to the map, the last part of the continental United States that was added was

    (1) the Louisiana Purchase.
    (2) the Mexican Cession.
    (3) Oregon Country.
    (4) the Gadsden Purchase.
    (5) Florida.

34. The Mexican War of 1846–1848 was ended by the Treaty of Guadalupe Hidalgo, which gave what large area of land to the United States?

    (1) The Louisiana Purchase
    (2) The Mexican Cession
    (3) Oregon Country
    (4) The Gadsden Purchase
    (5) Florida

35. The Louisiana Purchase was made during the presidency of which of the following men?

    (1) George Washington (1789–1797)
    (2) Millard Fillmore (1850–1853)
    (3) Thomas Jefferson (1801–1809)
    (4) James Polk (1845–1849)
    (5) Franklin Pierce (1853–1857)

36. Which sentence is the best summary of the map's content?

    (1) Texas was annexed before the Gadsden Purchase was made.
    (2) The Louisiana Purchase extended from the Gulf of Mexico to the Canadian border.
    (3) At the time of the Constitutional Convention, the territory of the United States was all east of the Mississippi River.
    (4) The Oregon Country is north and west of the Louisiana Purchase.
    (5) The expansion of the continental United States was made up of adjoining pieces of land that were added during the nineteenth century.

37. "During the decade 1840–1850 they left their native land in large numbers because of the famine and came to the United States to settle, for the greater part, in seaboard cities." This description best applies to immigrants from

    (1) Germany.
    (2) Ireland.
    (3) Russia.
    (4) Italy.
    (5) Denmark.

Items 38 and 39 refer to the following passage.

Although people sometimes think of the earth as unchanging and solid, this is not really true. In fact, the earth is changing constantly, both on and beneath the surface. Evidence of this activity can be seen in the United States today. Active volcanoes are found in both Oregon and Hawaii. Earthquakes are common in California, especially along the San Andreas Fault. The New Madrid Fault, a less active but well-known fault, runs from southern Illinois through Missouri, Tennessee, and Arkansas.

Weather has a big effect on the shape and form of the earth's surface. Tornadoes are common during some seasons in Iowa, Nebraska, Kansas, Illinois, Wisconsin, and other states in the Midwest. Heavy rains sometimes cause flash floods in Texas, Arizona, New Mexico, and California. Hurricanes are annual events and sometimes strike Florida, the Carolinas, and other states along the eastern seaboard.

38. Someone who lives near the San Andreas Fault probably worries most about the danger from

    (1) hurricanes.
    (2) tornadoes.
    (3) earthquakes.
    (4) volcanoes.
    (5) flash floods.

39. In 1811 and 1812, the Mississippi River changed its course through Tennessee, Missouri, and Arkansas. What most likely forced this change?

    (1) Hurricanes
    (2) Tornadoes
    (3) Earthquakes
    (4) Volcanoes
    (5) Flash floods

Items 40 and 41 refer to the following cartoon.

The NORTH ATLANTIC TEA & ORIGAMI Society

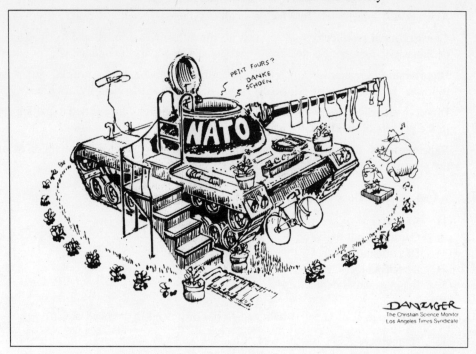

40. Which statement is the best summary of this 1990 cartoon's meaning?

(1) NATO has become too involved in Japanese affairs.
(2) NATO is not a well-managed organization.
(3) NATO has become ineffectual since the fall of communism.
(4) NATO needs to undertake joint training exercises with the former communist countries of Eastern Europe.
(5) NATO was a better organization when it had a strong adversary.

41. With which of the following statements would the cartoonist probably most agree?

(1) NATO needs a powerful enemy to be strong itself.
(2) France needs to rejoin NATO before the organization can become strong again.
(3) NATO has never been a useful organization for the United States to be a part of and it never will be.
(4) NATO should become a worldwide security group.
(5) NATO's benefit to the West has ended and it should be disbanded.

Listed below are five major present-day forms of government.

Aristocracy: government in which a small, privileged, hereditary group governs

Constitutional monarchy: government in which the real power is held by an elected parliament or congress but documents recognize a hereditary ceremonial king or queen

Dictatorship: government in which an individual and a small, trusted group of followers have all the power, usually to the detriment of the majority of citizens

Direct democracy: government in which all eligible citizens are entitled to participate in the process of making laws and setting policy

Representative democracy: government in which freely elected representatives of the great mass of citizens make laws and set policy

42. In Iraq, Saddam Hussein rules what type of government?

    (1) Aristocracy
    (2) Constitutional monarchy
    (3) Dictatorship
    (4) Direct democracy
    (5) Representative democracy

43. Queen Elizabeth II of Great Britain and Northern Ireland is the head of a(n)

    (1) aristocracy.
    (2) constitutional monarchy.
    (3) dictatorship.
    (4) direct democracy.
    (5) representative democracy.

44. Although many others would disagree, the Irish Republican Army would probably describe the government of Northern Ireland as a(n)

    (1) aristocracy.
    (2) constitutional monarchy.
    (3) dictatorship.
    (4) direct democracy.
    (5) representative democracy.

45. People in the United States tend to oppose dictatorships because

    (1) most Americans have a basic belief in the rights of all people to have a say in their government.
    (2) most known dictatorships have operated to the detriment of the majority of their citizens.
    (3) most people in the United States know little about forms of government other than democracy.
    (4) dictatorships often deny equal trading rights in their nations to U.S. companies.
    (5) the United States has never been governed by a dictatorship.

Items 46–48 refer to the following information.

Violence has become a major concern of many Americans in the 1990s. This violence includes: child abuse, spousal abuse, random shootings, assaults, and abuse of the elderly.

46. A member of a child welfare league would probably be most involved with finding solutions to which type of violence?

    (1) Child abuse
    (2) Spousal abuse
    (3) Abuse of the elderly
    (4) Random shootings
    (5) Assaults

47. A member of the American Association of Retired Persons would probably be most involved in finding solutions to which type of violence?

    (1) Child abuse
    (2) Spousal abuse
    (3) Abuse of the elderly
    (4) Random shootings
    (5) Assaults

48. Street gangs are most often associated with which type of criminal activity?

    (1) Anti-Semitic hate crimes
    (2) Thefts of information from computer systems
    (3) Retaliatory shootings
    (4) Rape
    (5) Credit card forgeries

49. An American student in London becomes friendly with the "wrong crowd" and soon is involved in a bungled bank robbery. The robbers are apprehended and the American student calls the American consulate for help. The consul can offer advice and encouragement to the jailed student but he *cannot*

    (1) request the release of the student, as a U.S. citizen, for trial in the United States.
    (2) attend the trial as an observer.
    (3) communicate with the student's parents to reassure them that the student is being treated fairly.
    (4) visit the student in prison if the student is convicted.
    (5) bring the student small gifts from home.

50. Sometimes "the impossible" can only be accomplished by the most "improbable" person. Thus, only a leader with well-established credentials as a hard-liner can get away with making overtures to "the other side." Of the following, which visit does *not* fit into this category.

    (1) Richard Nixon to China.
    (2) John Paul II to the Temple in Rome.
    (3) Willy Brandt to the United States.
    (4) Anwar Sadat to Jerusalem.
    (5) Saddam Hussein to the Israeli border.

ANSWERS AND EXPLANATIONS

1. **The correct answer is (3). (Comprehension)** According to the table, open communication is the most highly valued job factor, with 65 percent of respondents saying they rate it "very important."

2. **The correct answer is (3). (Comprehension)** The table indicates that the size of the company is the least important factor.

3. **The correct answer is (2). (Analysis)** The flow of communication within the company and the management style of the supervisor are two of the three most highly rated qualities in their importance to workers.

4. **The correct answer is (2). (Application)** Because open communication is highly desired by most employees, the interviewer would be wise to talk about the company's ability to fulfill this desire.

5. **The correct answer is (1). (Comprehension)** The drawing shows gangs growing out of poverty, drugs, and ignorance.

6. **The correct answer is (4). (Evaluation)** The correct answer is choice (4), because the cartoonist, who sees poverty, drugs, and ignorance as the causes of gangs, would probably agree that the only way to end gang violence is to eliminate these causes.

7. **The correct answer is (2). (Analysis)** A retired individual living on an insurance annuity has a fixed income. As the second inflation starts, the value of his or her income depreciates. The other four choices would feel little or no immediate effect from inflation.

8. **The correct answer is (1). (Analysis)** On February 27, 1991, President Bush ordered a cease fire. At the time Saddam Hussein was left in control of Iraq. Although Kurds in the north and Shi'ite Muslims in the south attempted to overthrow Saddam, he was able to put down both rebellions.

9. **The correct answer is (3). (Comprehension)** The War Powers Act of 1973 places the following limits on the president's use of the military. He must report in writing to Congress within 48 hours after he sends troops into any conflict. Congress then has sixty days to declare war or provide for the continued use of those troops. If Congress fails to provide such authorization, the president must remove the troops, so choice (3) is correct.

10. **The correct answer is (3). (Analysis)** Korea was divided into North and South Korea, Vietnam into North and South Vietnam, and Germany into East and West Germany. Japan was the only nation not to be divided into Communist and non-Communist spheres of influence, so choice (3) is the correct answer.

11. **The correct answer is (3). (Comprehension)** New York City is three time zones to the east of San Francisco, so it is 3 hours later in New York.

12. **The correct answer is (5). (Application)** Because Washington, D.C., is in the Eastern time zone and Portland, Oregon, is in the Pacific time zone, the time difference is three hours, so when it is 9 a.m. in Portland, it is noon in Washington.

13. **The correct answer is (2). (Analysis)** Originally, each town across the country set its own time by the position of the sun, so it was impossible to figure the arrival and departure times of trains. The creation of time zones solved this problem.

14. **The correct answer is (3). (Comprehension)** According to the graph, the year of highest profits was 1989.

15. **The correct answer is (1). (Evaluation)** Reducing costs (i.e., salaries) would have helped increase profits. The other four choices would not have increased the profitability of the store; in fact, choices (2) and (3) would have actually added to the problem.

16. **The correct answer is (2). (Analysis)** The year the business opened, 1984, would have been the one during which the most employees would have been hired, because it can be assumed that a full staff would have been put in place that year.

17. **The correct answer is (3). (Comprehension)** This answer can be derived by looking only at the latitudes of the various options. Only choices (3) and (5), points C and E, are in the south latitudes, so the other three choices can be eliminated immediately. Choice (5) is at 60 degrees south latitude, so choice (3), point C, can be determined to be the correct answer by the process of elimination.

18. **The correct answer is (1). (Application)** By locating points B and D on the globe, it should become apparent that point B is both west and north of point D, so choice (1) is correct.

19. **The correct answer is (4). (Comprehension)** Between 1965 and 1971, spending declined for only one category—training of federal personnel—so choice (4) is correct.

20. **The correct answer is (3). (Analysis)** Choices (1), (2), (4), and (5) may or may not be true statements; they cannot be verified by the information in the bar graph. Only choice (3) contains information that can be verified by the bar graph.

21. **The correct answer is (2). (Comprehension)** While the United States remains the largest financial contributor to the UN peacekeeping efforts, smaller or non-aligned nations supply the majority of the troops. The top five troop contributors are: India, Nigeria, Jordan, Bangladesh, and Australia. The number of peacekeeping missions escalated in 1993, then declined from 1996 to 1999, but rose again in 2000.

22. **The correct answer is (3). (Analysis)** The Electoral College is established in article II, section 1.2. Bills of attainder are prohibited in article 1, section 9.3. An "Acting President" is established by the twenty-fifth Amendment. Nowhere in the Constitution is there any provision for the creation of national political parties.

23. **The correct answer is (3). (Analysis)** The series of events best describes the political changes within Japan during the time period given. It begins with the removal of the Tokugawa Shogun and the beginning of the Meiji Restoration (1868). It ends with the American occupation of Japan at the end of World War II (1945) .

24. **The correct answer is (2). (Comprehension)** Executive agreements in foreign affairs are made between the president and other heads of state. They do not require Senate approval. Many have secret provisions, so Congress is bypassed. Over 9,000 Executive Agreements have been issued by presidents.

25. **The correct answer is (4). (Comprehension)** The problem of repeat offenders who had been released early by parole boards is shown in the cartoon as the responsibility of the boards themselves.

26. **The correct answer is (1). (Application)** The cartoonist would probably tell the parole board to be less lenient and more cautious about whom they release, because such leniency is the issue of the cartoon.

27. **The correct answer is (5). (Analysis)** Choice (5) is the only one that describes the situation regarding immigration from Japan and China to America.

28. **The correct answer is (5). (Comprehension)** More than 90 percent of the immigrants were from Europe.

29. **The correct answer is (1). (Evaluation)** The large number of immigrants from Europe, who, it must be assumed, were processed through Ellis Island, would indicate that choice (1) is the correct answer.

30. **The correct answer is (2). (Analysis)** The great racial tensions between African Americans and whites of European descent probably caused immigration from Africa to be almost nonexistent.

31. **The correct answer is (4). (Comprehension)** The Truman Doctrine requested $400 million from Congress to aid Turkey and Greece in their efforts to resist Soviet ambitions in their countries.

32. **The correct answer is (4). (Comprehension)** In the Monroe Doctrine, President Monroe in effect closed the Western Hemisphere to any further colonization or interference by European powers.

33. **The correct answer is (4). (Application)** The Gadsden Purchase was added in 1853, making it the final acquisition to the continental United States.

34. **The correct answer is (2). (Application)** The Mexican Cession was added to the United States in 1848 as a result of the Mexican War, which ended that year.

35. **The correct answer is (3). (Analysis)** The Louisiana Purchase was made in 1803, during the presidency of Thomas Jefferson.

36. **The correct answer is (5). (Analysis)** Choice (5) summarizes the entire map; each of the other choices describes only one part of it.

37. **The correct answer is (2). (Analysis)** Over a million people emigrated from Ireland after the devastating potato famines of 1846 and 1848. Many of them settled in the United States along the eastern seaboard.

38. **The correct answer is (3). (Application)** Because the San Andreas Fault is a major source of earthquakes, choice (3) is the correct answer.

39. **The correct answer is (3). (Application)** The passage describes the New Madrid Fault as running through the area, so choice (3) is the correct one.

40. **The correct answer is (3). (Comprehension)** The key word is *ineffectual,* because the drawing shows that the tank and its occupants have little to do except decorate a garden.

41. **The correct answer is (1). (Evaluation)** The cartoon implies that NATO's reason for existence (the Soviet Union) has disappeared. Therefore, the cartoonist would probably agree that a powerful enemy once again would lead to a stronger NATO.

42. **The correct answer is (3). (Application)** The Iraqi government under Saddam Hussein is a dictatorship.

43. **The correct answer is (2). (Application)** Great Britain and Northern Ireland are considered to be a model example of a constitutional monarchy. The current ruler is Queen Elizabeth II.

44. **The correct answer is (3). (Evaluation)** Because the Irish Republican Army strongly opposes British rule of Northern Ireland, the group would probably call the British government a dictatorship.

45. **The correct answer is (1). (Evaluation)** A belief in the right of people to have a say in their government is a traditional, strongly held American belief.

46. **The correct answer is (1). (Analysis)** Child abuse would probably be the major concern of someone involved in child welfare, so choice (1) is correct. The growth in the number of children who are involved in random shootings might also be a concern, particularly in terms of preventing such behavior, but this would still come under the overall heading of preventing child abuse.

47. **The correct answer is (3). (Analysis)** Of the types of violence listed, the AARP would probably be most interested in crimes directly targeted at its members, the elderly.

48. **The correct answer is (3). (Analysis)** Street gangs are most often associated with drive-by and random shootings of members of other such gangs, either in retribution for past incidents or as a way to gain territory.

49. **The correct answer is (1). (Analysis)** As signatory of the Universal Declaration of Human Rights, the United States is bound to the precept that all American citizens accused of a crime in a foreign nation are subject to the laws of that nation. Given this fact, the consul may not request the release of the student for trial in the United States as a U.S. citizen.

50. **The correct answer is (3). (Analysis)** As mayor of Berlin, Willy Brandt had stood fast against crises created by the Soviet Union. As a natural ally of the United States and its political ideology, he would not fit into the description of a hard-liner making overtures to "the other side."

ANALYSIS CHART

Use this table to determine your areas of strength and areas in which more work is needed. The numbers in the boxes refer to the multiple-choice questions in the practice test.

Content Area	Comprehension	Application	Analysis	Evaluation	Score
U.S. History	9, 21, 24, 31, 32	33, 34, 36	27, 30, 35, 37	29	_____ of 13
World History	28, 40, 8		10, 23, 50	41	_____ of 7
Geography	11, 17	12, 18, 38, 39	13		_____ of 7
Civics and Government	25	26, 42, 43	22, 46, 47, 48, 49	44, 45	_____ of 11
Economics	1, 2, 5, 14, 19	4	3, 7, 16, 20	6, 15	_____ of 12
Score	_____ of 16	_____ of 11	_____ of 17	_____ of 6	_____ of 50

Posttest

75 Minutes 50 Questions

Directions: Choose the <u>one best answer</u> for each item.

Items 1 and 2 are based on the following illustration.

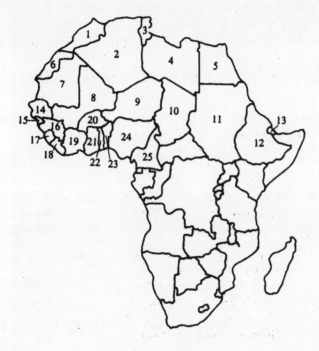

1. In an attempt to better the lot of his people by channeling funds from his military defense budget to his economic development budget, the leader of one country made an innovative and courageous peace overture to an enemy of long standing. This ruler came from

   (1) 1.
   (2) 5.
   (3) 12.
   (4) 20.
   (5) 4.

2. The influence of Italy on the African continent has been minimal, but in a show of his "superior military power," Mussolini invaded and easily conquered a weak, unprepared African country. That country was

   (1) 5.
   (2) 11.
   (3) 12.
   (4) 13.
   (5) 19.

Items 3–8 refer to the following passage.

Andrew Jackson (1767–1845) was elected president of the United States in 1828. Following are some highlights of his colorful life:

- At age thirteen, Jackson joined the Continental Army and fought the British in the Revolutionary War. When taken prisoner, Jackson refused to clean a British officer's boots, and the officer struck him in the head with a sword. The permanent scar became a lifelong reminder of his hatred for the British.

- In 1787, Jackson was admitted to the bar in North Carolina, where he practiced law for several years.

- In 1791, he married Rachel Donelson Robards, believing, as she herself believed, that she was legally divorced at the time. Three years later, this proved to be untrue and the couple had to remarry. The resulting scandal followed the pair for the rest of their lives.

- In 1796, Jackson was elected without opposition as Tennessee's first representative to the U.S. House of Representatives.

- In 1798, Jackson was elected to Tennessee's highest court, where he was noted for dispensing quick, fair justice.

- In 1806, he fought in a duel. Both men were shot, and his opponent died, although Jackson could have honorably prevented this death.

- In the War of 1812, Jackson rose to the rank of general and became a war hero through his successful leadership of American troops at the Battle of New Orleans. Later in his career, his political opponents charged him with murder for having approved the execution of several American soldiers for minor offenses during the war.

- As president, Jackson vetoed dozens of bills and grew powerful through the use of the spoils system.

- In 1835, he survived an assassination attempt. In 1837, he retired to his plantation after attending the inauguration of his handpicked successor, Martin Van Buren.

3. Jackson once said, "I believe that just laws can make no distinction of privilege between the rich and poor. . . ." What part of his life could he cite to prove that he followed this belief?

   (1) His marriage to Rachel Robards
   (2) His being charged with the murder of several American soldiers during the War of 1812
   (3) His time spent as a justice of the Tennessee Supreme Court
   (4) His use of the spoils system
   (5) His status as a hero of the War of 1812

4. Senator Henry Clay once described Jackson as "corrupt." What fact of Jackson's life might Clay have cited to prove his charge?

   (1)   His manipulation of the spoils system
   (2)   His joining of the Continental Army at age thirteen
   (3)   The duel he fought in which both he and his opponent were shot
   (4)   His almost lifelong hatred of the British
   (5)   His election as Tennessee's first representative to the U.S. Congress

5. Jackson was known throughout his life for sometimes behaving in a rash manner. Which of his actions could be cited to support this point of view?

   (1)   Studying law and being admitted to the bar
   (2)   Marrying a woman whose marital status was later questioned
   (3)   Retiring to his plantation after his two terms as president and hating the British
   (4)   Joining the army at thirteen and fighting a duel
   (5)   Becoming a hero of the War of 1812 and serving on the Tennessee Supreme Court

6. In which two American wars did Andrew Jackson participate?

   (1)   The Revolutionary War and the War of 1812
   (2)   The Civil War and the Spanish-American War
   (3)   World War I and World War II
   (4)   The Korean War and the Vietnam War
   (5)   The Crimean War and the Russo-Japanese War

7. In the Battle of New Orleans, British casualties numbered 2,000 whereas American casualties were only 21. What might be inferred about Jackson's military skills from this fact?

   (1)   The British troops were poorly trained
   (2)   The American troops had more and better weapons than the British did
   (3)   Jackson was an able military commander
   (4)   Jackson's infamous temper caused his chief military subordinates to do anything to win
   (5)   Jackson made a much better military leader than president

8. President Jackson vetoed the bill to recharter the Bank of the United States. As a result, "pet" banks began to print money and make new loans with little backing. Issuing new money and making loans in this way most likely resulted in

   (1)   a severe depression.
   (2)   severe inflation.
   (3)   more unemployment.
   (4)   decreased spending.
   (5)   a trade deficit.

Item 9 refers to the following cartoon.

'What it says isn't always what it means'

9. This cartoon refers to which principle of American government?

   (1) Separation of church and state
   (2) Checks and balances
   (3) Judicial review
   (4) Equality before the law
   (5) Bill of rights

10. Which of the following resulted from the Cuban Missile Crisis of October, 1963?

   (1) Cuba was subsequently invaded unsuccessfully by 1,000 U.S. trained anti-Castro troops.
   (2) Castro was temporarily removed from power, but then regained power several years later.
   (3) Soviet missiles were removed from Cuba, and U.S. Jupiter missiles were later removed from Turkey.
   (4) The United States diplomatically recognized Castro's Cuba.
   (5) Free travel between Cuba and the United States began.

11. For a treaty to be ratified in the American political system, what must happen?

    (1)   The president must include leaders of both houses of Congress in the negotiations.

    (2)   The House of Representatives and the U.S. Senate must approve the treaty by a majority vote.

    (3)   The Senate must approve by a three-quarters vote.

    (4)   The House must approve by a majority, the Senate must approve by a two-thirds vote.

    (5)   The Senate must approve by a two-thirds vote.

12. If you were to locate the majority of Americans on the "political spectrum"—left, center, or right—that majority would be found at or on the political

    (1)   left.
    (2)   center.
    (3)   right.
    (4)   far left.
    (5)   far right.

Items 13–17 are based on the following three graphs.

GROWTH   INFLATION   UNEMPLOYMENT

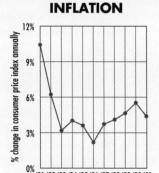
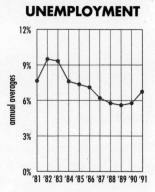

13. The two-year period with the greatest percent change in the rate of inflation was the period from

    (1)   1989–1991.
    (2)   1981–1983.
    (3)   1984–1986.
    (4)   1988–1990.
    (5)   1985–1987.

14. Which statement best describes the relationship shown by the charts between the growth of the gross domestic product and the rate of unemployment?

    (1)   A low rate of growth is often linked to high or rising unemployment.

    (2)   A high rate of growth is often linked to high or rising unemployment.

    (3)   A low or falling rate of unemployment is often linked to a low rate of growth.

    (4)   A high or rising rate of unemployment is often linked to moderate growth.

    (5)   A negative rate of growth is often linked to a low or falling rate of unemployment.

15. The greatest decrease in the growth of the gross domestic product was from

    (1) 1981–1982.
    (2) 1984–1985.
    (3) 1988–1990.
    (4) 1988–1991.
    (5) 1985–1987.

16. These graphs could help a person determine the best time to look for a new job. Such a time would be when

    (1) inflation is rising, unemployment is falling, and economic growth is rising.
    (2) inflation is falling, unemployment is rising, and economic growth is falling.
    (3) inflation is falling, unemployment is falling, and economic growth is rising.
    (4) inflation is falling, unemployment is falling, and economic growth is falling.
    (5) inflation is rising, unemployment is rising, and economic growth is rising.

17. The U.S. economy showed strong growth between 1983 and 1989. The most likely cause was

    (1) an increase in the number of immigrants to the United States between 1981 and 1990.
    (2) the falling rate of inflation between 1981 and 1986.
    (3) the reelection of President Ronald Reagan in 1984.
    (4) the falling rate of unemployment between 1983 and 1989.
    (5) the strengthening of the European Common Market in the 1980s.

Items 18–22 refer to the following passage.

In June 1991, Mount Pinatubo in the Philippines began one of the most violent volcanic eruptions of the twentieth century. More than 200,000 acres were covered with a thick coat of volcanic ash, pumice, and debris. In some places the coating grew to 15 feet thick. More than 600 people died. Some were killed by the ash itself. Many others died from inhaling the deadly gases Mount Pinatubo gave off. Experts believe that the gases and ash thrown into the upper atmosphere were the cause of below-average worldwide temperatures the following year. Each year's monsoon season for the decade following the 1991 explosion is expected to cause avalanches. About half of the 7 billion cubic meters of volcanic material deposited on Mount Pinatubo's slopes is likely to wash down into the plains below.

18. What was the major worldwide effect of Mount Pinatubo's explosion in 1991?

    (1) Avalanches
    (2) A thick coat of ash
    (3) Monsoons
    (4) Cooling temperatures
    (5) Deadly gases

19. According to the passage, avalanches are predicted during each monsoon season until at least what year?

    (1) 1991
    (2) 1992
    (3) 1995
    (4) 2000
    (5) 2001

20. To prevent more death and destruction from Mount Pinatubo's mud slides, a reasonable policy would be to

    (1) plant grasses and crops.
    (2) blow up the mountain.
    (3) pray for dry weather.
    (4) do nothing.
    (5) relocate people to a safe area.

21. The eruption created more than 60,000 refugees, many of them farmers and their families. The U.S. government sent $400 million in aid to help these people, but criticized the way some of it was spent by the Philippine government. Philippine officials used much of the money to build four-lane highways and tall concrete buildings. What was the probable reason for American criticism of this use of the money?

    (1) Not enough American contractors were used on the construction projects.
    (2) The $400 million was not enough to build all the highways that the Philippine officials wanted to construct.
    (3) The highways and tall buildings did not help the 60,000 refugees recover their lost farms and villages.
    (4) The highways were poorly constructed and were damaged in the next monsoon season.
    (5) American officials were not sure that the highways and tall buildings would withstand a possible future eruption of Mount Pinatubo.

22. According to the passage, people were killed by falling ash and

    (1) monsoons.
    (2) cooling temperatures.
    (3) avalanches.
    (4) falling buildings.
    (5) deadly gases.

23. From 1866 to 1915, around 25 million immigrants came to America.

    The main reason behind this massive influx was probably

    (1) the desire for economic betterment.
    (2) industrial expansion and increased use of farm machinery in Europe.
    (3) political and religious persecution.
    (4) improved transportation technology.
    (5) fear of the restrictive immigration laws soon to come.

24. Which of the following is a political characteristic found in both the United States and Great Britain?

    (1) A vote of "no confidence"
    (2) Popular elections
    (3) A unitary system
    (4) The fusion of executive and legislative branches
    (5) A hereditary ruler

25. The concept of "collective security" is most closely associated with

   (1)   North Atlantic Treaty Organization.
   (2)   League of Nations.
   (3)   United Nations General Assembly.
   (4)   European Union.
   (5)   NAFTA.

26. The names of Colin Powell, Henry Kissinger, Cyrus Vance, John Foster Dulles, and Dean Rusk are all associated with the position of

   (1)   National Security Adviser.
   (2)   Secretary of Defense.
   (3)   Secretary of the Treasury.
   (4)   Secretary of State.
   (5)   U.N. Ambassador.

27. The nine justices of the U.S. Supreme Court all receive lifetime appointments. In which of the following ways are their decisions probably most affected by this fact?

   (1)   Because they have federal appointments, they probably favor the federal government over state governments when the two are on opposite sides of an issue.
   (2)   They work more slowly and carefully than they might if some oversight group could set the pace.
   (3)   They probably tend to follow the beliefs of the president who nominated them.
   (4)   They probably tend to become independent thinkers because they are not accountable to any politician or party.
   (5)   They probably rely more heavily on initial drafts of decisions that are written by their law clerks.

Items 28–31 refer to the following chart.

U.S. NATIONAL PARKS AND THEIR VISITORS

Year	No. of Parks	No. of Visitors (in thousands)
1970	35	45,879
1960	29	26,630
1950	28	13,919
1940	26	7,358
1930	22	2,775
1920	19	920
1910	13	119

28. How many visits were made to U.S. national parks in 1960?

    (1) 29
    (2) 26,630
    (3) 12,711
    (4) 26.63 million
    (5) 29 million

29. The number of national parks almost tripled between 1910 and 1970, but the number of visits increased at a much higher rate. Two of the oldest parks, Yellowstone and Yosemite, continue to have among the largest numbers of visitors per year. What factors probably best account for this great increase in visits?

    (1) A general increase in the U.S. population and more leisure time
    (2) A vastly improved transportation system and more leisure time
    (3) Creation of new parks close to large metropolitan areas and a general increase in U.S. population
    (4) Better advertising about improved park facilities and an increased interest nationally in ecology and the environment
    (5) Improved security services within the parks and an increase in the amount of disposable income available to most Americans

30. Between which years did the smallest actual increase in visits take place?

    (1) 1960 and 1970
    (2) 1920 and 1930
    (3) 1910 and 1920
    (4) 1950 and 1960
    (5) 1930 and 1940

31. The factor that has contributed most to the growth in the number of national parks, as well as in the numbers of national historic sites, battlefields, and monuments, has been

    (1) the general growth of the federal government in the twentieth century.
    (2) the growth of the amount of leisure time for most Americans in the twentieth century.
    (3) a general American belief that national historic and natural sites of interest should be preserved for future generations to enjoy.
    (4) the increasing number of states in the western United States that were admitted to the Union in the first half of the twentieth century.
    (5) the inability of state governments to care adequately for various sites because of local financial problems.

32. The consumer price index (CPI) is used to measure inflation, or a general rise in prices. The index measures the prices of a "typical consumer's market basket" of goods and services. Which of the following items would not be in this market basket?

    (1) Mortgage payment
    (2) Meat
    (3) Automobiles
    (4) Medical care
    (5) Wages

33. For years, the United States took a hard-line stance against the communist Soviet Union. Now we are friendly and helpful toward Russia, the largest republic to result from the breakup of the Soviet Union. This change shows that U.S. foreign policy

    (1) is flexible enough to change when circumstances change.
    (2) reflects a wishy-washy attitude toward world events.
    (3) is staunchly against communism.
    (4) is subject to the whims of the president.
    (5) has not changed for at least fifty years.

34. During the last half of the nineteenth century, an important aim of Japan in modernizing itself was to

    (1) improve the living conditions of the peasants.
    (2) remove the Western European nations from China.
    (3) resist threats of foreign domination.
    (4) increase the power of the feudal lords.
    (5) extend equal rights to Japanese women.

35. Which of the following is an "intangible component" of national/international power?

    (1) National will
    (2) Number of troops in the army
    (3) Economic productivity and growth rates
    (4) The trade balance—export vs. import revenue
    (5) The Gross Domestic Product

36. In which one of the following paired events, did the *first* lead directly to the *second*?

    (1) Assassination of John Kennedy—immediate swearing-in of Gerald Ford
    (2) Bombing of Pearl Harbor—annexing Hawaii by the United States of America
    (3) Failure of the League of Nations—World War I
    (4) Purchase of Alaska—cold war with Russia
    (5) Assassination of President Garfield—passage of the Pendleton Civil Service Act

Item 37 is based on the following table.

PROJECTED POPULATION OF SOME GROUPS OF PEOPLE
WITHIN THE UNITED STATES
(number in millions)

Group	Year 2000	Year 2050	Year 2080
Male, White	108.8	105.6	103.6
Female, White	112.7	116.2	108.7
Male, Black	16.7	22.4	22.6
Female, Black	18.3	24.7	25.0

37. Which statement best summarizes the content of the table?

(1) The number of blacks in the United States will increase between the years 2000 and 2080.
(2) The number of blacks in the United States will show the greatest percentage of increase between the years 2000 and 2050.
(3) The number of white females in the United States will increase between the years 2000 and 2050.
(4) The number of whites in the United States will be greater than the number of blacks in the years between 2000 and 2080.
(5) The total number of blacks in the United States will increase between the years 2000 and 2080 both in actual numbers and in relation to the total number of whites.

38. George Washington set a precedent by not running for a third term as president. Later this practice became law. Why is a two-term limit a good policy for the country?

(1) Most people are too tired after two terms as president to be effective during a third term.
(2) Many people want to be president, and it's not fair to them if one person has the job too long.
(3) One person should not have so much power for such a long period of time.
(4) Members of Congress object to the predictable policies of one president.
(5) Most citizens get tired of listening to one leader after eight years and need to hear from someone else.

39. U.S. senators are elected for six-year terms. They are expected to represent the interests of their states and to take a long-range view of the needs of the entire country. Which qualities or experiences would be least useful for a U.S. senator to have?

(1) An ability to reach compromises on important issues
(2) A clear understanding of the meaning of the Constitution
(3) Strong financial and business skills
(4) Strong ties to a foreign government
(5) A good public speaking style

40. If the demand for automobiles increases, but the supply does not change, what will happen to the price and the quantity exchanged?

(1) They will stay the same.
(2) The price and the quantity exchanged will increase.
(3) The price will increase and the quantity exchanged will decrease.
(4) The price will decrease and the quantity exchanged will increase.
(5) The price will stay the same and the quantity exchanged will increase.

Items 41 and 42 refer to the following information.

The table below shows the number of widgets produced by ABC Widget Company if it adds workers without changing any other economic resource.

Number of Workers	Total Widgets Produced	Number Added
1	50	—
2	110	60
3	160	50
4	200	40
5	230	30

41. Based on the table, which added worker makes the greatest contribution to the total output of widgets?

(1) First
(2) Second
(3) Third
(4) Fourth
(5) Fifth

42. The law of diminishing returns takes effect with the addition of which worker?

(1) First
(2) Second
(3) Third
(4) Fourth
(5) Fifth

43. The right to use the airways is controlled by the government in which of the following countries?

I. the former Soviet Union
II. the United States
III. Great Britain
IV. Lebanon
V. Israel

(1) I and IV only
(2) I and III only
(3) I, II, and III only
(4) I and II only
(5) I, II, III, IV, and V

44. In which United Nations body are all member states represented?

  (1)   Security Council
  (2)   Economic and Social Council
  (3)   General Assembly
  (4)   Trusteeship Council
  (5)   World Bank

45. All of the following former or current world leaders are correctly matched with his or her nation EXCEPT

  (1)   Vladimir Putin—Russia
  (2)   Saddam Hussein—Iraq
  (3)   Andres Pastrana—Mexico
  (4)   Anwar Sadat—Egypt
  (5)   Margaret Thatcher—England

46. During the Cold War, many Americans believed that communism, if allowed to spread, would threaten democracy. To prevent the spread of communism, the United States pursued a policy of

  (1)   intervention in the affairs of communist countries.
  (2)   brinkmanship, or risking war to maintain peace.
  (3)   containment, or keeping communism within its current borders.
  (4)   massive retaliation against any threat or action by a communist country.
  (5)   covert operations, or secret activities aimed at undermining communist governments.

Items 47 and 48 refer to the following passage.

From 1848 to 1919, American women fought for a constitutional amendment giving them suffrage, or the right to vote. Year after year, more and more women attended rallies and marched in the streets. In one parade, a reporter noted that "women doctors, women lawyers, women architects, women artists, actresses and sculptors; women waitresses, domestics; a huge division of industrial workers . . . all marched with an intensity and purpose that astonished the crowds that lined the streets." In 1919, Congress passed the Nineteenth Amendment, giving women the right to vote. A year later, the states ratified it, and female suffrage became the law of the land.

47. Attending speeches, rallies, and marches are activities that

    (1)   are protected by the First Amendment.
    (2)   were unbecoming for women at the time.
    (3)   convinced lawmakers to pass the Nineteenth Amendment.
    (4)   did little to further the cause of suffrage.
    (5)   showed how determined all women were.

48. Which conclusion is best supported by the reporter's description of a suffragist parade?

    (1)   Only a handful of women wanted suffrage and were willing to take a stand.
    (2)   Only wealthy women had time to take part in marches and parades supporting suffrage.
    (3)   Voting was not a serious issue for most women.
    (4)   Women from many different walks of life took a stand in favor of women's suffrage.
    (5)   Working women were interested in voting because the stakes were higher for them.

49. Which of the following is not consistent with the writings of Karl Marx?

    (1)   The concept of the "wage slave"
    (2)   The primacy of class struggle
    (3)   The growing poverty of the proletariat
    (4)   The withering away of the state
    (5)   The accumulation of individual profit

50. Which of the following can be best classified as nations marked by low birthrates and low death rates?

    (1)   Communist China, India, the United Arab Republic
    (2)   United States, India, Lebanon
    (3)   Brazil, Indonesia, Sudan
    (4)   Great Britain, France, Austria
    (5)   Ghana, Mexico, Spain

ANSWERS AND EXPLANATIONS

1. **The correct answer is (2). (Comprehension).** In 1977 Anwar el-Sadat, President of Egypt, became the first Arab head of state to visit Israel. Two years later, Egypt and Israel signed a peace treaty at the Camp David Accords.

2. **The correct answer is (3). (Comprehension)** In 1935 Italy invaded Ethiopia and occupied the country until 1941.

3. **The correct answer is (3). (Analysis)** Because the passage states that while a judge, Jackson was noted for his fairness, choice (3) is correct. None of the other choices is related to his beliefs about justice and fairness.

4. **The correct answer is (1). (Application)** Jackson's manipulation of the spoils system, which was in and of itself corrupt, would be a justification for Clay's description. The other four choices are in no way related to Jackson's corruptibility.

5. **The correct answer is (4). (Application)** Going off to fight a war as a youngster and becoming involved in a duel are clearly not well-thought-out actions. None of the other events, as described, could be called rash.

6. **The correct answer is (1). (Comprehension)** According to the passage, Jackson fought in the Revolutionary War in the late 1700s and in the War of 1812.

7. **The correct answer is (3). (Analysis)** The success of the Americans in the Battle of New Orleans and the extremely low number of American casualties are strong indicators that Jackson was a good military commander. Nothing in the passage supports any of the other four choices.

8. **The correct answer is (2). (Application)** Increasing the money supply and giving loans without increasing production would result in inflation.

9. **The correct answer is (3). (Application)** The power of the judicial system to review the constitutionality of laws is the principle of American government to which the cartoon refers.

10. **The correct answer is (3). (Analysis)** The Bay of Pigs invasion occurred in 1961 prior to the Cuban Missile Crisis. Castro was never removed from power, the United States has never diplomatically recognized Castro's Cuba, nor has free travel been allowed between the two countries. Soviet missiles were removed from Cuba, and later the United States removed the Jupiter missiles from Turkey.

11. **The correct answer is (5). (Analysis)** Only the United States Senate is involved in the ratification process, and according to Article II, section 2.2, of the Constitution, a two-thirds vote of the Senate is required for ratification of a treaty.

12. **The correct answer is (2). (Application)** The majority of Americans today would be at or on the political center. Given the large number of issues involved in American politics today, political divisions become less rigidly defined. Therefore the majority of Americans are at or on the center of the spectrum.

13. **The correct answer is (2). (Application)** The greatest percent change in inflation was a decrease of approximately 7.5 percent from 1981–1983, making choice (2) the best answer.

14. **The correct answer is (1). (Analysis)** A low rate of growth often means that employers are not expanding their businesses and therefore not hiring additional employees, and the employers may actually be laying off some workers in response to sluggish sales.

15. **The correct answer is (4). (Application)** The greatest decrease—about 5 percent—was from 1988–1991.

16. **The correct answer is (3). (Evaluation)** The best time to look for a job would be when the economy was growing (so that businesses might be in need of additional workers), unemployment was falling (so that there would be fewer available workers for employers to choose from), and inflation was falling (so that businesses would not be afraid of future monetary problems).

17. **The correct answer is (2). (Analysis)** Falling inflation is good for both business and employment because business can better predict the costs of its materials and supplies and people have a consistent amount of money to spend. Choice (4) was an effect, not a cause, of economic growth. Choices (1), (3), and (5) represent factors not included in the graph.

18. **The correct answer is (4). (Comprehension)** All of the choices describe the effects of the Mount Pinatubo eruption, but only choice (4) describes an effect that touched the whole world.

19. **The correct answer is (5). (Application)** Because the effects of the 1991 eruption are expected to last for a decade, avalanches are predicted until at least the year 2001.

20. **The correct answer is (5). (Analysis)** The safest plan would be to move people out of the danger zone. Planting grasses and crops, choice (1), is often a good long-term solution to prevent mudslides on slopes, but plants are not likely to grow in volcanic ash. Meanwhile, the destructive slides would continue. Choices (2), (3), and (4) are not reasonable options.

21. **The correct answer is (3). (Evaluation)** Because most of those who were displaced were farmers from small towns and villages, the creation of highways and tall buildings clearly did not help them regain what they had lost.

22. **The correct answer is (5). (Comprehension)** The passage states that deadly gases and falling ash were the elements that killed the most people.

23. **The correct answer is (1). (Analysis)** The main reason for the post-Civil War influx of immigrants was the attraction of economic opportunities in the United States. Labor-recruiting agents, steamship companies, and land-grant railroads all advertised the abundant opportunities available in the United States.

24. **The correct answer is (2). (Analysis)** Of the choices provided, the only characteristic shared by both nations is the use of the popular election for the selection of political representatives.

25. **The correct answer is (1). (Analysis)** NATO was formed out of a desire by the Western nations to form a measure of "collective security" against the spread of Communism following the conclusion of World War II. NATO is the only choice that is applicable to this goal.

26. **The correct answer is (4). (Analysis).** Colin Powell is the current Secretary of State and is linked to the other men who previously served in this position.

27. **The correct answer is (4). (Evaluation)** This independence has led some justices, including some of the most famous, to follow their consciences, regardless of previous tilts toward liberal or conservative platforms.

28. **The correct answer is (4). (Comprehension)** The chart lists numbers of visits in thousands, and 26,630 times 1,000 equals 26.63 million.

29. **The correct answer is (2). (Evaluation)** The twentieth century has seen a great improvement in transportation systems worldwide. In addition, a shortened work week and more work-saving machines for both the home and the factory have led to an increase in leisure time. These two factors have allowed Americans to take more vacations and to visit national parks more frequently.

30. **The correct answer is (3). (Comprehension)** The smallest number of increased visits was 801,000, which occurred between 1910 and 1920.

31. **The correct answer is (3). (Analysis)** The belief in the preservation of valuable sites in America has contributed to the increase in the numbers of national parks, historic sites, battlefields, and monuments.

32. **The correct answer is (5). (Analysis)** Housing (rent and mortgage payments), food, cars, and medical care are all goods or services purchased by typical consumers. Wages represent income, not spending.

31. **The correct answer is (3). (Analysis)** The belief in the preservation of valuable sites in America has contributed to the increase in the numbers of national parks, historic sites, battlefields, and monuments.

34. **The correct answer is (3). (Analysis)** Having witnessed what happened to China as a result of imperialism, one of Japan's primary aims following the Meiji Restoration was to retain their sovereignty by resisting foreign dominance. Modernization would best fulfill this goal.

35. **The correct answer is (1). (Analysis)** National will is an intangible component of national/international power. All of the other choices are tangible factors that can be quantifiably measured.

36. **The correct answer is (5). (Comprehension)** President Garfield believed appointments should be made on merit rather than the spoils system. He was assassinated by Charles J. Guiteau who had asked for an appointment which Garfield did not feel was merited. The direct result of these events was the passage of the Pendleton Civil Service Act.

37. **The correct answer is (5). (Analysis)** Choice (5) gives the most complete description of the relationship between the black population and the white population. Each of the other choices describes only one portion of the facts presented in the chart.

38. **The correct answer is (3). (Analysis)** The two-term limit is part of the system of checks and balances, which prevents any one group or individual from gaining too much power in the nation.

39. **The correct answer is (4). (Analysis)** Strong ties to a foreign government might make it impossible for an elected American official to operate with the best interests of the United States in mind.

40. **The correct answer is (2). (Analysis)** An increase in demand means that more will be purchased at every possible price. Hence, if demand increases and supply does not change, the demand curve will shift outward from the price axis, resulting in a higher price and more quantity exchanged.

41. **The correct answer is (2). (Application)** The second worker adds 60 units to output; all other workers, including the first one, add fewer than 60 units.

42. **The correct answer is (3). (Application)** Total output increases, but the third worker adds 50 units, fewer than the 60 units added by the second worker.

43. **The correct answer is (5). (Comprehension)** The Paris Convention of 1919 granted sovereignty to each nation for the air space above it. Given that fact, the only logical choice would be all of the countries listed.

44. **The correct answer is (3). (Analysis)** The term "General Assembly" is a clue to the fact that this is indeed the only choice where all member-states are represented.

45. **The correct answer is (3). (Analysis)** Andreas Pastrana became the President of Columbia in June of 1998. The other pairs are correctly matched.

46. **The correct answer is (3). (Analysis)** To prevent the spread of communism is to contain it, so containment, choice (3), is the only possible answer. In its fight against communism, the United States has since pursued the other policies listed, except choice (4), massive retaliation.

47. **The correct answer is (1). (Application)** The activities described are protected by the rights of free speech and assembly guaranteed in the First Amendment.

48. **The correct answer is (4). (Evaluation)** The description of the parade indicates that all sorts of women participated in pro-suffrage marches and other activities, so choice (4) is the best conclusion. The other choices assume that only certain groups of women marched or make incorrect assumptions about the womens' support of suffrage.

49. **The correct answer is (5). (Analysis)** Marx believed that all history could be defined as a class struggle over the control of the means of production. The only choice that does not fit with this concept of history is the idea of individual profit.

50. **The correct choice is (4). (Analysis)** This is the only group that does not contain a nation with a high birth rate and/or higher death rate. Therefore it is the best choice.

Appendix

The following are historical documents that are important in the development of the United States of America.

1. The Declaration of Independence (1776)
2. The Constitution of the United States of America (1787)
3. The Federalist Paper No. 10 (1787)
4. The Federalist Paper No. 51 (1788)
5. The Monroe Doctrine (1823)
6. Declaration of Sentiments, Women's Rights (1848)
7. The Emancipation Proclamation (1863)

ROAD MAP

- *The Declaration of Independence*
- *The Constitution of the United States of America*
- *The Federalist Papers*
- *The Monroe Doctrine*
- *Report of the Woman's Rights Convention*
- *The Emancipation Proclamation (1863)*

THE DECLARATION OF INDEPENDENCE
IN CONGRESS, JULY 4, 1776

The Unanimous Declaration of the Thirteen United States of America

When in the Course of human events, it becomes necessary for one people to dissolve the political bands which have connected them with another, and to assume among the powers of the earth, the separate and equal station to which the Laws of Nature and of Nature's God entitle them, a decent respect to the opinions of mankind requires that they should declare the causes which impel them to the separation.

We hold these truths to be self-evident, that all men are created equal, that they are endowed by their Creator with certain unalienable Rights, that among these are Life, Liberty and the pursuit of Happiness—That to secure these rights, Governments are instituted among Men, deriving their just powers from the consent of the governed, —That whenever any Form of Government becomes destructive of these ends, it is the Right of the People to alter or to abolish it, and to institute new Government, laying its foundation on such principles and organizing its powers in such form, as to them shall seem most likely to effect their Safety and Happiness. Prudence, indeed, will dictate that Governments long established should not be changed for light and transient causes; and accordingly all experience hath shown, that mankind are more disposed to suffer, while evils are sufferable, than to right themselves by abolishing the forms to which they are accustomed. But when a long train of abuses and usurpations, pursuing invariably the same Object evinces a design to reduce them under absolute Despotism, it is their right, it is their duty, to throw off such Government, and to provide new Guards for their future security—Such has been the patient sufferance of these Colonies; and such is now the necessity which constrains them to alter their former Systems of Government. The history of the present King of Great Britain is a history of repeated injuries and usurpations, all having in direct object the establishment of an absolute Tyranny over these States. To prove this, let Facts be submitted to a candid world.

He has refused his Assent to Laws, the most wholesome and necessary for the public good.

He has forbidden his Governors to pass Laws of immediate and pressing importance, unless suspended in their operation till his Assent should be obtained; and when so suspended, he has utterly neglected to attend to them.

He has refused to pass other Laws for the accommodation of large districts of people, unless those people would relinquish the right of Representation in the Legislature, a right inestimable to them and formidable to tyrants only.

He has called together legislative bodies at places unusual, uncomfortable, and distant from the depository of their public Records, for the sole purpose of fatiguing them into compliance with his measures.

He has dissolved Representative Houses repeatedly, for opposing with manly firmness his invasions on the rights of the people.

He has refused for a long time, after such dissolutions, to cause others to be elected; whereby the Legislative powers, incapable of Annihilation, have returned to the People at large for their exercise; the State remaining in the mean time exposed to all the dangers of invasion from without, and convulsions within.

He has endeavored to prevent the population of these States; for that purpose obstructing the Laws for Naturalization of Foreigners; refusing to pass others to encourage their migrations hither, and raising the conditions of new Appropriations of Lands.

He has obstructed the Administration of Justice, by refusing his Assent to Laws for establishing Judiciary powers.

He has made Judges dependent on his Will alone, for the tenure of their offices, and the amount and payment of their salaries.

He has erected a multitude of New Offices, and sent hither swarms of Officers to harass our people, and eat out their substance.

He has kept among us, in times of peace, Standing Armies without the Consent of our legislatures.

He has affected to render the Military independent of and superior to the Civil power.

He has combined with others to subject us to a jurisdiction foreign to our constitution, and unacknowledged by our laws; giving his Assent to their Acts of pretended Legislation:

For Quartering large bodies of armed troops among us:

For protecting them, by a mock Trial, from punishment for any Murders which they should commit on the Inhabitants of these States:

For cutting off our Trade with all parts of the world:

For imposing Taxes on us without our Consent:

For depriving us in many cases, of the benefits of Trial by Jury:

For transporting us beyond Seas to be tried for pretended offences:

For abolishing the free System of English Laws in a neighboring Province, establishing therein an Arbitrary government, and enlarging its Boundaries so as to render it at once an example and fit instrument for introducing the same absolute rule into these Colonies:

For taking away our Charters, abolishing our most valuable Laws, and altering fundamentally the Forms of our Governments:

For suspending our own Legislatures, and declaring themselves invested with power to legislate for us in all cases whatsoever.

He has abdicated Government here, by declaring us out of his Protection and waging War against us.

He has plundered our seas, ravaged our Coasts, burnt our towns, and destroyed the lives of our people.

He is at this time transporting large Armies of foreign Mercenaries to complete the works of death, desolation and tyranny, already begun with circumstances of Cruelty & perfidy scarcely paralleled in the most barbarous ages, and totally unworthy the Head of a civilized nation.

He has constrained our fellow Citizens taken Captive on the high Seas to bear Arms against their Country, to become the executioners of their friends and Brethren, or to fall themselves by their Hands.

He has excited domestic insurrections amongst us, and has endeavored to bring on the inhabitants of our frontiers, the merciless Indian Savages, whose known rule of warfare, is an undistinguished destruction of all ages, sexes and conditions.

In every stage of these Oppressions We have Petitioned for Redress in the most humble terms: Our repeated Petitions have been answered only by repeated injury. A Prince whose character is thus marked by every act which may define a Tyrant, is unfit to be the ruler of a free people.

Nor have We been wanting in attentions to our British brethren. We have warned them from time to time of attempts by their legislature to extend an unwarrantable jurisdiction over us. We have reminded them of the circumstances of our emigration and settlement here. We have appealed to their native justice and magnanimity, and we have conjured them by the ties of our common kindred to disavow these usurpations, which, would inevitably interrupt our connections and correspondence. They too have been deaf to the voice of justice and of consanguinity. We must, therefore, acquiesce in the necessity, which denounces our Separation, and hold them, as we hold the rest of mankind, Enemies in War, in Peace Friends.

We, therefore, the Representatives of the United States of America, in General Congress, Assembled, appealing to the Supreme Judge of the world for the rectitude of our intentions, do, in the Name, and by Authority of the good People of these Colonies, solemnly publish and declare, That these United Colonies are, and of Right ought to be Free and Independent States; that they are Absolved from all Allegiance to the British Crown, and that all political connection between them and the State of Great Britain, is and ought to be totally dissolved; and that as Free and Independent States, they have full Power to levy War, conclude Peace, contract Alliances, establish Commerce, and to do all other Acts and Things which Independent States may of right do. And for the support of this Declaration, with a firm reliance on the protection of divine Providence, we mutually pledge to each other our Lives, our Fortunes and our sacred Honor.

THE CONSTITUTION OF THE UNITED STATES OF AMERICA

We the People of the United States, in Order to form a more perfect Union, establish Justice, insure domestic Tranquility, provide for the common defence, promote the general Welfare, and secure the Blessings of Liberty to ourselves and our Posterity, do ordain and establish this Constitution for the United States of America.

ARTICLE I.

Section 1. All legislative Powers herein granted shall be vested in a Congress of the United States, which shall consist of a Senate and House of Representatives.

Section 2. The House of Representatives shall be composed of Members chosen every second Year by the People of the several States, and the Electors in each State shall have the Qualifications requisite for Electors of the most numerous Branch of the State Legislature.

No Person shall be a Representative who shall not have attained to the Age of twenty five Years, and been seven Years a Citizen of the United States, and who shall not, when elected, be an Inhabitant of that State in which he shall be chosen.

Representatives and direct Taxes shall be apportioned among the several States which may be included within this Union, according to their respective Numbers, which shall be determined by adding to the whole Number of free Persons, including those bound to Service for a Term of Years, and excluding Indians not taxed, three fifths of all other Persons.

The actual Enumeration shall be made within three Years after the first Meeting of the Congress of the United States, and within every subsequent Term of ten Years, in such Manner as they shall by Law direct. The Number of Representatives shall not exceed one for every thirty Thousand, but each State shall have at Least one Representative; and until such enumeration shall be made, the State of New Hampshire shall be entitled to choose three, Massachusetts eight, Rhode Island and Providence Plantations one, Connecticut five, New York six, New Jersey four, Pennsylvania eight, Delaware one, Maryland six, Virginia ten, North Carolina five, South Carolina five and Georgia three.

When vacancies happen in the Representation from any State, the Executive Authority thereof shall issue Writs of Election to fill such Vacancies.

The House of Representatives shall choose their Speaker and other Officers; and shall have the sole Power of Impeachment.

Section 3. The Senate of the United States shall be composed of two Senators from each State, chosen by the Legislature thereof, for six Years; and each Senator shall have one Vote.

Immediately after they shall be assembled in Consequence of the first Election, they shall be divided as equally as may be into three Classes. The Seats of the Senators of the first Class shall be vacated at the Expiration of the second Year, of the second Class at the Expiration of the fourth Year, and of the third Class at the Expiration of the sixth Year, so that one third may be chosen every second Year; and if Vacancies happen by Resignation, or otherwise, during the Recess of the Legislature of any State, the Executive thereof may make temporary Appointments until the next Meeting of the Legislature, which shall then fill such Vacancies.

No person shall be a Senator who shall not have attained to the Age of thirty Years, and been nine Years a Citizen of the United States, and who shall not, when elected, be an Inhabitant of that State for which he shall be chosen.

The Vice President of the United States shall be President of the Senate, but shall have no Vote, unless they be equally divided.

The Senate shall choose their other Officers, and also a President pro tempore, in the absence of the Vice President, or when he shall exercise the Office of President of the United States.

The Senate shall have the sole Power to try all Impeachments. When sitting for that Purpose, they shall be on Oath or Affirmation. When the President of the United States is tried, the Chief Justice shall preside: And no Person shall be convicted without the Concurrence of two thirds of the Members present.

Judgment in Cases of Impeachment shall not extend further than to removal from Office, and disqualification to hold and enjoy any Office of honor, Trust or Profit under the United States: but the Party convicted shall nevertheless be liable and subject to Indictment, Trial, Judgment and Punishment, according to Law.

Section 4. The Times, Places and Manner of holding Elections for Senators and Representatives, shall be prescribed in each State by the Legislature thereof; but the Congress may at any time by Law make or alter such Regulations, except as to the Place of Choosing Senators.

The Congress shall assemble at least once in every Year, and such Meeting shall be on the first Monday in December, unless they shall by Law appoint a different Day.

Section 5. Each House shall be the Judge of the Elections, Returns, and Qualifications of its own Members, and a Majority of each shall constitute a Quorum to do Business; but a smaller number may adjourn from day to day, and may be authorized to compel the Attendance of absent Members, in such Manner, and under such Penalties as each House may provide.

Each House may determine the Rules of its Proceedings, punish its Members for disorderly Behavior, and, with the Concurrence of two thirds, expel a Member.

Each House shall keep a Journal of its Proceedings, and from time to time publish the same, excepting such Parts as may in their Judgment require Secrecy; and the Yeas and Nays of the Members of either House on any question shall, at the Desire of one fifth of those Present, be entered on the Journal.

Neither House, during the Session of Congress, shall, without the Consent of the other, adjourn for more than three days, nor to any other Place than that in which the two Houses shall be sitting.

Section 6. The Senators and Representatives shall receive a Compensation for their Services, to be ascertained by Law, and paid out of the Treasury of the United States. They shall in all Cases, except Treason, Felony, and Breach of the Peace, be privileged from Arrest during their Attendance at the Session of their respective Houses, and in going to and returning from the same; and for any Speech or Debate in either House, they shall not be questioned in any other Place.

No Senator or Representative shall, during the Time for which he was elected, be appointed to any civil Office under the Authority of the United States which shall have been created, or the Emoluments whereof shall have been increased during such time; and no Person holding any Office under the United States, shall be a Member of either House during his Continuance in Office.

Section 7. All bills for raising Revenue shall originate in the House of Representatives; but the Senate may propose or concur with Amendments as on other Bills.

Every Bill which shall have passed the House of Representatives and the Senate, shall, before it become a Law, be presented to the President of the United States; If he approve he shall sign it, but if not he shall return it, with his Objections to that House in which it shall have originated, who shall enter the Objections at large on their Journal, and proceed to reconsider it. If after such Reconsideration two thirds of that House shall agree to pass the Bill, it shall be sent, together with the Objections, to the other House, by which it shall likewise be reconsidered, and if approved by two thirds of that House, it shall become a Law. But in all such Cases the Votes of both Houses shall be determined by Yeas and Nays, and the Names of the Persons voting for and against the Bill shall be entered on the Journal of each House respectively. If any Bill shall not be returned by the President within ten Days (Sundays excepted) after it shall have been presented to him, the Same shall be a Law, in like Manner as if he had signed it, unless the Congress by their Adjournment prevent its Return, in which Case it shall not be a Law.

Every Order, Resolution, or Vote to which the Concurrence of the Senate and House of Representatives may be necessary (except on a question of Adjournment) shall be presented to the President of the United States; and before the Same shall take Effect, shall be approved by him, or being disapproved by him, shall be repassed by two thirds of the Senate and House of Representatives, according to the Rules and Limitations prescribed in the Case of a Bill.

Section 8. The Congress shall have Power To lay and collect Taxes, Duties, Imposts and Excises, to pay the Debts and provide for the common Defence and general Welfare of the United States; but all Duties, Imposts and Excises shall be uniform throughout the United States;

To borrow money on the credit of the United States;

To regulate Commerce with foreign Nations, and among the several States, and with the Indian Tribes;

To establish an uniform Rule of Naturalization, and uniform Laws on the subject of Bankruptcies throughout the United States;

To coin Money, regulate the Value thereof, and of foreign Coin, and fix the Standard of Weights and Measures;

To provide for the Punishment of counterfeiting the Securities and current Coin of the United States;

To establish Post Offices and Post Roads;

To promote the Progress of Science and useful Arts, by securing for limited Times to Authors and Inventors the exclusive Right to their respective Writings and Discoveries;

To constitute Tribunals inferior to the supreme Court;

To define and punish Piracies and Felonies committed on the high Seas, and Offenses against the Law of Nations;

To declare War, grant Letters of Marque and Reprisal, and make Rules concerning Captures on Land and Water;

To raise and support Armies, but no Appropriation of Money to that Use shall be for a longer Term than two Years;

To provide and maintain a Navy;

To make Rules for the Government and Regulation of the land and naval Forces;

To provide for calling forth the Militia to execute the Laws of the Union, suppress Insurrections and repel Invasions;

To provide for organizing, arming, and disciplining the Militia, and for governing such Part of them as may be employed in the Service of the United States, reserving to the States respectively, the Appointment of the Officers, and the Authority of training the Militia according to the discipline prescribed by Congress;

To exercise exclusive Legislation in all Cases whatsoever, over such District (not exceeding ten Miles square) as may, by Cession of particular States, and the acceptance of Congress, become the Seat of the Government of the United States, and to exercise like Authority over all Places purchased by the Consent of the Legislature of the State in which the Same shall be, for the Erection of Forts, Magazines, Arsenals, dock-Yards, and other needful Buildings; And

To make all Laws which shall be necessary and proper for carrying into Execution the foregoing Powers, and all other Powers vested by this Constitution in the Government of the United States, or in any Department or Officer thereof.

Section 9. The Migration or Importation of such Persons as any of the States now existing shall think proper to admit, shall not be prohibited by the Congress prior to the Year one thousand eight hundred and eight, but a tax or duty may be imposed on such Importation, not exceeding ten dollars for each Person.

The privilege of the Writ of Habeas Corpus shall not be suspended, unless when in Cases of Rebellion or Invasion the public Safety may require it.

No Bill of Attainder or *ex post facto* Law shall be passed. No capitation, or other direct, Tax shall be laid, unless in Proportion to the Census or Enumeration herein before directed to be taken.

No Tax or Duty shall be laid on Articles exported from any State.

No Preference shall be given by any Regulation of Commerce or Revenue to the Ports of one State over those of another: nor shall Vessels bound to, or from, one State, be obliged to enter, clear, or pay Duties in another.

No Money shall be drawn from the Treasury, but in Consequence of Appropriations made by Law; and a regular Statement and Account of the Receipts and Expenditures of all public Money shall be published from time to time.

No Title of Nobility shall be granted by the United States: And no Person holding any Office of Profit or Trust under them, shall, without the Consent of the Congress, accept of any present, Emolument, Office, or Title, of any kind whatever, from any King, Prince, or foreign State.

Section 10. No State shall enter into any Treaty, Alliance, or Confederation; grant Letters of Marque and Reprisal; coin Money; emit Bills of Credit; make any Thing but gold and silver Coin a Tender in Payment of Debts; pass any Bill of Attainder, *ex post facto* Law, or Law impairing the Obligation of Contracts, or grant any Title of Nobility.

No State shall, without the Consent of the Congress, lay any Imposts or Duties on Imports or Exports, except what may be absolutely necessary for executing it's inspection Laws: and the net Produce of all Duties and Imposts, laid by any State on Imports or Exports, shall be for the Use of the Treasury of the United States; and all such Laws shall be subject to the Revision and Control of the Congress.

No State shall, without the Consent of Congress, lay any duty of Tonnage, keep Troops, or Ships of War in time of Peace, enter into any Agreement or Compact with another State, or with a foreign Power, or engage in War, unless actually invaded, or in such imminent Danger as will not admit of delay.

ARTICLE II.

Section 1. The executive Power shall be vested in a President of the United States of America. He shall hold his Office during the Term of four Years, and, together with the Vice-President chosen for the same Term, be elected, as follows:

Each State shall appoint, in such Manner as the Legislature thereof may direct, a Number of Electors, equal to the whole Number of Senators and Representatives to which the State may be entitled in the Congress: but no Senator or Representative, or Person holding an Office of Trust or Profit under the United States, shall be appointed an Elector.

[The Electors shall meet in their respective States, and vote by Ballot for two persons, of whom one at least shall not lie an Inhabitant of the same State with themselves. And they shall make a List of all the Persons voted for, and of the Number of Votes for each; which List they shall sign and certify, and transmit sealed to the Seat of the Government of the United States, directed to the President of the Senate. The President of the Senate shall, in the Presence of the Senate and House of Representatives, open all the Certificates, and the Votes shall then be counted. The Person having the greatest Number of Votes shall be the President, if such Number be a Majority of the whole Number of Electors appointed; and if there be more than one who have such Majority, and have an equal Number of Votes, then the House of Representatives shall immediately choose by Ballot one of them for President; and if no Person have a Majority, then from the five highest on the List the said House shall in like Manner choose the President. But in choosing the President, the Votes shall be taken by States, the Representation from each State having one Vote; a quorum for this Purpose shall consist of a Member or Members from two thirds of the States, and a Majority of all the States shall be necessary to a Choice. In every Case, after the Choice of the President, the Person having the greatest Number of Votes of the Electors shall be the Vice President. But if there should remain two or more who have equal Votes, the Senate shall choose from them by Ballot the Vice President.]

The Congress may determine the Time of choosing the Electors, and the Day on which they shall give their Votes; which Day shall be the same throughout the United States.

No person except a natural born Citizen, or a Citizen of the United States, at the time of the Adoption of this Constitution, shall be eligible to the Office of President; neither shall any Person be eligible to that Office who shall not have attained to the Age of thirty-five Years, and been fourteen Years a Resident within the United States.

In Case of the Removal of the President from Office, or of his Death, Resignation, or Inability to discharge the Powers and Duties of the said Office, the same shall devolve on the Vice President, and the Congress may by Law provide for the Case of Removal, Death, Resignation or Inability, both of the President and Vice President, declaring what Officer shall then act as President, and such Officer shall act accordingly, until the Disability be removed, or a President shall be elected.

The President shall, at stated Times, receive for his Services, a Compensation, which shall neither be increased nor diminished during the Period for which he shall have been elected, and he shall not receive within that Period any other Emolument from the United States, or any of them.

Before he enter on the Execution of his Office, he shall take the following Oath or Affirmation:—"I do solemnly swear (or affirm) that I will faithfully execute the Office of President of the United States, and will to the best of my Ability, preserve, protect and defend the Constitution of the United States."

Section 2. The President shall be Commander in Chief of the Army and Navy of the United States, and of the Militia of the several States, when called into the actual Service of the United States; he may require the Opinion, in writing, of the principal Officer in each of the executive Departments, upon any subject relating to the Duties of their respective Offices, and he shall have Power to Grant Reprieves and Pardons for Offenses against the United States, except in Cases of Impeachment.

He shall have Power, by and with the Advice and Consent of the Senate, to make Treaties, provided two thirds of the Senators present concur; and he shall nominate, and by and with the Advice and Consent of the Senate, shall appoint Ambassadors, other public Ministers and Consuls, Judges of the Supreme Court, and all other Officers of the United States, whose Appointments are not herein otherwise provided for, and which shall be established by Law: but the Congress may by Law vest the Appointment of such inferior Officers, as they think proper, in the President alone, in the Courts of Law, or in the Heads of Departments.

The President shall have Power to fill up all Vacancies that may happen during the Recess of the Senate, by granting Commissions which shall expire at the End of their next Session.

Section 3. He shall from time to time give to the Congress Information of the State of the Union, and recommend to their Consideration such Measures as he shall judge necessary and expedient; he may, on extraordinary Occasions, convene both Houses, or either of them, and in Case of Disagreement between them, with Respect to the Time of Adjournment, he may adjourn them to such Time as he shall think proper; he shall receive Ambassadors and other public Ministers; he shall take Care that the Laws be faithfully executed, and shall Commission all the Officers of the United States.

Section 4. The President, Vice President, and all civil Officers of the United States, shall be removed from Office on Impeachment for, and Conviction of, Treason, Bribery, or other high Crimes and Misdemeanors.

ARTICLE III.

Section 1. The judicial Power of the United States, shall be vested in one Supreme Court, and in such inferior Courts as the Congress may from time to time ordain and establish. The Judges, both of the supreme and inferior Courts, shall hold their Offices during good Behavior, and shall, at stated Times, receive for their Services a Compensation which shall not be diminished during their Continuance in Office.

Section 2. The judicial Power shall extend to all Cases, in Law and Equity, arising under this Constitution, the Laws of the United States, and Treaties made, or which shall be made, under their Authority; to all Cases affecting Ambassadors, other public Ministers and Consuls; to all Cases of admiralty and maritime Jurisdiction; to Controversies to which the United States shall be a Party; to Controversies between two or more States; between a State and Citizens of another State; between Citizens of different States; between Citizens of the same State claiming Lands under Grants of different States, and between a State, or the Citizens thereof, and foreign States, Citizens or Subjects.

In all Cases affecting Ambassadors, other public Ministers and Consuls, and those in which a State shall be Party, the Supreme Court shall have original Jurisdiction. In all the other Cases before mentioned, the Supreme Court shall have appellate Jurisdiction, both as to Law and Fact, with such Exceptions, and under such Regulations as the Congress shall make.

Trial of all Crimes, except in Cases of Impeachment, shall be by Jury; and such Trial shall be held in the State where the said Crimes shall have been committed; but when not committed within any State, the Trial shall be at such Place or Places as the Congress may by Law have directed.

Section 3. Treason against the United States, shall consist only in levying War against them, or in adhering to their Enemies, giving them Aid and Comfort. No Person shall be convicted of Treason unless on the Testimony of two Witnesses to the same overt Act, or on Confession in open Court.

The Congress shall have power to declare the Punishment of Treason, but no Attainder of Treason shall work Corruption of Blood, or Forfeiture except during the Life of the Person attainted.

ARTICLE IV.

Section 1. Full Faith and Credit shall be given in each State to the public Acts, Records, and judicial Proceedings of every other State. And the Congress may by general Laws prescribe the Manner in which such Acts, Records, and Proceedings shall be proved, and the Effect thereof.

Section 2. The Citizens of each State shall be entitled to all Privileges and Immunities of Citizens in the several States.

A Person charged in any State with Treason, Felony, or other Crime, who shall flee from Justice, and be found in another State, shall on demand of the executive Authority of the State from which he fled, be delivered up, to be removed to the State having Jurisdiction of the Crime.

No Person held to Service or Labour in one State, under the Laws thereof, escaping into another, shall, in Consequence of any Law or Regulation therein, be discharged from such Service or Labour, But shall be delivered up on Claim of the Party to whom such Service or Labour may be due.

Section 3. New States may be admitted by the Congress into this Union; but no new States shall be formed or erected within the Jurisdiction of any other State; nor any State be formed by the Junction of two or more States, or parts of States, without the Consent of the Legislatures of the States concerned as well as of the Congress.

The Congress shall have Power to dispose of and make all needful Rules and Regulations respecting the Territory or other Property belonging to the United States; and nothing in this Constitution shall be so construed as to Prejudice any Claims of the United States, or of any particular State.

Section 4. The United States shall guarantee to every State in this Union a Republican Form of Government, and shall protect each of them against Invasion; and on Application of the Legislature, or of the Executive (when the Legislature cannot be convened) against domestic Violence.

ARTICLE V.

The Congress, whenever two thirds of both Houses shall deem it necessary, shall propose Amendments to this Constitution, or, on the Application of the Legislatures of two thirds of the several States, shall call a Convention for proposing Amendments, which, in either Case, shall be valid to all Intents and Purposes, as part of this Constitution, when ratified by the Legislatures of three fourths of the several States, or by Conventions in three fourths thereof, as the one or the other Mode of Ratification may be proposed by the Congress; Provided that no Amendment which may be made prior to the Year One thousand eight hundred and eight shall in any Manner affect the first and fourth Clauses in the Ninth Section of the first Article; and that no State, without its Consent, shall be deprived of its equal Suffrage in the Senate.

ARTICLE VI.

All Debts contracted and Engagements entered into, before the Adoption of this Constitution, shall be as valid against the United States under this Constitution, as under the Confederation.

This Constitution, and the Laws of the United States which shall be made in Pursuance thereof; and all Treaties made, or which shall be made, under the Authority of the United States, shall be the supreme Law of the Land; and the Judges in every State shall be bound thereby, any Thing in the Constitution or Laws of any State to the Contrary notwithstanding.

The Senators and Representatives before mentioned, and the Members of the several State Legislatures, and all executive and judicial Officers, both of the United States and of the several States, shall be bound by Oath or Affirmation, to support this Constitution; but no religious Test shall ever be required as a Qualification to any Office or public Trust under the United States.

ARTICLE VII.

The Ratification of the Conventions of nine States, shall be sufficient for the Establishment of this Constitution between the States so ratifying the Same.

Done in Convention by the Unanimous Consent of the States present the Seventeenth Day of September in the Year of our Lord one thousand seven hundred and Eighty seven and of the Independence of the United States of America the Twelfth. In Witness whereof We have hereunto subscribed our Names.

Articles in Addition to, and Amendment of, the Constitution of the United States of America, Proposed by Congress, and Ratified by the Legislatures of the Several States, Pursuant to the Fifth Article of the Original Constitution.

[The first ten amendments went into effect in 1791.]

AMENDMENT I

Congress shall make no law respecting an establishment of religion, or prohibiting the free exercise thereof; or abridging the freedom of speech, or of the press; or the right of the people peaceably to assemble, and to petition the Government for a redress of grievances.

AMENDMENT II

A well regulated Militia, being necessary to the security of a free State, the right of the people to keep and bear Arms, shall not be infringed.

AMENDMENT III

No Soldier shall, in time of peace be quartered in any house, without the consent of the Owner, nor in time of war, but in a manner to be prescribed by law.

AMENDMENT IV

The right of the people to be secure in their persons, houses, papers, and effects, against unreasonable searches and seizures, shall not be violated, and no Warrants shall issue, but upon probable cause, supported by Oath or affirmation, and particularly describing the place to be searched, and the persons or things to be seized.

AMENDMENT V

No person shall be held to answer for a capital, or otherwise infamous crime, unless on a presentment or indictment of a Grand Jury, except in cases arising in the land or naval forces, or in the Militia, when in actual service in time of War or public danger; nor shall any person be subject for the same offense to be twice put in jeopardy of life or limb; nor shall be compelled in any criminal case to be a witness against himself, nor be deprived of life, liberty, or property, without due process of law; nor shall private property be taken for public use, without just compensation.

AMENDMENT VI

In all criminal prosecutions, the accused shall enjoy the right to a speedy and public trial, by an impartial jury of the State and district wherein the crime shall have been committed, which district shall have been previously ascertained by law, and to be informed of the nature and cause of the accusation; to be confronted with the witnesses against him; to have compulsory process for obtaining witnesses in his favor, and to have the Assistance of Counsel for his defence.

AMENDMENT VII

In Suits at common law, where the value in controversy shall exceed twenty dollars, the right of trial by jury shall be preserved, and no fact tried by a jury, shall be otherwise re-examined in any Court of the United States, than according to the rules of the common law.

AMENDMENT VIII

Excessive bail shall not be required, nor excessive fines imposed, nor cruel and unusual punishments inflicted.

AMENDMENT IX

The enumeration in the Constitution, of certain rights, shall not be construed to deny or disparage others retained by the people.

AMENDMENT X

The powers not delegated to the United States by the Constitution, nor prohibited by it to the States, are reserved to the States respectively, or to the people.

AMENDMENT XI

The Judicial power of the United States shall not be construed to extend to any suit in law or equity, commenced or prosecuted against one of the United States by Citizens of another State, or by Citizens or Subjects of any Foreign State.

AMENDMENT XII

The Electors shall meet in their respective states, and vote by ballot for President and Vice President, one of whom, at least, shall not be an inhabitant of the same state with themselves; they shall name in their ballots the person voted for as President, and in distinct ballots the person voted for as Vice President, and they shall make distinct lists of all persons voted for as President, and of all persons voted for as Vice President and of the number of votes for each, which lists they shall sign and certify, and transmit sealed to the seat of the government of the United States, directed to the President of the Senate;

The President of the Senate shall, in the presence of the Senate and House of Representatives, open all the certificates and the votes shall then be counted;

The person having the greatest Number of votes for President, shall be the President, if such number be a majority of the whole number of Electors appointed; and if no person have such majority, then from the persons having the highest numbers not exceeding three on the list of those voted for as President, the House of Representatives shall choose immediately, by ballot, the President. But in choosing the President, the votes shall be taken by states, the representation from each state having one vote; a quorum for this purpose shall consist of a member or members from two thirds of the states, and a majority of all the states shall be necessary to a choice. And if the House of Representatives shall not choose a President whenever the right of choice shall devolve upon them, before the fourth day of March next following, then the Vice-President shall act as President, as in the case of the death or other constitutional disability of the President.

The person having the greatest number of votes as Vice President, shall be the Vice President, if such number be a majority of the whole number of Electors appointed, and if no person have a majority, then from the two highest numbers on the list, the Senate shall choose the Vice President; a quorum for the purpose shall consist of two thirds of the whole number of Senators, and a majority of the whole number shall be necessary to a choice. But no person constitutionally ineligible to the office of President shall be eligible to that of Vice President of the United States.

AMENDMENT XIII

1. Neither slavery nor involuntary servitude, except as a punishment for crime whereof the party shall have been duly convicted, shall exist within the United States, or any place subject to their jurisdiction.

2. Congress shall have power to enforce this article by appropriate legislation.

AMENDMENT XIV

1. All persons born or naturalized in the United States, and subject to the jurisdiction thereof, are citizens of the United States and of the State wherein they reside. No State shall make or enforce any law which shall abridge the privileges or immunities of citizens of the United States; nor shall any State deprive any person of life, liberty, or property, without due process of law; nor deny to any person within its jurisdiction the equal protection of the laws.

2. Representatives shall be apportioned among the several States according to their respective numbers, counting the whole number of persons in each State, excluding Indians not taxed. But when the right to vote at any election for the choice of electors for President and Vice President of the United States, Representatives in Congress, the Executive and Judicial officers of a State, or the members of the Legislature thereof, is denied to any of the male inhabitants of such State, being twenty-one years of age, and citizens of the United States, or in any way abridged, except for participation in rebellion, or other crime, the basis of representation therein shall be reduced in the proportion which the number of such male citizens shall bear to the whole number of male citizens twenty-one years of age in such State.

3. No person shall be a Senator or Representative in Congress, or elector of President and Vice President, or hold any office, civil or military, under the United States, or under any State, who, having previously taken an oath, as a member of Congress, or as an officer of the United States, or as a member of any State legislature, or as an executive or judicial officer of any State, to support the Constitution of the United States, shall have engaged in insurrection or rebellion against the same, or given aid or comfort to the enemies thereof. But Congress may by a vote of two thirds of each House, remove such disability.

4. The validity of the public debt of the United States, authorized by law, including debts incurred for payment of pensions and bounties for services in suppressing insurrection or rebellion, shall not be questioned. But neither the United States nor any State shall assume or pay any debt or obligation incurred in aid of insurrection or rebellion against the United States, or any claim for the loss or emancipation of any slave; but all such debts, obligations and claims shall be held illegal and void.

5. The Congress shall have power to enforce, by appropriate legislation, the provisions of this article.

AMENDMENT XV

1. The right of citizens of the United States to vote shall not be denied or abridged by the United States or by any State on account of race, color, or previous condition of servitude.

2. The Congress shall have power to enforce this article by appropriate legislation.

AMENDMENT XVI

The Congress shall have power to lay and collect taxes on incomes, from whatever source derived, without apportionment among the several States, and without regard to any census or enumeration.

AMENDMENT XVII

The Senate of the United States shall be composed of two Senators from each State, elected by the people thereof, for six years; and each Senator shall have one vote. The electors in each State shall have the qualifications requisite for electors of the most numerous branch of the State legislatures.

When vacancies happen in the representation of any State in the Senate, the executive authority of such State shall issue writs of election to fill such vacancies: Provided, That the legislature of any State may empower the executive thereof to make temporary appointments until the people fill the vacancies by election as the legislature may direct.

This amendment shall not be so construed as to affect the election or term of any Senator chosen before it becomes valid as part of the Constitution.

AMENDMENT XVIII

1. After one year from the ratification of this article the manufacture, sale, or transportation of intoxicating liquors within, the importation thereof into, or the exportation thereof from the United States and all territory subject to the jurisdiction thereof for beverage purposes is hereby prohibited.

2. The Congress and the several States shall have concurrent power to enforce this article by appropriate legislation.

3. This article shall be inoperative unless it shall have been ratified as an amendment to the Constitution by the legislatures of the several States, as provided in the Constitution, within seven years from the date of the submission hereof to the States by the Congress.

AMENDMENT XIX

The right of citizens of the United States to vote shall not be denied or abridged by the United States or by any State on account of sex.

Congress shall have power to enforce this article by appropriate legislation.

AMENDMENT XX

1. The terms of the President and Vice President shall end at noon on the 20th day of January, and the terms of Senators and Representatives at noon on the 3rd day of January, of the years in which such terms would have ended if this article had not been ratified; and the terms of their successors shall then begin.

2. The Congress shall assemble at least once in every year, and such meeting shall begin at noon on the 3rd day of January, unless they shall by law appoint a different day.

3. If, at the time fixed for the beginning of the term of the President, the President elect shall have died, the Vice President elect shall become President. If a President shall not have been chosen before the time fixed for the beginning of his term, or if the President elect shall have failed to qualify, then the Vice President elect shall act as President until a President shall have qualified; and the Congress may by law provide for the case wherein neither a President elect nor a Vice President elect shall have qualified, declaring who shall then act as President, or the manner in which one who is to act shall be selected, and such person shall act accordingly until a President or Vice President shall have qualified.

4. The Congress may by law provide for the case of the death of any of the persons from whom the House of Representatives may choose a President whenever the right of choice shall have devolved upon them, and for the case of the death of any of the persons from whom the Senate may choose a Vice President whenever the right of choice shall have devolved upon them.

5. Sections 1 and 2 shall take effect on the 15th day of October following the ratification of this article.

6. This article shall be inoperative unless it shall have been ratified as an amendment to the Constitution by the legislatures of three fourths of the several States within seven years from the date of its submission.

AMENDMENT XXI

1. The eighteenth article of amendment to the Constitution of the United States is hereby repealed.

2. The transportation or importation into any State, Territory, or possession of the United States for delivery or use therein of intoxicating liquors, in violation of the laws thereof, is hereby prohibited.

3. The article shall be inoperative unless it shall have been ratified as an amendment to the Constitution by conventions in the several States, as provided in the Constitution, within seven years from the date of the submission hereof to the States by the Congress.

AMENDMENT XXII

1. No person shall be elected to the office of the President more than twice, and no person who has held the office of President, or acted as President, for more than two years of a term to which some other person was elected President shall be elected to the office of the President more than once. But this Article shall not apply to any person holding the office of President, when this Article was proposed by the Congress, and shall not prevent any person who may be holding the office of President, or acting as President, during the term within which this Article becomes operative from holding the office of President or acting as President during the remainder of such term.

2. This article shall be inoperative unless it shall have been ratified as an amendment to the Constitution by the legislatures of three fourths of the several States within seven years from the date of its submission to the States by the Congress.

AMENDMENT XXIII

1. The District constituting the seat of Government of the United States shall appoint in such manner as the Congress may direct: A number of electors of President and Vice President equal to the whole number of Senators and Representatives in Congress to which the District would be entitled if it were a State, but in no event more than the least populous State; they shall be in addition to those appointed by the States, but they shall be considered, for the purposes of the election of President and Vice President, to be electors appointed by a State; and they shall meet in the District and perform such duties as provided by the twelfth article of amendment.

2. The Congress shall have power to enforce this article by appropriate legislation.

AMENDMENT XXIV

1. The right of citizens of the United States to vote in any primary or other election for President or Vice President, for electors for President or Vice President, or for Senator or Representative in Congress, shall not be denied or abridged by the United States or any State by reason of failure to pay any poll tax or other tax.

2. The Congress shall have power to enforce this article by appropriate legislation.

AMENDMENT XXV

1. In case of the removal of the President from office or of his death or resignation, the Vice President shall become President.

2. Whenever there is a vacancy in the office of the Vice President, the President shall nominate a Vice President who shall take office upon confirmation by a majority vote of both Houses of Congress.

3. Whenever the President transmits to the President pro tempore of the Senate and the Speaker of the House of Representatives his written declaration that he is unable to discharge the powers and duties of his office, and until he transmits to them a written declaration to the contrary, such powers and duties shall be discharged by the Vice President as Acting President.

4. Whenever the Vice President and a majority of either the principal officers of the executive departments or of such other body as Congress may by law provide, transmit to the President pro tempore of the Senate and the Speaker of the House of Representatives their written declaration that the President is unable to discharge the powers and duties of his office, the Vice President shall immediately assume the powers and duties of the office as Acting President.

Thereafter, when the President transmits to the President pro tempore of the Senate and the Speaker of the House of Representatives his written declaration that no inability exists, he shall resume the powers and duties of his office unless the Vice President and a majority of either the principal officers of the executive department or of such other body as Congress may by law provide, transmit within four days to the President pro tempore of the Senate and the Speaker of the House of Representatives their written declaration that the President is unable to discharge the powers and duties of his office. Thereupon Congress shall decide the issue, assembling within 48 hours for that purpose if not in session. If the Congress, within twenty-one days after receipt of the latter written declaration, or, if Congress is not in session, within twenty-one days after Congress is required to assemble, determines by two thirds vote of both Houses that the President is unable to discharge the powers and duties of his office, the Vice President shall continue to discharge the same as Acting President; otherwise, the President shall resume the powers and duties of his office.

AMENDMENT XXVI

1. The right of citizens of the United States, who are 18 years of age or older, to vote shall not be denied or abridged by the United States or by any State on account of age.

2. The Congress shall have power to enforce this article by appropriate legislation.

AMENDMENT XXVII

No law, varying the compensation for the services of the Senators and Representatives, shall take effect, until an election of Representatives shall have intervened.

THE FEDERALIST PAPERS

[The Federalist Papers were written by Alexander Hamilton, James Madison, and John Jay. They were originally conceived as a series of letters to the New York newspapers to encourage support for the ratification of the Constitution. The signature, "Publius" is a pseudonym that they all shared in their 51 letters.]

FEDERALIST NO. 10
The Same Subject Continued

(The Union as a Safeguard Against Domestic Faction and Insurrection)

To the People of the State of New York:

AMONG the numerous advantages promised by a well-constructed Union, none deserves to be more accurately developed than its tendency to break and control the violence of faction. The friend of popular governments never finds himself so much alarmed for their character and fate, as when he contemplates their propensity to this dangerous vice. He will not fail, therefore, to set a due value on any plan which, without violating the principles to which he is attached, provides a proper cure for it. The instability, injustice, and confusion introduced into the public councils, have, in truth, been the mortal diseases under which popular governments have everywhere perished; as they continue to be the favorite and fruitful topics from which the adversaries to liberty derive their most specious declamations. The valuable improvements made by the American constitutions on the popular models, both ancient and modern, cannot certainly be too much admired; but it would be an unwarrantable partiality, to contend that they have as effectually obviated the danger on this side, as was wished and expected. Complaints are everywhere heard from our most considerate and virtuous citizens, equally the friends of public and private faith, and of public and personal liberty, that our governments are too unstable, that the public good is disregarded in the conflicts of rival parties, and that measures are too often decided, not according to the rules of justice and the rights of the minor party, but by the superior force of an interested and overbearing majority. However anxiously we may wish that these complaints had no foundation, the evidence of known facts will not permit us to deny that they are in some degree true. It will be found, indeed, on a candid review of our situation, that some of the distresses under which we labor have been erroneously charged on the operation of our governments; but it will be found, at the same time, that other causes will not alone account for many of our heaviest misfortunes; and, particularly, for that prevailing and increasing distrust of public engagements, and alarm for private rights, which are echoed from one end of the continent to the other. These must be chiefly, if not wholly, effects of the unsteadiness and injustice with which a factious spirit has tainted our public administrations.

By a faction, I understand a number of citizens, whether amounting to a majority or a minority of the whole, who are united and actuated by some common impulse of passion, or of interest, adversed to the rights of other citizens, or to the permanent and aggregate interests of the community.

There are two methods of curing the mischiefs of faction: the one, by removing its causes; the other, by controlling its effects.

There are again two methods of removing the causes of faction: the one, by destroying the liberty which is essential to its existence; the other, by giving to every citizen the same opinions, the same passions, and the same interests.

It could never be more truly said than of the first remedy, that it was worse than the disease. Liberty is to faction what air is to fire, an aliment without which it instantly expires. But it could not be less folly to abolish liberty, which is essential to political life, because it nourishes faction, than it would be to wish the annihilation of air, which is essential to animal life, because it imparts to fire its destructive agency.

The second expedient is as impracticable as the first would be unwise. As long as the reason of man continues fallible, and he is at liberty to exercise it, different opinions will be formed. As long as the connection subsists between his reason and his self-love, his opinions and his passions will have a reciprocal influence on each other; and the former will be objects to which the latter will attach themselves. The diversity in the faculties of men, from which the rights of property originate, is not less an insuperable obstacle to a uniformity of interests. The protection of these faculties is the first object of government. From the protection of different and unequal faculties of acquiring property, the possession of different degrees and kinds of property immediately results; and from the influence of these on the sentiments and views of the respective proprietors, ensues a division of the society into different interests and parties.

The latent causes of faction are thus sown in the nature of man; and we see them everywhere brought into different degrees of activity, according to the different circumstances of civil society. A zeal for different opinions concerning religion, concerning government, and many other points, as well of speculation as of practice; an attachment to different leaders ambitiously contending for pre-eminence and power; or to persons of other descriptions whose fortunes have been interesting to the human passions, have, in turn, divided mankind into parties, inflamed them with mutual animosity, and rendered them much more disposed to vex and oppress each other than to co-operate for their common good. So strong is this propensity of mankind to fall into mutual animosities, that where no substantial occasion presents itself, the most frivolous and fanciful distinctions have been sufficient to kindle their unfriendly passions and excite their most violent conflicts. But the most common and durable source of factions has been the various and unequal distribution of property. Those who hold and those who are without property have ever formed distinct interests in society. Those who are creditors, and those who are debtors, fall under a like discrimination. A landed interest, a manufacturing interest, a mercantile interest, a moneyed interest, with many lesser interests, grow up of necessity in civilized nations, and divide them into different classes, actuated by different sentiments and views. The regulation of these various and interfering interests forms the principal task of modern legislation, and involves the spirit of party and faction in the necessary and ordinary operations of the government.

No man is allowed to be a judge in his own cause, because his interest would certainly bias his judgment, and, not improbably, corrupt his integrity. With equal, nay with greater reason, a body of men are unfit to be both judges and parties at the same time; yet what are many of the most important acts of legislation, but so many judicial determinations, not indeed concerning the rights of single persons, but concerning the rights of large bodies of citizens? And what are the different classes of legislators but advocates and parties to the causes which they determine? Is a law proposed concerning private debts? It is a question to which the creditors are parties on one side and the debtors on the other. Justice ought to hold the balance between them. Yet the parties are, and must be, themselves the judges; and the most numerous party, or, in other words, the most powerful faction must be expected to prevail. Shall domestic manufactures be encouraged, and in what degree, by restrictions on foreign manufactures? are questions which would be differently decided by the landed and the manufacturing classes, and probably by neither with a sole regard to justice and the public good. The apportionment of taxes on the various descriptions of property is an act which seems to require the most exact impartiality; yet there is, perhaps, no legislative act in which greater opportunity and temptation are given to a predominant party to trample on the rules of justice. Every shilling with which they overburden the inferior number, is a shilling saved to their own pockets.

It is in vain to say that enlightened statesmen will be able to adjust these clashing interests, and render them all subservient to the public good. Enlightened statesmen will not always be at the helm. Nor, in many cases, can such an adjustment be made at all without taking into view indirect and remote considerations, which will rarely prevail over the immediate interest which one party may find in disregarding the rights of another or the good of the whole.

The inference to which we are brought is, that the CAUSES of faction cannot be removed, and that relief is only to be sought in the means of controlling its EFFECTS.

If a faction consists of less than a majority, relief is supplied by the republican principle, which enables the majority to defeat its sinister views by regular vote. It may clog the administration, it may convulse the society; but it will be unable to execute and mask its violence under the forms of the Constitution. When a majority is included in a faction, the form of popular government, on the other hand, enables it to sacrifice to its ruling passion or interest both the public good and the rights of other citizens. To secure the public good and private rights against the danger of such a faction, and at the same time to preserve the spirit and the form of popular government, is then the great object to which our inquiries are directed. Let me add that it is the great desideratum by which this form of government can be rescued from the opprobrium under which it has so long labored, and be recommended to the esteem and adoption of mankind.

By what means is this object attainable? Evidently by one of two only. Either the existence of the same passion or interest in a majority at the same time must be prevented, or the majority, having such coexistent passion or interest, must be rendered, by their number and local situation, unable to concert and carry into effect schemes of oppression. If the impulse and the opportunity be suffered to coincide, we well know that neither moral nor religious motives can be relied on as an adequate control. They are not found to be such on the injustice and violence of individuals, and lose their efficacy in proportion to the number combined together, that is, in proportion as their efficacy becomes needful.

From this view of the subject it may be concluded that a pure democracy, by which I mean a society consisting of a small number of citizens, who assemble and administer the government in person, can admit of no cure for the mischiefs of faction. A common passion or interest will, in almost every case, be felt by a majority of the whole; a communication and concert result from the form of government itself; and there is nothing to check the inducements to sacrifice the weaker party or an obnoxious individual. Hence it is that such democracies have ever been spectacles of turbulence and contention; have ever been found incompatible with personal security or the rights of property; and have in general been as short in their lives as they have been violent in their deaths. Theoretic politicians, who have patronized this species of government, have erroneously supposed that by reducing mankind to a perfect equality in their political rights, they would, at the same time, be perfectly equalized and assimilated in their possessions, their opinions, and their passions.

A republic, by which I mean a government in which the scheme of representation takes place, opens a different prospect, and promises the cure for which we are seeking. Let us examine the points in which it varies from pure democracy, and we shall comprehend both the nature of the cure and the efficacy which it must derive from the Union.

The two great points of difference between a democracy and a republic are: first, the delegation of the government, in the latter, to a small number of citizens elected by the rest; secondly, the greater number of citizens, and greater sphere of country, over which the latter may be extended.

The effect of the first difference is, on the one hand, to refine and enlarge the public views, by passing them through the medium of a chosen body of citizens, whose wisdom may best discern the true interest of their country, and whose patriotism and love of justice will be least likely to sacrifice it to temporary or partial considerations. Under such a regulation, it may well happen that the public voice, pronounced by the representatives of the people, will be more consonant to the public good than if pronounced by the people themselves, convened for the purpose. On the other hand, the effect may be inverted. Men of factious tempers, of local prejudices, or of sinister designs, may, by intrigue, by corruption, or by other means, first obtain the suffrages, and then betray the interests, of the people. The question resulting is, whether small or extensive republics are more favorable to the election of proper guardians of the public weal; and it is clearly decided in favor of the latter by two obvious considerations:

In the first place, it is to be remarked that, however small the republic may be, the representatives must be raised to a certain number, in order to guard against the cabals of a few; and that, however large it may be, they must be limited to a certain number, in order to guard against the confusion of a multitude. Hence, the number of representatives in the two cases not being in proportion to that of the two constituents, and being proportionally greater in the small republic, it follows that, if the proportion of fit characters be not less in the large than in the small republic, the former will present a greater option, and consequently a greater probability of a fit choice.

In the next place, as each representative will be chosen by a greater number of citizens in the large than in the small republic, it will be more difficult for unworthy candidates to practice with success the vicious arts by which elections are too often carried; and the suffrages of the people being more free, will be more likely to centre in men who possess the most attractive merit and the most diffusive and established characters.

It must be confessed that in this, as in most other cases, there is a mean, on both sides of which inconveniences will be found to lie. By enlarging too much the number of electors, you render the representatives too little acquainted with all their local circumstances and lesser interests; as by reducing it too much, you render him unduly attached to these, and too little fit to comprehend and pursue great and national objects. The federal Constitution forms a happy combination in this respect; the great and aggregate interests being referred to the national, the local and particular to the State legislatures.

The other point of difference is, the greater number of citizens and extent of territory which may be brought within the compass of republican than of democratic government; and it is this circumstance principally which renders factious combinations less to be dreaded in the former than in the latter. The smaller the society, the fewer probably will be the distinct parties and interests composing it; the fewer the distinct parties and interests, the more frequently will a majority be found of the same party; and the smaller the number of individuals composing a majority, and the smaller the compass within which they are placed, the more easily will they concert and execute their plans of oppression. Extend the sphere, and you take in a greater variety of parties and interests; you make it less probable that a majority of the whole will have a common motive to invade the rights of other citizens; or if such a common motive exists, it will be more difficult for all who feel it to discover their own strength, and to act in unison with each other. Besides other impediments, it may be remarked that, where there is a consciousness of unjust or dishonorable purposes, communication is always checked by distrust in proportion to the number whose concurrence is necessary.

Hence, it clearly appears, that the same advantage which a republic has over a democracy, in controlling the effects of faction, is enjoyed by a large over a small republic,—is enjoyed by the Union over the States composing it. Does the advantage consist in the substitution of representatives whose enlightened views and virtuous sentiments render them superior to local prejudices and schemes of injustice? It will not be denied that the representation of the Union will be most likely to possess these requisite endowments. Does it consist in the greater security afforded by a greater variety of parties, against the event of any one party being able to outnumber and oppress the rest? In an equal degree does the increased variety of parties comprised within the Union, increase this security. Does it, in fine, consist in the greater obstacles opposed to the concert and accomplishment of the secret wishes of an unjust and interested majority? Here, again, the extent of the Union gives it the most palpable advantage.

The influence of factious leaders may kindle a flame within their particular States, but will be unable to spread a general conflagration through the other States. A religious sect may degenerate into a political faction in a part of the Confederacy; but the variety of sects dispersed over the entire face of it must secure the national councils against any danger from that source. A rage for paper money, for an abolition of debts, for an equal division of property, or for any other improper or wicked project, will be less apt to pervade the whole body of the Union than a particular member of it; in the same proportion as such a malady is more likely to taint a particular county or district, than an entire State.

In the extent and proper structure of the Union, therefore, we behold a republican remedy for the diseases most incident to republican government. And according to the degree of pleasure and pride we feel in being republicans, ought to be our zeal in cherishing the spirit and supporting the character of Federalists.

PUBLIUS.

FEDERALIST NO. 51

The Structure of the Government Must Furnish the Proper Checks and Balances between the Different Departments

To the People of the State of New York:

TO WHAT expedient, then, shall we finally resort, for maintaining in practice the necessary partition of power among the several departments, as laid down in the Constitution? The only answer that can be given is, that as all these exterior provisions are found to be inadequate, the defect must be supplied, by so contriving the interior structure of the government as that its several constituent parts may, by their mutual relations, be the means of keeping each other in their proper places. Without presuming to undertake a full development of this important idea, I will hazard a few general observations, which may perhaps place it in a clearer light, and enable us to form a more correct judgment of the principles and structure of the government planned by the convention.

In order to lay a due foundation for that separate and distinct exercise of the different powers of government, which to a certain extent is admitted on all hands to be essential to the preservation of liberty, it is evident that each department should have a will of its own; and consequently should be so constituted that the members of each should have as little agency as possible in the appointment of the members of the others. Were this principle rigorously adhered to, it would require that all the appointments for the supreme executive, legislative, and judiciary magistracies should be drawn from the same fountain of authority, the people, through channels having no communication whatever with one another. Perhaps such a plan of constructing the several departments would be less difficult in practice than it may in contemplation appear. Some difficulties, however, and some additional expense would attend the execution of it. Some deviations, therefore, from the principle must be admitted. In the constitution of the judiciary department in particular, it might be inexpedient to insist rigorously on the principle: first, because peculiar qualifications being essential in the members, the primary consideration ought to be to select that mode of choice which best secures these qualifications; secondly, because the permanent tenure by which the appointments are held in that department, must soon destroy all sense of dependence on the authority conferring them.

It is equally evident, that the members of each department should be as little dependent as possible on those of the others, for the emoluments annexed to their offices. Were the executive magistrate, or the judges, not independent of the legislature in this particular, their independence in every other would be merely nominal.

But the great security against a gradual concentration of the several powers in the same department, consists in giving to those who administer each department the necessary constitutional means and personal motives to resist encroachments of the others. The provision for defense must in this, as in all other cases, be made commensurate to the danger of attack. Ambition must be made to counteract ambition. The interest of the man must be connected with the constitutional rights of the place. It may be a reflection on human nature, that such devices should be necessary to control the abuses of government. But what is government itself, but the greatest of all reflections on human nature? If men were angels, no government would be necessary. If angels were to govern men, neither external nor internal controls on government would be necessary. In framing a government which is to be administered by men over men, the great difficulty lies in this: you must first enable the government to control the governed; and in the next place oblige it to control itself. A dependence on the people is, no doubt, the primary control on the government; but experience has taught mankind the necessity of auxiliary precautions.

This policy of supplying, by opposite and rival interests, the defect of better motives, might be traced through the whole system of human affairs, private as well as public. We see it particularly displayed in all the subordinate distributions of power, where the constant aim is to divide and arrange the several offices in such a manner as that each may be a check on the other that the private interest of every individual may be a sentinel over the public rights. These inventions of prudence cannot be less requisite in the distribution of the supreme powers of the State.

But it is not possible to give to each department an equal power of self-defense. In republican government, the legislative authority necessarily predominates. The remedy for this inconveniency is to divide the legislature into different branches; and to render them, by different modes of election and different principles of action, as little connected with each other as the nature of their common functions and their common dependence on the society will admit. It may even be necessary to guard against dangerous encroachments by still further precautions. As the weight of the legislative authority requires that it should be thus divided, the weakness of the executive may require, on the other hand, that it should be fortified. An absolute negative on the legislature appears, at first view, to be the natural defense with which the executive magistrate should be armed. But perhaps it would be neither altogether safe nor alone sufficient. On ordinary occasions it might not be exerted with the requisite firmness, and on extraordinary occasions it might be perfidiously abused. May not this defect of an absolute negative be supplied by some qualified connection between this weaker department and the weaker branch of the stronger department, by which the latter may be led to support the constitutional rights of the former, without being too much detached from the rights of its own department?

If the principles on which these observations are founded be just, as I persuade myself they are, and they be applied as a criterion to the several State constitutions, and to the federal Constitution it will be found that if the latter does not perfectly correspond with them, the former are infinitely less able to bear such a test.

There are, moreover, two considerations particularly applicable to the federal system of America, which place that system in a very interesting point of view.

First. In a single republic, all the power surrendered by the people is submitted to the administration of a single government; and the usurpations are guarded against by a division of the government into distinct and separate departments. In the compound republic of America, the power surrendered by the people is first divided between two distinct governments, and then the portion allotted to each subdivided among distinct and separate departments. Hence a double security arises to the rights of the people. The different governments will control each other, at the same time that each will be controlled by itself.

Second. It is of great importance in a republic not only to guard the society against the oppression of its rulers, but to guard one part of the society against the injustice of the other part. Different interests necessarily exist in different classes of citizens. If a majority be united by a common interest, the rights of the minority will be insecure. There are but two methods of providing against this evil: the one by creating a will in the community independent of the majority that is, of the society itself; the other, by comprehending in the society so many separate descriptions of citizens as will render an unjust combination of a majority of the whole very improbable, if not impracticable. The first method prevails in all governments possessing an hereditary or self-appointed authority. This, at best, is but a precarious security; because a power independent of the society may as well espouse the unjust views of the major, as the rightful interests of the minor party, and may possibly be turned against both parties. The second method will be exemplified in the federal republic of the United States. Whilst all authority in it will be derived from and dependent on the society, the society itself will be broken into so many parts, interests, and classes of citizens, that the rights of individuals, or of the minority, will be in little danger from interested combinations of the majority. In a free government the security for civil rights must be the same as that for religious rights. It consists in the one case in the multiplicity of interests, and in the other in the multiplicity of sects. The degree of security in both cases will depend on the number of interests and sects; and this may be presumed to depend on the extent of country and number of people comprehended under the same government. This view of the subject must particularly recommend a proper federal system to all the sincere and considerate friends of republican government, since it shows that in exact proportion as the territory of the Union may be formed into more circumscribed Confederacies, or States oppressive combinations of a majority will be facilitated: the best security, under the republican forms, for the rights of every class of citizens, will be diminished: and consequently the stability and independence of some member of the government, the only other security, must be proportionately increased. Justice is the end of government. It is the end of civil society. It ever has been and ever will be pursued until it be obtained, or until liberty be lost in the pursuit. In a society under the forms of which the stronger faction can readily unite and oppress the weaker, anarchy may as truly be said to reign as in a state of nature, where the weaker individual is not secured against the violence of the stronger; and as, in the latter state, even the stronger individuals are prompted, by the uncertainty of their condition, to submit to a government which may protect the weak as well as themselves; so, in the former state, will the more powerful factions or parties be gradually induced, by a like motive, to wish for a government which will protect all parties, the weaker as well as the more powerful. It can be little doubted that if the State of Rhode Island was separated from the Confederacy and left to itself, the insecurity of rights under the popular form of government within such narrow limits would be displayed by such reiterated oppressions of factious majorities that some power altogether independent of the people would soon be called for by the voice of the very factions whose misrule had proved the necessity of it. In the extended republic of the United States, and among the great variety of interests, parties, and sects which it embraces, a coalition of a majority of the whole society could seldom take place on any other principles than those of justice and the general good; whilst there being thus less danger to a minor from the will of a major party, there must be less pretext, also, to provide for the security of the former, by introducing into the government a will not dependent on the latter, or, in other words, a will independent of the society itself. It is no less certain than it is important, notwithstanding the contrary opinions which have been entertained, that the larger the society, provided it lie within a practical sphere, the more duly capable it will be of self-government. And happily for the REPUBLICAN CAUSE, the practicable sphere may be carried to a very great extent, by a judicious modification and mixture of the FEDERAL PRINCIPLE.

PUBLIUS.

THE MONROE DOCTRINE

December 2, 1823

The Monroe Doctrine was expressed during President Monroe's seventh annual message to Congress, December 2, 1823:

. . . At the proposal of the Russian Imperial Government, made through the minister of the Emperor residing here, a full power and instructions have been transmitted to the minister of the United States at St. Petersburg to arrange by amicable negotiation the respective rights and interests of the two nations on the northwest coast of this continent. A similar proposal has been made by His Imperial Majesty to the Government of Great Britain, which has likewise been acceded to. The Government of the United States has been desirous by this friendly proceeding of manifesting the great value which they have invariably attached to the friendship of the Emperor and their solicitude to cultivate the best understanding with his Government. In the discussions to which this interest has given rise and in the arrangements by which they may terminate the occasion has been judged proper for asserting, as a principle in which the rights and interests of the United States are involved, that the American continents, by the free and independent condition which they have assumed and maintain, are henceforth not to be considered as subjects for future colonization by any European powers . . .

It was stated at the commencement of the last session that a great effort was then making in Spain and Portugal to improve the condition of the people of those countries, and that it appeared to be conducted with extraordinary moderation. It need scarcely be remarked that the results have been so far very different from what was then anticipated. Of events in that quarter of the globe, with which we have so much intercourse and from which we derive our origin, we have always been anxious and interested spectators. The citizens of the United States cherish sentiments the most friendly in favor of the liberty and happiness of their fellow-men on that side of the Atlantic. In the wars of the European powers in matters relating to themselves we have never taken any part, nor does it comport with our policy to do so. It is only when our rights are invaded or seriously menaced that we resent injuries or make preparation for our defense. With the movements in this hemisphere we are of necessity more immediately connected, and by causes which must be obvious to all enlightened and impartial observers. The political system of the allied powers is essentially different in this respect from that of America. This difference proceeds from that which exists in their respective Governments; and to the defense of our own, which has been achieved by the loss of so much blood and treasure, and matured by the wisdom of their most enlightened citizens, and under which we have enjoyed unexampled felicity, this whole nation is devoted. We owe it, therefore, to candor and to the amicable relations existing between the United States and those powers to declare that we should consider any attempt on their part to extend their system to any portion of this hemisphere as dangerous to our peace and safety. With the existing colonies or dependencies of any European power we have not interfered and shall not interfere. But with the Governments who have declared their independence and maintain it, and whose independence we have, on great consideration and on just principles, acknowledged, we could not view any interposition for the purpose of oppressing them, or controlling in any other manner their destiny, by any European power in any other light than as the manifestation of an unfriendly disposition toward the United States. In the war between those new Governments and Spain we declared our neutrality at the time of their recognition, and to this we have adhered, and shall continue to adhere, provided no change shall occur which, in the judgment of the competent authorities of this Government, shall make a corresponding change on the part of the United States indispensable to their security.

The late events in Spain and Portugal show that Europe is still unsettled. Of this important fact no stronger proof can be adduced than that the allied powers should have thought it proper, on any principle satisfactory to themselves, to have interposed by force in the internal concerns of Spain. To what extent such interposition may be carried, on the same principle, is a question in which all independent powers whose governments differ from theirs are interested, even those most remote, and surely none of them more so than the United States. Our policy in regard to Europe, which was adopted at an early stage of the wars which have so long agitated that quarter of the globe, nevertheless remains the same, which is, not to interfere in the internal concerns of any of its powers; to consider the government de facto as the legitimate government for us; to cultivate friendly relations with it, and to preserve those relations by a frank, firm, and manly policy, meeting in all instances the just claims of every power, submitting to injuries from none. But in regard to those continents circumstances are eminently and conspicuously different. It is impossible that the allied powers should extend their political system to any portion of either continent without endangering our peace and happiness; nor can anyone believe that our southern brethren, if left to themselves, would adopt it of their own accord. It is equally impossible, therefore, that we should behold such interposition in any form with indifference. If we look to the comparative strength and resources of Spain and those new Governments, and their distance from each other, it must be obvious that she can never subdue them. It is still the true policy of the United States to leave the parties to themselves, in hope that other powers will pursue the same course. . . .

REPORT OF THE WOMAN'S RIGHTS CONVENTION

Seneca Falls, NY

July 19th and 20th, 1848

DECLARATION OF SENTIMENTS

When, in the course of human events, it becomes necessary for one portion of the family of man to assume among the people of the earth a position different from that which they have hitherto occupied, but one to which the laws of nature and of nature's God entitle them, a decent respect to the opinions of mankind requires that they should declare the causes that impel them to such a course.

We hold these truths to be self-evident; that all men and women are created equal; that they are endowed by their Creator with certain inalienable rights; that among these are life, liberty, and the pursuit of happiness; that to secure these rights governments are instituted, deriving their just powers from the consent of the governed. Whenever any form of Government becomes destructive of these ends, it is the right of those who suffer from it to refuse allegiance to it, and to insist upon the institution of a new government, laying its foundation on such principles, and organizing its powers in such form as to them shall seem most likely to effect their safety and happiness. Prudence, indeed, will dictate that governments long established should not be changed for light and transient causes; and accordingly, all experience hath shown that mankind are more disposed to suffer, while evils are sufferable, than to right themselves, by abolishing the forms to which they are accustomed. But when a long train of abuses and usurpations, pursuing invariably the same object, evinces a design to reduce them under absolute despotism, it is their duty to throw off such government, and to provide new guards for their future security. Such has been the patient sufferance of the women under this government, and such is now the necessity which constrains them to demand the equal station to which they are entitled.

The history of mankind is a history of repeated injuries and usurpations on the part of man toward woman, having in direct object the establishment of an absolute tyranny over her. To prove this, let facts be submitted to a candid world.

He has never permitted her to exercise her inalienable right to the elective franchise.

He has compelled her to submit to laws, in the formation of which she had no voice.

He has withheld from her rights which are given to the most ignorant and degraded men—both natives and foreigners.

Having deprived her of this first right of a citizen, the elective franchise, thereby leaving her without representation in the halls of legislation, he has oppressed her on all sides.

He has made her, if married, in the eye of the law, civilly dead.

He has taken from her all right in property, even to the wages she earns.

He has made her, morally, an irresponsible being, as she can commit many crimes, with impunity, provided they be done in the presence of her husband. In the covenant of marriage, she is compelled to promise obedience to her husband, he becoming, to all intents and purposes, her master—the law giving him power to deprive her of her liberty, and to administer chastisement.

He has so framed the laws of divorce, as to what shall be the proper causes of divorce; in case of separation, to whom the guardianship of the children shall be given, as to be wholly regardless of the happiness of women—the law, in all cases, going upon the false supposition of the supremacy of man, and giving all power into his hands.

After depriving her of all rights as a married woman, if single and the owner of property, he has taxed her to support a government which recognizes her only when her property can be made profitable to it.

He has monopolized nearly all the profitable employments, and from those she is permitted to follow, she receives but a scanty remuneration.

He closes against her all the avenues to wealth and distinction, which he considers most honorable to himself. As a teacher of theology, medicine, or law, she is not known.

He has denied her the facilities for obtaining a thorough education—all colleges being closed against her.

He allows her in Church as well as State, but a subordinate position, claiming Apostolic authority for her exclusion from the ministry, and with some exceptions, from any public participation in the affairs of the Church.

He has created a false public sentiment, by giving to the world a different code of morals for men and women, by which moral delinquencies which exclude women from society, are not only tolerated but deemed of little account in man.

He has usurped the prerogative of Jehovah himself, claiming it as his right to assign for her a sphere of action, when that belongs to her conscience and her God.

He has endeavored, in every way that he could to destroy her confidence in her own powers, to lessen her self-respect, and to make her willing to lead a dependent and abject life.

Now, in view of this entire disfranchisement of one-half the people of this country, their social and religious degradation—in view of the unjust laws above mentioned, and because women do feel themselves aggrieved, oppressed, and fraudulently deprived of their most sacred rights, we insist that they have immediate admission to all the rights and privileges which belong to them as citizens of these United States.

In entering upon the great work before us, we anticipate no small amount of misconception, misrepresentation, and ridicule; but we shall use every instrumentality within our power to effect our object. We shall employ agents, circulate tracts, petition the State and national Legislatures, and endeavor to enlist the pulpit and the press in our behalf. We hope this Convention will be followed by a series of Conventions, embracing every part of the country.

Firmly relying upon the final triumph of the Right and the True, we do this day affix our signatures to this declaration.

THE EMANCIPATION PROCLAMATION (1863)
By the President of the United States of America: Abraham Lincoln

A PROCLAMATION

Whereas on the 22nd day of September, A.D. 1862, a proclamation was issued by the President of the United States, containing, among other things, the following, to wit:

"That on the 1st day of January, A.D. 1863, all persons held as slaves within any State or designated part of a State the people whereof shall then be in rebellion against the United States shall be then, thenceforward, and forever free; and the executive government of the United States, including the military and naval authority thereof, will recognize and maintain the freedom of such persons and will do no act or acts to repress such persons, or any of them, in any efforts they may make for their actual freedom.

"That the executive will on the 1st day of January aforesaid, by proclamation, designate the States and parts of States, if any, in which the people thereof, respectively, shall then be in rebellion against the United States; and the fact that any State or the people thereof shall on that day be in good faith represented in the Congress of the United States by members chosen thereto at elections wherein a majority of the qualified voters of such States shall have participated shall, in the absence of strong countervailing testimony, be deemed conclusive evidence that such State and the people thereof are not then in rebellion against the United States."

Now, therefore, I, Abraham Lincoln, President of the United States, by virtue of the power in me vested as Commander in Chief of the Army and Navy of the United States in time of actual armed rebellion against the authority and government of the United States, and as a fit and necessary war measure for suppressing said rebellion, do, on this 1st day of January, A.D. 1863, and in accordance with my purpose so to do, publicly proclaimed for the full period of one hundred days from the first day above mentioned, order and designate as the States and parts of States wherein the people thereof, respectively, are this day in rebellion against the United States the following, to wit:

Arkansas, Texas, Louisiana (except the parishes of St. Bernard, Palquemines, Jefferson, St. John, St. Charles, St. James, Ascension, Assumption, Terrebone, Lafourche, St. Mary, St. Martin, and Orleans, including the city of New Orleans), Mississippi, Alabama, Florida, Georgia, South Carolina, North Carolina, and Virginia (except the forty-eight counties designated as West Virginia, and also the counties of Berkeley, Accomac, Northhampton, Elizabeth City, York, Princess Anne, and Norfolk, including the cities of Norfolk and Portsmouth), and which excepted parts are for the present left precisely as if this proclamation were not issued.

And by virtue of the power and for the purpose aforesaid, I do order and declare that all persons held as slaves within said designated States and parts of States are, and henceforward shall be, free; and that the Executive Government of the United States, including the military and naval authorities thereof, will recognize and maintain the freedom of said persons.

And I hereby enjoin upon the people so declared to be free to abstain from all violence, unless in necessary self-defence; and I recommend to them that, in all case when allowed, they labor faithfully for reasonable wages.

And I further declare and make known that such persons of suitable condition will be received into the armed service of the United States to garrison forts, positions, stations, and other places, and to man vessels of all sorts in said service.

And upon this act, sincerely believed to be an act of justice, warranted by the Constitution upon military necessity, I invoke the considerate judgment of mankind and the gracious favor of Almighty God.

NOTES

NOTES

NOTES

NOTES

Need Help Paying for School?
We'll Show You the Money!

Peterson's offers students like you a wide variety of comprehensive resources to help you meet all your financial planning needs.

Scholarships, Grants & Prizes 2002

ISBN 0-7689-0695-4, with CD,
$26.95 pb/$39.95 CAN/£18.99 UK,
August 2001

College Money Handbook 2002

ISBN 0-7689-0694-6,
$26.95 pb/$39.95 CAN/£18.99 UK,
August 2001

Scholarship Almanac 2002

ISBN 0-7689-0692-X
$12.95 pb/$18.95 CAN/£9.99 UK,
August 2001

The Insider's Guide to Paying for College

ISBN 0-7689-0230-4,
$9.95 pb/$14.95 CAN/£11.99 UK,
1999

Scholarships and Loans for Adult Students

ISBN 0-7689-0296-7,
$19.95 pb/$29.95 CAN/£16.99 UK,
1999

Grants for Graduate & Postdoctoral Study

ISBN 0-7689-0019-0,
$32.95 pb/$45.95 CAN/£25 UK,
1998

Scholarships for Study in the USA & Canada

ISBN 0-7689-0266-5,
$21.95 pb/$32.95 CAN/£16.99 UK,
1999

Visit your local bookstore or call to order: **800-338-3282.** To order online, go to **www.petersons.com** and head for the bookstore!

PETERSON'S™
THOMSON LEARNING